SAUCERS, SWASTIKAS AND PSYOPS

A History of a Breakaway Civilization:
Hidden Aerospace Technologies and Pyschological Operations

Other Books by Joseph P. Farrell:

LBJ and the Conspiracy to Kill Kennedy
Roswell and the Reich
Nazi International
Reich of the Black Sun
The S.S. Brotherhood of the Bell
Secrets of the Unified Field
The Cosmic War
The Giza Death Star
The Giza Death Star Deployed
The Giza Death Star Destroyed
The Grid of the Gods (with Scott de Hart)

SAUCERS, SWASTIKAS AND PSYOPS

Joseph P. Farrell

Adventures Unlimited Press

Saucers, Swastikas and Psyops

ISBN: 978-1-935487-75-3

Published by:
Adventures Unlimited Press
One Adventure Place
Kempton, Illinois 60946 USA
auphq@frontiernet.net

www.adventuresunlimitedpress.com

Cover by Terry Lamb

10 9 8 7 6 5 4 3 2 1

Above all, to
Scott Douglas de Hart:
A true master, adept, and poet of deep mysteries,
who crossed the Rubicon with me:
Anything I could say, any gratitude I could express, are simply inadequate for
you; thank you for so many years of friendship, so many inspirations through
so many conversations,

You are a true

And to:
George Ann Hughes,
Constant in prayer, in encouragement, and in love;

And to
Tracy S. Fisher:
You are, and will always be, sorely missed;

"For we are opposed around the world by a monolithic and ruthless conspiracy that relies primarily on covert means for expanding its sphere of influence—on infiltration instead of invasion, on subversion instead of elections, on intimidation instead of free choice, on guerrillas by night instead of armies by day. It is a system which has conscripted vast human and material resources into the building of a tightly knit, highly efficient machine that combines military, diplomatic, intelligence, economic, scientific and political operations. Its preparations are concealed, not published. Its mistakes are buried, not headlined. Its dissenters are silenced, not praised. No expenditure is questioned, no rumor is printed, no secret is revealed. It conducts the Cold War, in short, with a war-time discipline no democracy would ever hope or wish to match."
President John F. Kennedy,
Waldorf-Astoria Hotel, New York City,
April 27, 1961

TABLE OF CONTENTS

Table of Contents

Table of Contents

Table of Contents

Table of Contents

PREFACE

This is not an "exciting" book, but it *is* a necessary one. In it, we will enter a Hall of Mirrors filled with fog, for unlike all of my other books, this is not even a case of argued speculation; it is rather more like the Cliff Notes version of a very complicated story, told with footnotes. Imagine a world in chaos; there is economic displacement; the richer get richer, more idle, and more corrupt, insane with the lust for power and yet, addle-minded and scarcely able to coordinate the grand schemes by which they presume to enslave the world. There is rising resentment against them. Violence against the old order steps into the streets. Chaos reigns and there is a growing longing and yearning for a return to order, peace, and stability. Now imagine that, into this picture, steps a break-away civilization, propelled by ancient doctrines and an advanced and almost magical technology. This underground, breakaway civilization steps into the previously described chaotic condition, promising brotherhood, peace, prosperity, and to share its advanced and almost magical technologies; all of this, it says, can be ours, if we but trust its peaceful intentions and leadership, and abandon our warlike ways.

No. I am not talking about our "space brothers" here, nor about our situation at the beginning of the second decade of the twenty-first century of the third millennium, but about the Nazis, the world's first "breakaway" civilization, representing an underground stream from which it emerged, and to which, upon the conclusion of the world's biggest and bloodiest war, it returned again. In that, there lies a tale, the tale contained, in part, in this book.

You are about to embark on reading a book populated by a whole host of bizarre characters, strange concepts, and sources that are of dubious standing, from Neo-Nazis, to famous early UFO "contactees," to more reputable sources such as engineers in the loftiest reaches of the military-industrial complex, tenured historians in academia, UFOlogists, and the even stranger relationships between all of them. For the past few years now, I have written a series of books exploring exotic Nazi technology and have attempted to rationalize its achievements on the basis of terrestrial science and engineering principles that were known at the time. In pursuing this story, I have also attempted to survey in many previous books the implications of this technology for history.

In presenting the conclusions of this research throughout those books,[1] and then as a guest speaker at some conferences, I have invariably been asked by a certain type of what may best be called "UFO-ET religionist" if all this explosion of technology during the Nazi era was not best explained by them having recovered a crashed UFO and reverse-engineered it. Needless to say, after having written several books on the Nazi Bell story and attempting to rationalize its various details as best as I can, I find such questions irritating at one level and—to be honest—insulting at another, for why bother to research the subject at all if any claims for the existence of an exotic technology, Nazi or otherwise, is to be explained by such a procedure?

Yet, the questions did raise to my mind a disturbing possibility concerning the statements of the Nazi scientists made after the war, when they were pressed to account for the extraordinary development of technology during the Third Reich's thankfully short twelve-year existence, statements quickly pointed out to me by the faithful apologists of the extraterrestrial hypothesis of UFOs. One such UFO fundamentalist, indignant that I should question the Roswell extraterrestrial dogma and the self-appointed magisterium defending it, confronted me with the reverse-engineering hypothesis, i.e., that the Nazis had recovered a crashed extraterrestrial UFO and had reverse engineered it. When I responded that I simply did not accept that explanation, he then pointed out that both Drs. Von Braun and Oberth indicated that the Nazis had "had help" from "out there." This he did as if playing a high trump card that would carry the day and end any discussion of entirely terrestrial explanations for Nazi technological achievements. To my rejoinder—that I did not see how Von Braun's and Oberth's

---

[1] *Reich of the Black Sun: Nazi Secret Weapons and the Cold War Allied Legend* (Adventures Unlimited Press, 2005); *The SS Brotherhood of the Bell: NASA's Nazis, JFK, and Majic-12*(Adventures Unlimited Press, 2006); *Secrets of the Unified Field: The Philadelphia Experiment, the Nazi Bell, and the Discarded Theory* (Adventures Unlimited Press, 2007); *The Philosophers' Stone: Alchemy and the Secret Research for Exotic Matter* (Feral House, 2009); *The Nazi International: The Nazis' Postwar Plan to Control Finance, Conflict, Physics and Space* (Adventures Unlimited Press, 2008); *Roswell and the Reich: The Nazi Connection* (Adventures Unlimited Press, 2010).

rockets could possibly represent advanced reversed engineered extraterrestrial saucer technology recovered from a crashed UFO (for which there is but threadbare evidence to begin with), and to my rejoinder that why should we trust Nazis or anything they said *after* the war when we did not trust them before or during it—he had no response, other than to say "Well, then, why did they make that statement?"

The question hovered over the end of our conversation as we explored various ideas, and indeed, the question has long bothered me as well, and my suspicion has always been, that the answers of the postwar Paperclip Nazis were deliberately disingenuous—not entirely false, but not entirely true—and that they may have been made in the service of some hidden agenda, an agenda that can only be qualified as a psychological operation and disinformation campaign.

That, in part, is what *this* book is about.

Anyone familiar with the subject of UFOlogy from the immediate postwar period into the early and mid-1950s, will at once be aware of some peculiar things, not the least of which is the curious resemblance between the "spaceships" 1950s contactee George Adamski, and the alleged Nazi saucer called the "Hannebu." I have long maintained, in numerous interviews and in private conversations, that the latter is, at best, a bit of misdirection and at worst, disinformation for which there is no clear chain of evidence for the documents that purport to certify it. But the question remains: *why the resemblance in the first place?*

Other questions only heighten the dilemma.

For example, why are Adamski's "extraterrestrials" entirely human in appearance? Why are a small number of other early UFO contactee reports explicit in their claims that their occupants spoke German?[2] What is the nature of the "message" these occupants are

---

[2] For the famous Reinhold Schmidt case, see my *Nazi International*, pp. 29-43. Another case is mentioned by Dr. Frank E. Stranges in a self-published pamphlet entitled *Nazi UFO Secrets and Bases Exposed* (I.E.C. Publishing Company: 1982). While Stranges' work must be evaluated against its non-critical repetition of the whole Hannebu-Vril Nazi flying saucer legend, it is worth noting what he records of another alleged UFO contact event involving German-speaking occupants:

> "The following event took place in Reno, Nevada, during a UFO Convention, July 1966, at the Centennial Coliseum.

"This 'Amalgamated Flying Saucer Clubs of America' Convention included leading researchers: Wayne Aho, Orfeo Angelucci, Dr. Dan Fry, Carl Anderson, George Van Tassel, Gabriel Green, and myself, Dr. Frank E. Stranges.

"On Thursday morning, July 7th, the phone rang in my hotel room. THe caller (wishing to remain anonymous) asked me to meet with him before the convention convened at the Centennial Coliseum.

"When I met with him, he stated that he had followed my career for many years, and was pleased with my work. He cautioned me to look straight forward, and not to look at him directly at any time during our conversation.

"His first question was, 'Do you know anything about German Saucers?' I informed him that all I knew was what I had readin UFOP accounts from magazines and newspapers."

Here it is worth interrupting Stranges' account, to recall the fact that at *that* time, nothing was known of the Bell project, nor of the Schauberger saucers, nor much about alleged suction saucers. The alleged Hannebu-Vril field propulsion saucers were the core of the story. Resuming:

"He then requested that I brief him on the 'German UFO Crash' that took place in Helgoland, West Germany. This question was directed to the account that was written and reported at length in my book *Saucerama*.

"He seemed quite satisfied with my narrative on the Helgoland matter. Without warning he said, 'Do you know that there will be a German Saucer about one-quarter of a mile from the Reno Airport Control Tower in the morning? It has already arrived in this area!' (Gabriel Green and several others had reported sighting a UFO high above the city early that morning.)

"He further stated that the German Saucer would LAND near the Airport (sic) in the morning. Then he turned and left the auditorium.

"The following morning I took a taxi to the Reno Airport with a friend of mine. We had the driver let us off on the outskirts of the Airport. Trudging along a dusty road we approached an area that rose slightly and suddenly dropped into a shallow ravine.

"To our great surprise, there it was... a saucer-shaped craft sitting on the ground on three short legs.

"As we approached the craft, it appeared to be 50 feet in diameter, with a large outer rim. We noticed a ladder leading to a door that slid open.

"A heavily built man with a deep scar on his cheek and dark heavy eyebrows stood at the opening. There was a brief exchange of German between my companion and him. He tried to hand us some U.S. currency as he explained that he wanted us to purchase some food for him.

"He continued to speak in German and I concluded that he was very desperate. As he spoke, he continued to watch the sky like a hawk.

communicating to the contactees? And why pick *those particular* contactees to begin with? And who are their associates?

And most importantly, why—if the stories of the Nazi Bell device and other advanced aerodyne technologies emanating from the Third Reich are true—did that nation pursue *both* technologies: the obsolescent rocket technology of Von Braun's V-2s, and the exotic technologies represented by the alleged Nazi saucers and, more importantly, the Bell device?

As I concluded in my previous book *The SS Brotherhood of the Bell*, these two very disparate types of technologies seemed to resemble the outlines of two nascent space programs, one, a "secret" one employing rockets and other conventional technologies, and another, a *genuinely* secret one, one lying in truly abyssal black depths of classification, employing much more exotic technologies with, perhaps, an entirely different agenda. So, why assert that all the *public* technology, came from "ETs" after the war? We are dealing with a two track space program, and an extraterrestrial mythology. The question is: *why*?

"Suddenly, he waved us off and the door slid shut. We heard a hissing sound similar to that of equipment run by hydraulic power. My companion and I turned around and saw a police car approaching us.

"The saucer wined like a jet plane coming in for a landing. The outer rim revolved and kicked up dust, dirt and gravel. It left the ground swiftly, hover, there was an intense vibration. It then shot over toward the Control Tower and continued on until it was out of sight.

...

"This type of sighting has been reported not only by myself but many other responsible people from all walks of life in numerous parts of the world.

"During my recent visit to West Germany, I was not too surprised to meet certain gentlemen who were familiar with my Reno UFO sighting.

"They stated that before long, attempts would be make to contact South American Government officials, to establish a trade agreement that would be honored on an International level.

...

"Eyewitnesses claim to have seen Nazi Swastikas painted on the exterior of landed craft."(pp. 27-29).

The reader may make of these fantastic claims what he will. But if true(and it's a mighty big if), a question immediately occurs: why do we *not* hear of such reports in the UFOlogy community?

The answer to that question is also, in part, what this book is about.

But if there *is* such a two-track program, the question is *why?* Why go to such lengths and expenditure? What is the *agenda?*

Part of the answer is contained in the title of this work itself: *Saucers, Swastikas, Psyops: A History of a Breakaway Civilization: Hidden Aerospace Technologies and Psychological Operations.* For our purposes here, the two key words in the title are "hidden technologies" and "psychological warfare." In the main text of this work, I mean "psychological warfare" to encompass all the techniques employed by intelligence agencies (and for that matter, advertizing agencies and corporations) to *manage perceptions.* But as the psychological operations component of the title also suggests, we are here concerned with the *activities* of that breakaway civilization as well.

In the case of *perception management* our principal foci in the coming pages will be twofold, as we shall discover a certain amount of evidence that suggests that perceptions are being managed for two purposes:

1) a "narrow" purpose of the concealment of various technologies being tested in public, or being accidentally seen by the public, and to manage the *interpretation* of what it is seeing. In this case, there are two *types* of technologies possibly being seen, implying that two possible "programs" are being tested or deployed in closely-held circumstances:
   a) technologies implying advanced *physics* principles, whether those principles have to deal with aerospace, aerodynamic, or other fields of physics and technical applications;
   b) technologies implying a *biological* or even *genetic* program(which unfortunately is beyond the immediate scope of this book); and,
   c) this concealment may also be for the purpose of hiding an actual *covert war* being waged in part by means of these programs by, and against, "whomever";
2) a much broader "cultural" purpose of the implanting of certain "memes" in society at large, memes inclusive of extraterrestrials, invasions, abductions, apocalyptic

scenarios, revelations (or, to call it by its popular term within ufology, "disclosure").

Others have written about various aspects of these problems, but the only ones who have attempted to combine them into a large and coherent picture of scholarly examinations of the record are the seminal and critically important works of Richard Dolan and Dr. Jacques Vallee.

It seems to me, therefore, that a fresh approach was warranted, taking into account the possible Nazi component of this breakaway ci civilization, not so much to displace the works of these scholars and researchers, but rather, to supplement them with more information, and with the exposition of the possibilities of new connections between already well-known dots, and by delving even deeper into the mystery of why so many of these possibilities and connections seem to originate in the dark and terrible time and place of the Third Reich.

As always, my thanks to my dear friend George Ann Hughes of *The Byte Show* for endless prayers and encouragement. And above all, my thanks to my friend of nearly twenty years, Dr. Scott D. de Hart, for the inspirations of so many conversations, some of the contents of which are reflected in the observations on religion herein.

Joseph P Farrell,
From somewhere
2011

Preface

PART ONE:
SAUCERS

"In this section we penetrate an international Hall of Mirrors that will give us new insights into a process that could be called mythological engineering—the deliberate creation of social movements to serve either as opportunities for experiment, as outlets for personal fantasy, or as a vehicle for more down-to-earth political purposes...
Therefore, I have taken special pains to move step-by-step through a mass of evidence that, in my opinion, points to the deliberate exploitation of the belief in extraterrestrials by human groups."
Jacques Vallee
Revelations: Alien Contact and Human Deception
(Ballantine Books, 1991), p. 96.

1

OF CIVILIZATIONS, BREAKAWAY AND OTHERWISE:
RICHARD DOLAN AND CARROLL QUIGLEY

"Oh no, oh my God, they are going to kill us all."
Texas Governor John Connally, during the assassination of President John F. Kennedy[1]

I magine a civilization here on earth that exists covertly inside and alongside of those we know about, with access to the most advanced technologies, technologies straight off the drawing boards of Hollywood production companies and special effects artists, a civilization with nearly bottomless sources of funding, staging events for the gullible, torturing others and driving them into mental and emotional breakdown, and waging a covert war with its own members using its own "apocalyptic technologies," and masking that war behind the perfect plausible deniability: mother nature. This breakaway civilization, moreover, has its own ideology, and its own dubious "morality", as was evidenced by its first real incarnation: Nazi Germany. Unlike Nazi Germany, or for that matter, civilizations in general, it has no "core area" where it is centered; it comprises not one nation, but many; its peoples are drawn from all groups and languages, for it speaks but one language, the language of power. It is, in part, the resurrection of Atlantis, and in part, like a bad nightmare version of superhero comic books, with the villains, and not the superheroes, possessing all the superhuman powers and technologies.

If the idea of such a breakaway civilization sounds fanciful or even absurd, then hold on, because this book attempts to outline its *components, structure, and initial postwar history.*

The concept of such a breakaway civilization is intimately tied, moreover, to the subject of UFOs, for it was first propounded by the well-known and scholarly ufologist Richard M. Dolan, in his landmark documents study *UFOs and the National Security State.*

---

[1] Cited in my book *LBJ and the Conspiracy to Kill Kennedy: A Coalescence of Interests* (Adventures Unlimited Press, 2011), p. 277.

Of Civilizations, Breakaway and Otherwise

A. The Breakaway Civilization Concept of Richard M. Dolan

Dolan first mentions the idea of a breakaway civilization with implied access to advanced aerospace technologies in connection with the well-known phenomenon of UFOs "buzzing" the various defense installations of the U.S.A. and other countries, and with it, he begins to suspect, and then to dismiss, a Nazi connection:

> Is one to believe that this was a demonstration of secret Nazi power emanating from Antarctica? No tangible evidence has ever emerged to support this thesis. Or, were all the early UFOs manufactured by the Americans and Soviets? If so, who was buzzing the American military pilots and bases with such regularity? Since there is no evidence that it was the Soviets, does this mean that a secret American flying saucer program was charged with provoking an unsuspecting American defense establishment? For more than fifty years? No proponent of the man-made UFO thesis has been able to come to terms with this issue, although one could do it by postulating the existence of a completely separate breakaway civilization. [2]

Dolan is, of course, entirely correct: no evidence of any secret Nazi flying saucer research base has ever been forthcoming from Antarctica, or, for that matter, anywhere else. Indeed, as this author has observed on numerous occasions, such a base would have required enormous electrical power, if the Nazi Bell project is any measure, for that project required an entire electrical power plant to be built close to its test installations,[3] a fact ruling out Antarctica as a source for such craft. Additionally, construction of such a research center would have taxed the German Navy—or any other navy for that matter—beyond its operational and logistical resources during World War Two, and would have required a large logistical effort to support it *after* the war, resources that the postwar Nazi organization did not have.

These caveats notwithstanding, Dolan speculates further on the parameters that such a conception implies:

---

[2] Richard M. Dolan, *UFOs and the National Security State: The Cover-Up Exposed, 1973-1991* (Keyhole Publishing Company, 2009), p. 61.

[3] See my *SS Brotherhood of the Bell* (Adventures Unlimited Press, 2006), pp. 141-191, and my *Secrets of the Unified Field* (Adventures Unlimited Press, 2008), pp. 242-252, 280-281.

If we also consider the possibility of covert breakthroughs in propulsion technology, and the "off the grid" nature of the deep-black world itself, we come to the possibility that we are dealing with, in effect, a "breakaway civilization." One with *loose connections at various points to the open civilization of humanity, but, with great independence, secrecy, and a monopoly of certain key scientific secrets.* The history of the Cold War showed that separate infrastructures could, to some extent, evolve. Western politics, economy, science, and culture developed along paths that were very different from those in the Soviet Union or China. Important breakthroughs occurred in secrecy—stealth being a prominent example. Granted, the level of separation implied for a breakaway civilization would be vastly greater than any Cold War examples. In principle, however, such a development is possible, and responsible research must consider the strength of the supporting evidence and clues.[4]

Note the things that Dolan implies are clear markers of such a civilization:

1) It has "loose connections at various points" to the open civilization(s) of humanity;
2) It possesses "great independence" from them;
3) It is secret, that is to say, its structure, components, and activities are largely hidden from the open civilizations of humanity; and finally and most importantly,
4) It holds a monopoly over certain scientific concepts and the technologies that result from them.

These points form the structural outline of this book, for we will investigate the points of overlap or contact between this "breakaway civilization", its putative structure, components, or factions, and activities, and the implied scientific concepts and technologies, with a view to arguing a prima facie case that such a breakaway civilization indeed exists. Additionally, our contention will be that this civilization is fundamentally Fascist in its outlook and ideology.

For Dolan, the concept of a breakaway civilization is intimately connected to the subject of UFOs and, moreover, the persistent

---

[4] Dolan, op. cit. , pp. 565-565, emphasis added.

stories and evidence that at least *some* UFO artifacts were recovered. It is worth citing Dolan's remarks here at length:

> It looks as though the UFO secret involved more than mere knowledge of the presence of aliens of some sort. During the 1970s and 1980s, researchers made a strong case that alien artifacts were recovered and studied by the U.S. military. Conceding that such exotic technology would be vastly ahead of anything developed by human civilization, how long would it take before some clever team of (human) scientists developed major new insights that might transform existing technologies, or even create new fields of study altogether? It is not evident that all black world developments would eventually become public. On the contrary, it is entirely feasible that some breakthroughs would in turn lead to other breakthroughs, and so on in the manner very typical of science, in which successes build upon each other with ever greater speed and effectiveness.
>
> Thus, there exists the possibility of what I have come to call a "breakaway civilization." *This would entail a situation in which black world science and technology has reached a sufficient level beyond the "official" world, in which its foundational areas of knowledge are so different (understanding of non-terrestrial intelligences, spacetime, dimensionality, etc), that it can fairly be* called a separate civilization. Throughout human history, multiple civilizations often existed simultaneously, possessing disparate levels of technology and operating on vastly different assumptions of the world. There is no inherent reason to doubt that something like this can happen again—or has already happened.[5]

Dolan is clearly implying here that his "breakaway civilization" also possesses a completely different *physics*—and a technology based upon it—than the public civilization with its known physics models and technologies. So we may add to Dolan's checklist of "indicators" of such a civilization a fifth marker:

> 5) It possesses a different, and perhaps even a *radically* different physics than the standard models of "public consumption" physics, and thus, possesses different principles of engineering and technology.

---

[5] Dolan, op. cit., p. 580, emphasis added.

1. The 1988 Affair of the "Alien Reproduction Vehicle"

Dolan then mentions the case of the so-called "Alien Reproduction Vehicle," a vehicle that, according to whistleblower testimony, was back-engineered from off-the-shelf terrestrial components to emulate the performance of an alleged captured alien flying saucer:

> Indeed, the 1988 demonstration of the "Alien Reproduction Vehicle" (ARV) points to the existence of such a major breakthrough. Supporting this even further is the complete absence, even two decades later, of anything like the ARV in the arsenal of the U.S. military. The object was reportedly described as having gone into space on many occasions, and even to have explored the solar system. The person who carefully observed it and described it to friends noted that it looked as though it had been in service for a long time. This would indicate that the ARV had nothing at all to do with U.S. military mandates, at least not in any conventional geopolitical sense. Just as clearly, its mission would logically have something to do with the presence of non-human intelligences.[6]

The story of the "Alien Reproduction Vehicle" or ARV was first reported by Mark McCandlish in 1988.

According to McCandlish, on November 12, 1988 a major open house and air show was held at Norton Air Force Base in California, while at nearby Palmdale, at Lockheed's celebrated "Skunk Works" facility, three of the ARVs were on display. McCandlish, who had worked in aerospace as a conceptual artist, holding several security clearances, planned to attend but was unable to do so. The story and description of the ARVs was related to him by his friend Brad Sorenson, who attended the show and saw the ARVs in Lockheed's Skunk Works hanger because he attended the show with a high ranking Defense department personage, probably a secretary or under-secretary. Sorensen gained access by accompanying this personage.[7]

McCandlish was subsequently able to verify the description of these ARVs by hearing similar and independent descriptions of a

---

[6] Dolan, op. cit., pp. 580-581.
[7] Ibid., pp. 457-458.

vehicle from yet another contact within the aerospace world, Kent Sellen.[8] Sorensen, who had seen three such vehicles hovering above the ground, also heard a general—the rank and service branch are unclear but it is assumed an U.S. Air Force general—speaking to a group of people. According to what Sorensen told McCandlish, the general

> (Referred) to the vehicles as "Alien Reproduction Vehicles," also as the Flux Liner (because they used high voltage electricity). He mentioned several fascinating features of the ARV. One was that it could perform at "light speed or better." Another was that it ran on energy obtained through the vacuum—presumably the zero point energy field, better described scientifically as the "quantum zero point fluctuations of the vacuum." It had extraordinary acceleration and maneuverability, able to move from a ground-level hovering position to 80,000 feet within 2.5 seconds. It was also apparently stated that the ARV had by this time already performed a general reconnaissance of all the planets of the solar system in a search for life, and that no life was found. Sorensen noted that the ARV looked "ancient" and as though it had been used extensively.[9]

Dolan notes that if this story is true, then it has certain implications for the hypothesis of a breakaway civilization, for "it would mean that 'black world' science had achieved a substantial, revolutionary breakthrough on this matter well ahead of 'white world' science."[10]

Dolan is correct, but the story also carries further implications. First, the science behind the alleged craft—use of the vacuum flux or zero point energy as an energy source—is *entirely terrestrial*, in other words, it is not the *concepts* that are advanced, since the idea of the zero point energy stems from work of the physicists in the 1930s. As I have also pointed out elsewhere, this conception was made the central area of inquiry for a postwar Nazi fusion research project in Argentina in the 1950s, headed by the scientist Dr. Ronald Richter.[11] Thus, we may be dealing, even with the story itself, with a layer of disinformation or obfuscation, for by that time, the word "alien" had come to mean, within the wider culture,

---

[8] Dolan, op. cit., p. 460.

[9] Ibid., p. 459.

[10] Ibid., p. 460.

[11] See my *The Nazi International* (Adventures Unlimited Press, 2008), pp. 314-343.

"extraterrestrial," with its original meaning, "foreign," being left far behind.

More importantly, it is to be noted that there are two things that would indicate, as Dolan rightly points out, that if the story is true then two breakthroughs have occurred: (1) the "relativistic speed limit" of the velocity of light has been overcome, and (2) the craft, if it were manned (as McCandlish's drawings clearly show), then it would have had to generate its own gravitational field, otherwise the occupants would have been crushed to death by the severe accelerations reported for it. The story, in other words, is *consistent* with the markers of a breakaway civilization that Dolan has laid down, *whether or not the ultimate source of the technology was human or extraterrestrial.*

Finally, it is to be noted that the technology in question was employed for a *hidden purpose*, namely, the covert manned exploration of space. If so, this would rationalize rather well why the U.S.A. has recently sworn off any further manned exploration of space by means of conventional rockets; if elements within the U.S.A. did possess such technology, rockets are as obsolete as the Pony Express. We thus have two more markers of a "breakaway civilization," and these, I think, are Dolan's real points in mentioning the story:

6) A breakaway civilization, having monopolies over advanced technologies and theoretical science, will likely employ that technology in covert activities;

7) It will seek to *cloak* those activities, if discovered, behind stories and fabrications of a different origin for the technologies, lest the knowledge become accessible publicly, and end the monopoly of the breakaway civilization.

Cutaway of the Alleged Alien Reproduction Vehicle Based on McCandlish's Drawings. Note the Chairs in the Top

2. How A Breakaway Civilization Might Evolve

By pinpointing the world of "black projects," Dolan is putting his finger on a unique feature of Western civilization that would allow such a breakaway civilization to arise with comparative ease, as compared to a similar development in a nation comprising a non-Western civilization. That feature is the fact that most of the western world's "black projects" occur in nations with (1) a broad revenue-gathering tax base, (2) a government military, as distinguished from private or mercenary militaries, and most importantly (3) corporations contracted to do the actual research and development of the technologies. It is this public-private *mixture* that is a crucial component of the possibility of a breakaway civilization as we shall see.

There is, however, another component, equally crucial to the development of a breakaway civilization: *compartmentalization*. Black projects are so tightly organized and compartmentalized that a low level technician, working on a particular piece or component of a project, may not even know what that component is ultimately for, nor what others involved in the project are working on. Only senior level managers will know the larger picture. This fact allows the possibility that *any given project can be infiltrated or co-opted from an outside source, infiltrating personnel into the various levels of the project.*

The private corporation-public military mixture characteristic is thus the fertile ground on which a breakaway civilization can grow, and the most obvious potential candidates for the core of the breakaway civilization hypothesis would be the very corporations engaged in the research themselves, and behind them, the holders of public debt securities from a given nation, if those holders be corporations or banks of sufficient size.

When these two facts are considered *historically*, the best two candidates for the core group or groups exercising covert control over such projects, their technologies, and the military personnel engaged in using them, are the corporate and banking centers of High Capital in the West, and the Nazis, and indeed, as we shall discover in later chapters of this book, there are abundant connections between the two and black projects, and abundant indications that they employ these in a variety of black operations roles, among them, psychological operations.

B. Dr. Carroll Quigley on the Markers of Civilizations

However, in order to sharpen our analysis of the markers and indicators of the breakaway civilization, it will be helpful to have a standard historiographical approach to the subject, and for this, no one serves our purposes better than the late, and famous, Georgetown Professor, Dr. Carroll Quigley. Quigley is well-known both to conventional historians and to researchers of "conspiracy theory," for Quigley literally wrote the "bibles" of modern conspiracy theory in two works that outlined the vast, and largely hidden and secretive maneuverings of international banking and corporations during the twentieth century to achieve a state of total control over the world and over the masses of humanity. These two works are *The Anglo-American Establishment*, and a massive—and unfootnoted—academic tome of twentieth century history, *Tragedy and Hope: A History of the World in Our Time.* In the latter book, Quigley even admits that he was able to expose details of these secret maneuverings because he had been given access to the secret papers and files of the very families, banks, and corporations

9

involved. Quigley was even mentioned by former President Bill Clinton in his nomination acceptance speech at the 1992 Democratic Party National Convention as having been one of the key figures who helped shape his world view, a mention that, at the time, gave conspiracy theorists much grist for speculation.

But Quigley was also the author of numerous peer-reviewed academic papers, and of yet a third book, little appreciated by conspiracy theory researchers, but which we shall rely upon heavily here. After all, if Quigley wrote the "bibles" for conspiracy theory in the above two works, then what he has to say about the markers of civilizations and of their historical analysis ought to be of importance for analysis of the possibilities of the idea of a breakaway civilization. That book is *The Evolution of Civilizations: An Introduction to Historical Analysis.*

Georgetown History Professor Dr. Carroll Quigley (1910-1977)

It was Quigley's conviction "that civilization is an object that can be studied in a scientific way just as a quartz crystal can be studied."[12] To this end, Quigley devised a number of criteria by which to analyze civilizations, and to categorize them.

1. The Six Areas of Potential and the Four Types of Groups

According to Quigley, human potential organizes itself within civilizations into six levels or categories of activity:

1) military,
2) political,
3) economic,
4) social,
5) religious, or as we shall see in this book, ideological,
6) intellectual.[13]

As can be seen from this list, there are four areas already implicated in the notion of a breakaway civilization as Dolan outlined it; these are the military, political, economic, and intellectual categories of organizing human potential.

These considerations lead Quigley to an analysis of the types of groups that form around these areas of potential. There are four types of groups:

1) social groups,
2) societies,
3) producing societies, and
4) civilizations.[14]

With respect to the first of these categories, social groups, Quigley notes that what distinguishes them from societies and civilizations proper is the fact that members of groups can determine "who is in it and who is not."[15]

Dolan has already hinted at this unique feature of his breakaway civilization idea, but it is worth emphasizing it here, for it is a feature that sharply distinguishes it from civilizations in the normal sense, for by the very nature of the case, such a breakaway civilization's members have to go through the normal security recruitment and

---

[12] Carroll Quigley, *The Evolution of Civilizations: An Introduction to Historical Analysis* (Liberty Fund, 1979), p. 85.

[13] Quigley, op. cit., p. 54,

[14] Ibid., p. 65.

[15] Ibid., p. 71.

vetting procedures, and to a certain extent, are *chosen* for their carefully defined roles.

This is a second distinguishing feature of the notion of a breakaway civilization, for in the case of an ordinary civilization, one is dealing with a relatively large population, whose interactions can only be statistically correlated.[16] In the case of a breakaway civilization, we are dealing with a much smaller "population", whose members are all selected, and who perform clearly defined roles, some of which we will be exploring in this book.

In other words, in Dolan's conception, we are dealing with a very different conception of a civilization, for in it, the notion of

---

[16] Quigley, op. cit., p. 67. The resemblance of aggregate social behavior of individual humans and the statistical modeling of quantum mechanics is something Quigley points out. It is worth mentioning here that Quigley, with his close association with and knowledge of international banking, also skirts close to the connection between closed systems of finance and closed systems of science and physics. While this is not yet the place to explore this in more detail, it is worth noting what Quigley says in this respect with regard to the Greek rationalists, i.e., those in the broad Pythagorean, Platonic, Hermetic tradition: "At that time the chief enemies of science were the rationalists. These men, with all the prestige of Pythagoras and Plato behind them, argued that the human senses are not dependable but are erroneous and misleading and that, accordingly, the truth must be sought without using the senses and observation, and by the use of reason and logic alone. The scientists of the day were trying to reduce the complexity of innumerable observed qualities to the simplicity of quantitative differences of a few fundamental elements." (p. 41). Accordingly, Quigley ascribes the Aristotelian philosophical outlook to be the broad basis behind modern science.

This view, in fact, was challenged—and severely so—by scholars of his day, among them Frances Yates, who demonstrated that the broad Platonic-Neoplatonic, and Hermetic tradition had far more to do with the rise of modern physics and mathematics in the hands Copernicus, Newton, and Leibniz, than most histories of science would care to admit. While this is not the place to explore the relationship between Aristotelianism and banking, it should be pointed out that the fundamental physics proposition of Platonism and Hermeticism is of open systems, and that of Aristotelianism, closed systems. It is also worth mentioning that the bankers of Venice, who promoted Aristotelianism, manipulated the trial and execution of the 16th century's premier Hermeticist, Giordano Bruno. In that, as they say, there lies a tale...

civilization is radically transformed. Just how radical this is may be glimpsed by Quigley's other analytical categories and markers.

2. Parasitic and Producing Societies, and the Breakaway Civilization

Quigley notes that there are three more essential markers of a civilization, and these, for our purposes, are quite important:

> The pattern of change in civilizations presented here consists of seven stages resulting from the fact that each civilization has an instrument of expansion that becomes an institution. The civilization rises while this organization is an instrument and declines as this organization becomes an institution.
>
> By the term "instrument of expansion" we mean that the society must be organized in such fashion that three things are true: (1) the society must be organized in such a way that it has an *incentive to invent* new ways of doing things; (2) it must be organized in such a way that somewhere in the society there is *accumulation of surplus*—that is, some persons in the society control more wealth than they wish to consume immediately; and (3) it must be organized in such a way that the surplus which is being accumulated is being used to pay for or to utilize the new inventions. All three of these things are essential to any civilization. Taken together, we call them an instrument of expansion....
>
> The three essential parts of an instrument of expansion are incentive to invent, accumulation of surplus, and application of this surplus to the new inventions.[17]

There are a number of crucial points here and it is best to summarize them, for these will become the areas of our investigation in subsequent chapters.

While it may seem that Quigley has presented but three characteristics of a civilization, he has in fact, presented four. There are the three obvious ones:

1) A civilization must be so organized as to invent new things or techniques of doing things. In terms of our analysis of a breakaway civilization, the obvious signal of this application

---

[17] Quigley, *The Evolution of Civilizations*, p. 132, emphasis in the original.

will be the invention of *new aerospace technologies* that are, by their very nature, the products of secret research projects;

2) A civilization must possess a *means of the accumulation of surplus*. For our purposes, this will mean that we must look for mechanisms or, as Quigley calls them, "instruments" of funding for such inventions that are relatively stable and secure, but, by the nature of the case, that are also relatively secret. In this case, we shall have to look for clues as to when and how such funding mechanisms or instruments arose, and then trace them historically as the breakaway civilization evolved and changed to meet new circumstances. Quigley again provides the clue of what to look for, for it is necessary to the accumulation of surplus that there be means of capital accumulation and investment; accordingly, we shall look for indications of covert capital accumulation and investment.[18] For our purposes, it is also worth noting that Quigley also explicitly states that the surplus-creating instrument or mechanisms do not "have to be an economic organization. In fact, (they) can be any kind of organization, military, political, social, religious, and so forth."[19] Obviously, our search will concentrate on the military instrument of surplus accumulation;

3) Any civilization, including a breakaway civilization, must also be organized so that accumulated surplus is used to pay for, or utilize, the invented technologies or techniques.

These are the obvious implications of Quigley's hallmarks of a civilization, but there is one other, implicit at the beginning of the previous quotation:

4) Any civilization *evolves*, that is, it changes to meet new circumstances, and it also changes as instruments evolve into institutions, which, according to Quigley, signals the beginning of the inevitable decline of that civilization. As we shall discover, Quigley notes that this evolutionary process of civilizations goes through seven distinct stages.

---

[18] Quigley, *The Evolution of Civilizations*, p. 137.
[19] Ibid, p. 138.

It is thus necessary to take a closer look at the distinction between "instruments" and "institutions" in Quigley's thought.

3. Instruments and Institutions, and Parasitic vs. Producing Societies

There are certain distinguishing features between instruments and institutions in Quigley's thought:

> An instrument is a social organization that is fulfilling effectively the purpose for which it arose. An institution is an instrument that has taken on activities and purposes of its own, separate from and different form the purposes for which it was intended. As a consequence, an institution achieves its original purposes with decreasing effectiveness.[20]

In other words, instruments become institutions when "the social conditions surrounding any such organization change in the course of time,"[21] leading such institutions to take on a bureaucratic inertia, a life of their own, whereby they seek to perpetuate their own power. They have become, Quigley notes, "vested interests."[22]

As this occurs, there occurs what Quigley calls the "tension of development," from which one of three outcomes is possible:

> ...reform, circumvention, or reaction. In the first case, reform, the institution is reorganized and its methods of action changed so that it becomes, relatively speaking, more of an instrument and achieves its purpose with sufficient facility to reduce tension to a socially acceptable level. In the second case, circumvention, the institution is left with more of its privileges and vested interests intact, but its duties are taken away and assigned to a new instrument within the same society. ...
>
> In the third possible outcome, reaction, the vested interests triumph in the struggle, and the people of that society are doomed to ineffective achievement of their needs on that level for an indefinite period.[23]

---

[20] Quigley, *The Evolution of Civilizations*, pp. 101-102.
[21] Ibid., pp. 102-103.
[22] Ibid., p. 103.
[23] Ibid., pp. 116-117.

As we shall see in the coming pages, the breakaway civilization has displayed remarkable dexterity in reforming itself to changing circumstances, creating ever new instruments for the performance of surplus accumulation and invention.

In his analysis of civilizations and societies, Quigley makes yet another important distinction for our purposes, namely, the distinction between parasitic and producing societies:

> The former are those which live from hunting, fishing, or merely gleaning. By their economic activities they do not increase, but rather decrease, the amount of wealth in the world. The second kind of societies, producing societies, live by agricultural and pastoral activities. By these activities they seek to increase the amount of wealth in the world.[24]

These are crucial to our analysis of the breakaway civilization, for as will be seen in coming chapters, the methods of its surplus accumulation are for the most part parasitic in nature *with respect to other societies and civilizations in the world, but productive with respect to itself.* It thus exists as a kind of *tertium quid* or "mixed" civilization.

4. The Five Dimensions of Civilization and the Sixfold Division of Culture

For Quigley, there are five "dimensions" of civilization, and here, again, we take careful note of these, for one of them bears direct implications for our analysis of the breakaway civilization and its history. Any civilization exists in the obvious three dimensions of space and a fourth dimension of time through which it evolves. But the fifth dimension is that of historical analysis and abstraction itself.

> All of these are easy to understand except the last. Let us look, for a moment, at this fifth dimension of abstraction. It is clear that every culture consists of concrete objects like clothes and weapons, of less tangible objects like emotions and feelings, and of quite abstract things like ideas. These form the dimension of abstraction.[25]

---

[24] Quigley, *The Evolution of Civilizations*, p. 76.
[25] Ibiid., p. 99.

This is quite the crucial point for our purposes, for Quigley was deeply concerned during his career to investigate the sociological consequences, the *ideological* consequences, of the changes indueced within a civilization by its *weaponry.*[26] The implications for our analysis are again obvious, for the types of technologies we shall be discussing also impose a certain worldview on *how best to utilize them to advance the causes and agendas of the breakaway civilization.* Indeed, as we shall discover, this became early on a major theme and concern as the breakaway civilization sought to distinguish itself from the very host civilization sustaining it.

In this respect, it is worth noting that for Quigley, there are six primary areas in which a civilization's culture manifest themselves:

1) the intellectual, or as we shall prefer to call it, the ideological, or the *world view*, that such a civilization has of itself;
2) religious; while this may seem the farthest removed area from the concerns of a breakaway civilization concerning itself with the invention of advanced technologies and the accumulation of surplus to sustain this invention, as we shall discover in the next chapter, the appearance or manifestation of advanced technologies was very early, and deliberately, coupled with an almost quasi-religious character in the experience and thought of one of the earliest, and most famous (or infamous) UFO contactees;
3) social, that is to say, the *organization* of the instruments of such accumulation and invention;
4) economic, or, for our purposes, the means of sustaining the financial requirements of the breakaway civilization;
5) political; and,
6) military.[27]

As we shall discover in the ensuing pages, the breakaway civilization blends or mixes the last two components of culture, producing a kind of society politically organized around a "chain of command" structure typical of military organizations.

---

[26] Quigley, *The Evolution of Civilizations*, p. 424.
[27] Ibid., p. 100.

5. The Seven Stages of Civilizations and "Core" vs "Peripheral" Societies

The most obvious feature of civilizations is that they evolve and change to meet changing circumstances, and here our concern will be to note how the parasitic breakaway civilization began under certain peculiar circumstances, arising in the Third Reich from a constellation of impulses, and then transplanted and changed itself to meet the new circumstances of a lost war and a new host. It is at this juncture that we will note the rise of *factions* within that breakaway civilization. These factions, we will discover, were present prior to the rise of that civilization in Nazi Germany, and re-emerged after the war, when the breakaway civilization reestablished contact with its separated components. With this in mind, we note that Quigley speaks of seven stages in the evolution of any civilization:

1) Mixture
2) Gestation
3) Expansion
4) Age of Conflict
5) Universal Empire
6) Decay
7) Invasion[28]

We may, for our purposes, overlay two distinct "periods" in the evolution of the breakaway civilization over Quigley's stages to clarify the history that will emerge in this book:

1) **Mixture:** The conditions of the breakaway civilization's rise in Nazi Germany are created by a mixture of components of the host civilization, i.e., Western civilization in general, and the unique ideology of Nazism;
2) **Gestation:** The elements of the breakaway civilization begin to emerge in the Third Reich with the creation of parallel and nested bureaucracies precisely concerned with
   a) the invention of new technologies in secret; and
   b) the means of the accumulation of surplus to sustain their development and utilization;

---

[28] Quigley, *The Evolution of Civilizations*, p. 146.

3) ***Expansion:*** At this stage, the breakaway civilization becomes a "state within a state", and is of exclusive Nazi character as the Reich itself expands;

4) ***Age of Conflict***: During this and the next stage, the breakaway civilization takes on new independence from the Nazi state, while remaining reliant upon it as its host;

5) ***Universal Empire***

6) ***Decay***: as the war will clearly be lost by the host, i.e., by the Third Reich, the breakaway civilization, which by now has transformed its instruments into institutions connected with the Third Reich, undergoes a process of self-reformation, transforming those institutions back into instruments for the express purpose of surviving the war and continuing its existence under changed circumstances;

7) ***Invasion:*** When the war ends, the breakaway civilization transplants itself into new hosts and redefines itself accordingly, regaining contact with the factions that originally helped create the conditions for its rise in the first place.

It is worth noting that Quigley states that during the fourth stage, the age of conflict, a growth of irrational belief systems and behaviors arises as a sign of that stage.[29] In this case, however, the irrationality is Fascism itself, and this ideological component becomes a stable feature of the breakaway civilization in all its stages, as we shall discover.

There is one final crucial element of civilizations in Quigley's thought, and it will become a core component of our analysis here. For Quigley, in every civilization, from Mesopotamian to modern Western civilizations, there are "core" and "peripheral" societies or states. We may illustrate what he means by pointing out that, in his analysis, the "core" societies or states of Western civilization emerged in France and England(and subsequently the United States), while peripheral states were societies or nations such as Germany.

Thus, "core" and "peripheral" states or societies are denoted by their geographical proximity to each other, by their location and *physical conditions of existence.* But in the case of a "breakaway"

---

[29] Quigley, *The Evolution of Civilizations*, p. 152.

civilization, we are not so lucky, for in the first instance, we are dealing with a society that is parasitic, i.e., living off a host, and in the second instance, its location, by its very nature, exists in several centers, many of these secret, or at least inaccessible to the general public of its host. How then does one define its "core" and "peripheral" areas? The answer, in the coming pages, is surprising, and disconcerting.

C. Conclusions and Implications

We are now in a position to summarize what we are looking for. By the nature of the case, we are looking for
1) A civilization existing within a host civilization,
2) With means of surplus accumulation that are a mixture of known and more covert sources, for the express purpose of,
3) the invention of advanced technologies which it intends to utilize in some fashion as yet to be ascertained,
4) with an ideology or world view of an almost quasi-religious character, an ideology in turn intimately coupled with the advanced technologies at its disposal, and with a basic Fascist world view of the mixture of corporations and governments; and,
5) a "core" and "peripheral" locations; and finally,
6) since much of this technology is of a military nature or of obvious military application, we may also look for the full panoply of military operations in connection with it, i.e., reconnaissance, psychological warfare, and so on.

Our entry into the exploration and analysis of the history of the breakaway civilization will be via the last of these components, for as already noted, there is an intimate and deep relationship between the military technologies of a civilization, and the world view that those technologies engender. We will enter the hall of mirrors of the breakaway civilization via its psychological operations performed in conjunction with those technologies, and via the suggestions of their first manifestation in the most famous—or, depending on one's lights—infamous of all UFO contactees.

George Adamski.

2

THE ADAMSKI ANOMALIES:
THE BEGINNINGS OF MURKY POSSIBILITIES

"Adamski was a self-styled friend of the Venusians; he published two books with obviously faked photographs in support of his claims."
Jacques Vallee[1]

"Nearly all discussions of the UFO contactees start with George Adamski, the most accomplished of the lot."
Greg Bishop[2]

By his own admission,[3] George Adamski was just about the *last* person anyone would expect extraterrestrials to make contact with, much less select as their ambassador to carry their "message" to humanity. Nor was this the only, nor the strangest, anomaly about the man's whole saga of alleged extraterrestrial contact, for the Adamski story fits little of the modern-day stereotype of extraterrestrial contact; there are no bug-eyed gray aliens, no reptilians, no gruesome kidnappings in the middle of the night with people being magically floated from their beds by beams of light into saucers to be subjected to a gruesome, bizarre, and downright sexual form of medical rape.

Instead, Adamski's "aliens" show up at the oddest times—like broad daylight[4]—and in the weirdest places—like restaurants and motel lobbies[5]—and they are entirely human in appearance, one is tempted to say "Nordic" or even Teutonic,[6]

---

[1] Jacques Vallee, *Revelations: Alien Contact and Human Deception* (Ballantine Books, 1991), p. 34.

[2] Greg Bishop, "My Bias Filter is Better than Your Bias Filter: or, Why I Like Contactees Better Than Abductees," *Wake Up Down There!: The **Excluded Middle** Collection*, ed. Gregory Bishop (Adventures Unlimited Press, 2000), p. 24.

[3] George Adamski, *Inside the Spaceships* (George Adamski Foundation, 1955), p. 78

[4] George Adamski, *Flying Saucers Have Landed* (George Adamski Foundation, 1995), pp. 215-231, 30-31.

[5] Adamski, *Inside the Spaceships*, p. 93.

[6] Ibid., p. 94.

and they communicate both telepathically[7] and by word of mouth.[8] And that's not all: they invite him aboard their distinctively "retro"-looking spaceships, there to have cordial discussions about theological matters[9] (that could have been looked up in any standard encyclopedia of the day) around conference tables[10] over what may best be described as a kind of informal high tea,[11] at which Adamski is tempted to smoke cigarettes, suggesting that in the high civilization of the extraterrestrial, anti-smoking fascism has not become the fad it is in the modern "free" West(perhaps they know something about tobacco our government isn't telling us).[12] To make matters very much worse, said telepathically-endowed humans travel in their decidedly retro-looking 1950s flying saucers and cigars, not so much from distant star systems, but from our celestial neighbors right here in our own solar system, such paradisial places as Venus,[13] Mars,[14] and Saturn,[15] all parts of a great Roddenberry-esque planetary Federation[16] enjoying the fruits of harmony, advanced technology, and enlightenment as they "boldly go where no man has gone before".

So *nutty* is all this nonsense—from any *number* of perspectives, not the least of which is planetary geology[17]—that few even in the UFOlogy community, suffused as it is by much more serious and plausible stories of middle-of-the-night

---

[7] Adamski, *Inside the Spaceships*, p. 96.

[8] Ibid., pp. 94-95.

[9] Ibid., pp. 136-159.

[10] Ibid., p. 135 ff.

[11] Ibid., p. 134.

[12] If so, I should be glad of any extraterrestrial "persuasion" to the nutty state governments of the USA, and also a recommendation for a good tobacconist, preferably one on this planet.

[13] Adamaski, *Inside the Spaceships*, p. 100.

[14] Ibid.

[15]. Ibid.

[16] Ibid., p. 121.

[17] Even Adamski admitted the bizarre nature of his claims to have meet humans from Venus, Mars, and Saturn conflicted with what was known of the geographies and climates of those planets at that time, See *Inside the Spaceships*, p. 96.

kidnappings and medical examinations by reptiles and little gray bug-eyed robots, take Adamski seriously at all anymore.

George Adamski

Worse still (yes, it *does* get worse!), Adamski bolstered all these fantastic tales by claiming that the military recruited him to photograph the saucers (which, we learn later, were from Venus, at least, in their initial contacts).

This is where the devil, as they say, is in the details.

A. Contact with Whom?

Adamski wrote two books recounting his alleged contact with extraterrestrials: *Flying Saucers Have Landed*, a prosaic account of his initial contact, and *Inside the Spaceships*, a wild Chopinesque fantasia about his subsequent visits to a "mothership" parked in Earth orbit. Though most now discount these wild fantasias, a closer look at them reveals many of the "memes" that have become a constant in the lore and mythology of contemporary UFOlogy, so a closer review is in order, for in that examination, as we shall see, are the beginnings of murky possibilities.

He begins his *Flying Saucers Have Landed* with the self-observation that he is a "philosopher, student, teacher," and "saucer researcher."[18] From there, he quickly moves to inform

---

[18] Adamski, *Flying Saucers Have Landed*, p. 9.

the reader that he owns two telescopes, a 15" reflector, and a more portable 6" reflector for which a camera is adapted to fit over the eyepiece.[19]

From here, the story moves quickly to a radio report of a cigar-shaped UFO over San Diego in 1946, a sighting discussed weeks later in Adamski's cafe on a Sunday:

> During this discussion six military officers who were sitting at another table listened intently to all points brought up. Then one of them spoke up and said, 'It is not as fantastic as it sounds. We know something about this.' I immediately asked what knowledge they had, but they would not reveal it. Yet they assured us all that the ship we had seen and were discussing was not of this world.[20]

Before pausing to analyze this encounter and what it might portend, it is worth noting that Adamski claims that he and members of his household had also seen a similar UFO at the time in question, and that Adamski described it as "a large black object, similar in shape to a dirigible, and apparently motionless."[21] The object appeared after an intense rain shower. Initially, we are told, Adamski thought nothing of it, but rather wrote it off to some sort of advanced though classified human technology: "I figured that during the war some new types of aircraft had been developed and that this was one of them."[22] As Adamski and his household were watching this strange "dirigible," the craft "pointed its nose upward and quickly shot up into space, *leaving a fiery trail behind it which remained visible for a good five minutes.*"[23]

Taking Adamski at his word here—and we shall see later that there are abundant reasons to question his assertions—then what we have is an unusual constellation of relationships:

1) Adamski sees a dirigible-shaped aircraft or UFO of some sort which *leaves a contrail* as it zips out of sight. As we

---

[19] Ibid.
[20] Adamski, *Flying Saucers Have Landed,,* p. 11.
[21] Ibid., p. 10.
[22] Ibid.
[23] Ibid., emphasis added.

have noted elsewhere, this signature was specifically mentioned in two US Air Force intelligence documents in the wake of the Roswell incident.[24] Adamski *himself* drew the logical conclusion that this, far from representing some sort of extra-terrestrial technology, represented some terrestrial one. Indeed, dirigibles *do* have the ability to seem to "hover," though they do not zip away leaving contrails. At best then, there is nothing about the sighting whose technological details compel to the conclusion that the origins of the craft were extraterrestrial;

2) The San Diego sighting of a similar craft was subsequently being discussed in Adamski's cafe, with "six military officers" in attendance. It is from these officers that Adamski learns the "fact" that the technology seen in San Diego—and by implication the one *he* had seen—was extraterrestrial, though the officers offer no substantiation for this assertion;

3) Thus, if one accepts Adamski at his word, then the "meme" of an extraterrestrial origin of this strange technology *did not originate from Adamski himself, but from the U.S. military.*

The significance of this "fact" cannot be pondered too long, for as I point out in *Roswell and the Reich*, a similar tactic of deflection of technological details to extraterrestrial origins for them might have been in play during the Roswell affair.[25]

Let it also be carefully noted that Adamski's first "contact" in connection with UFOs was not with "extraterrestrials", but with the military. One gets the sense, here, that the military might indeed have been doing "damage control" in the wake of the San

---

[24] Q.v. my *Roswell and the Reich: The Nazi Connection*, pp. 373-421.

[25] If the military was cloaking the possibly terrestrial origins for the technology displayed in these sightings, then the origins would have to be either from within an experimental American project, in which case the motivation would be simply to protect the technology concerned, or it would have to be from outside of America, in which case the motivation would be both technical *and political*, to deflect attention away from the potentially explosive political implications of the origins of such a technology outside of America, but from somewhere else on Earth.

Diego sighting, protecting an experimental technology with a cover story of its extraterrestrial origins, much like it would later do with the notorious Paul Bennewitz affair.[26]

In any case, Adamski's reaction to this revelation was somewhat predictable: "Naturally this made me take more stock in the situation,"[27] he writes, and it is from this moment that he began to try to use his telescopes to photograph UFOs. In other words, had the contact with the military *not* happened, he might never have pursued the course he subsequently did.

As if to reinforce this interest, in 1949, Adamski was—again by his own admission—paid a visit:

> Then late in 1949 four men came into the cafe at Palomar Gardens. Two of them had been in before and we had talked a little about the flying saucers. This day it was around noon, and raining—really pouring. They ordered some lunch and we began talking about flying saucers again. One of these men was Mr J.P. Maxfield, and another was his partner, Mr G.L. Bloom, both of the Point Loma Navy Electronics Laboratory near San Diego. The other two men were from a similar setup in Pasadena. One was in officer's uniform.
>
> They asked me if I would co-operate with them in trying to get photographs of strange craft moving through space, since I had smaller instruments than those at the big Observatory. I could maneuvre mine more easily than those on top could be moved, especially my 6-incher, which was without a dome. I could point it much as pointing a gun at ducks.
>
> ....
>
> I asked them then where I should look to be most likely to see the strange objects which they were asking me to try to photograph. We discussed the pros and cons of the possibility of bases being on the moon for inter-planetary craft. And finally the moon was decided upon as a good spot for careful observation.[28]

---

[26] For the best discussion of the Bennewitz affair, see Greg Bishop, *Project Beta: The Story of Paul Bennewitz, National Security, and the Creation of a Modern UFO Myth* (New York: Paraview Pocket Books, 2005). See especially pp. 154-198.

[27] Adamski, *Flying Saucers Have Landed*, p. 11.

[28] Adamski, *Flying Saucers Have Landed*, pp. 12-13.

One has difficulty believing the military would need an amateur astronomer and photographer to assist it with spotting UFOs on the Moon with 6" and 15" telescopes, much less "discuss" where Adamski should be pointing his telescopes to photograph the elusive craft, *unless it was trying to manipulate him.*

This initial contact was then followed by sightings of UFOs over Mexico City—phenomena continuing to this day—which, according to Adamksi, were reported on KMPC news of Beverly Hills. On this occasion, Mr. Bloom returned to Adamski's cafe and listened to the radio reports with Adamski. When the reporting was finished, Bloom informed Adamski that "they" did not have the "full story," creating the distinct impression that Mr. Bloom— of the Navy electronics laboratory in Point Loma—did.[29] At this juncture, Adamski reports that he handed Bloom a couple of UFO photographs he had taken through his telescope. Word of this somehow leaked to local media, and Adamski had to confirm that he had turned over photographs to the US military, which in turn, of course, denied that they showed "spaceships."[30] Contacted about the Adamski photos, the US Air Force denied ever having received them.[31]

Perhaps this was a bit of obfuscation, perhaps not, for Adamski had originally turned his photos over to Mr. Bloom, and as far as Adamski knew, Bloom worked not for the Air Force, but for the US Navy. There are three possibilities here: either Adamski's photos were simply lost in the inter-service rivalry and bureaucratic shuffle between the two services, or perhaps Adamski simply made up the story about meeting the men in the first place, or perhaps Adamski was being manipulated to believe his own photos and role had a greater significance than was really the case. In other words, perhaps Adamski was a component and unwitting player in a psychological operation. As we proceed, the evidence for the latter view will slowly accumulate.

[29] Ibid., p. 14.
[30] Adamski, *Flying Saucers Have Landed,,* p. 15.
[31] Ibid.

Indeed, Adamski himself obliquely suggests that the military's role in his photographs may have been part of some secret agenda, for remarking on his picture-taking, he then states that "I sent a set of them to the Wright Patterson Air Force Base. In the interest of national security they would have stopped me, if I was photographing our own secret craft. They never have."[32]

Perhaps they would have, perhaps they would not. Granting only for the sake of argument that Adamski's photos were genuine, the military could have easily managed the *perceptions* of what he was photographing by attributing extraterrestrial origins to them, and cloaking whatever technology might have been seen and photographed with a context that said "this is so far beyond terrestrial science that there is no need to investigate further."

But as is now readily granted in almost all ufological circles, the Adamski photographs were most likely simple hoaxes. In that case, the possibility arises that Adamski may have been helped in their concoction. But if so, then once again the question is, *why*?

Part of the answer to this might be indicated by two curious statements that Adamski makes in *Flying Saucers Have Landed*, statements that hover over its otherwise goofy landscape with a sinister significance, a significance that in the total context of his book is neither prepared nor resolved. *There is nothing leading up to these statements, and there is nothing, really, leading away from them. They are just there.*

The first of these is a statement that will become a familiar "indirect" argument that because of the sheer numbers of UFO sightings—in the early 1950s remember—the possibility that they all originate from experimental military projects cannot account for all of them.[33] What is interesting here is not so much the validity or the lack thereof of this line of reasoning, but the fact that it occurs almost for the first time in ufological literature in a book by one of ufology's most notorious contactees. Adamski, in other words, was one of the first to formulate the argument that "their numbers and frequencies of appearance took them out of (the) military experimental category."[34]

---

[32]Ibid., p. 18.
[33] Adamski, *Flying Saucers Have Landed*, p. 17.
[34] Ibid.

It is important to observe that this argument is an indirect one, for there are really only three ways such a conclusion for the extraterrestrial origins for UFOs could ever be advanced with anything approaching certitude:

1) The physics signatures of such objects must be exotic enough to compel to a conclusion that they are beyond the capabilities of any *known* or *conjectured* terrestrial science to embody;
2) Actual UFOs might be recovered and the technology might be determined to be so advanced as to be beyond human terrestrial science. In this eventuality, it is likely that such recovered technology would be deeply classified, and as such, any arguments for its off-world nature would depend on leaked information or descriptions of debris;
3) Actual UFO occupants might be recovered whose physiological features are so odd or unusual that they compel to the conclusion of an extraterrestrial origin.

Such is, of course, exactly what has been alleged in many famous UFO cases. We shall have occasion in this book to see that each of these three areas are themselves not entirely compelling, and that each are wide open to the management of perceptions.

The *second* statement that Adamski produced was even more unusual, and had even *less* preparation in the context of the book than the previous one, and again, there is absolutely no follow-up anywhere else in the book, or in its sequel, *Inside the Spaceships*. Here, it is best to cite the statement in its context:

> National security has many facets and the powers that be are themselves pushing out in the direction of space and of anti-gravity. *Also, they know they have an enemy.* And they do not know how far the enemy may have gone in this general field of a new form of power and propulsion. *They do know that at the close of the war all the German scientists with knowledge did not come to this country.*[35]

This is one of the most unusual statements in all of Adamski's output, and it is an oft-overlooked one.

---

[35] Adamski, *Flying Saucers Have Landed*, p. 21, emphasis added.

Note that at this period of time, antigravity was being written about in the open literature, *however*, the most *popular* articles would not be written until a few years *after* Adamski's book was actually published - just as a spate of popular articles on the subject of anti-gravity appeared in the mid-1950s - with some photographs that in turn appear to have been faked.[36] Thus, Adamski appears rather well-informed for a mere cafe owner who just happens to have been asked by people with military connections to photograph UFOs through his home telescopes! And who faked them? Adamski? or the military?

This only places the rest of his comments in an even more interesting light, for *how does Adamski know that the American military knows "they have an enemy"?* And *what enemy is it?* Adamski's words here are curiously ambiguous. Is the enemy the Soviet Union? Is the enemy extra-terrestrials? Or someone else? And then, from nowhere, unbidden, unprepared, and never followed-up, comes the statement that not all of the German scientists "with knowledge" came to this country, implying the "enemy" was the Nazis.

In the context of a series of statements about anti-gravity, unknown enemies, and American uncertainties about how far "the enemy may have gone in this general field of a new form of power and propulsion," it is a very sobering statement to make in an otherwise goofy book. Adamski seems to be implying that the "enemy" were Nazis, for why mention Germans in connection with all the preceding statements at all unless this was not his intention? As we shall see a little later, there may be a very subtle clue in Adamski's notorious photographs themselves.

1. The Nov 20, 1952 Contact: the Memes are Implanted

Just as quickly as Adamski makes these statements, he leaves them for the more familiar ufological territory of the weird and exotic, in this case, his alleged contact with an extraterrestrial. "It was," writes Adamski,

---

[36] See Nick Cook, *The Hunt For Zero Point* (London: Century, 2001), pp. 1-3.

about 12:30 in the noon hour on Thursday, 20 November 1952, that I first made personal contact with a man from another world. He came to Earth in his space craft, a flying saucer. He called it a Scout Ship.

This took place on the California desert 10.2 miles from Desert Center toward Parker, Arizona.[37]

Accompanying Adamski on this "historical occasion" were his secretary, Lucy McGinnis, another woman who was the owner of a cafe in Palomar Gardens,[38] and four people from Arizona who agreed to meet Adamski at the "contact site."

The four from Arizona were Mr. and Mrs. A.C. Bailey, and "Doctor" and Mrs. George H. Williamson.[39] We will return to George H. Williamson in a moment.

According to Adamski, shortly after noon the group heard the sound of an aircraft, a two engine plane "on a routine flight." Watching this airplane as it passed directly over their heads, the group continued to watch it until it was nothing but a speck.

Then, "it" happened:

Suddenly and simultaneously we all turned as one, looking again toward the closest mountain ridge where just a few minutes before the first plane had crossed. Riding high, and without sound, there was a gigantic cigar-shaped silvery ship, without wings or appendages of any kind. Slowly, almost as if it was drifting, it came in our direction; then seemed to stop, hovering motionless.

Excitedly Dr. Williamson exclaimed, 'Is that a space ship?'

At first glance it looked like a fuselage of a very large ship with the sun's rays reflecting brightly from its unpainted sides at an altitude and angle where wings might not be noticeable.

Schooled in caution against over-excitement and quick conclusions, especially in regard to aircraft, Lucy replied, 'No, George, I don't believe it is.'

'But that baby's high! And see how big it is!' exclaimed Al.

'And Lucy! It doesn't have wings or any other appendages like our planes do!' persisted George. And turning to me, 'What do you think Adamski?'

---

[37] Adamski, *Flying Saucers Have Landed*, p. 23.
[38] Ibid., p. 24.
[39] Ibid., pp. 23-24.

Before I could answer, Lucy interrupted, 'You're right, George! Look! It's orange on top—the whole length!'[40]

And thus began the event that would transform George Adamski, cafe owner, amateur UFO photographer and erstwhile "consultant" to the military, into Adamski the contactee.

Certain that the intention of the craft's occupants was to make contact, Adamski ordered his companions into the car in order to be driven closer to where he thought the "saucer" would land:

> ...(In) spite of all the excitement, I knew this was not the place; maybe not even the ship with which contact was to be made, if that was in the plan. But I did feel this ship had a definite 'something' to do with it all.
>
> Fully aware of the curiosity created by our party here in the desert where no one would normally picnic, I did not want to be more conspicuous by setting up my telescope and camera in such an open spot. Above all else, I didn't want to make the slightest mistake that might prevent a landing and personal contact being made, if such a possibility existed. And now I felt certain that it did.
>
> I said, 'Someone take me down the road—quick! That ship has come looking for me and I don't want to keep them waiting! Maybe the saucer is already up there somewhere— afraid to come down here where too many people would see them.'
>
> Don't ask me why I said this or how I knew. I have already said that I have a habit of following my feelings, and that is the way I felt.[41]

As the group drove in the car to the spot that Adamski designated, they observed the cigar-shaped object following them, stopping when the car stopped.[42]

Adamski then proceeded by himself with his six inch telescope and camera to a point a mile to a mile and a half from

---

[40] Adamski, *Flying Saucers Have Landed*, pp. 26-27.
[41] Ibid., p. 28.
[42] Ibid., pp. 28-29.

the car, ordering the rest of the group to drive back and observe carefully.[43]

> Not more than five minutes had elapsed after the car had left me when my attention was attracted by a flash in the sky and almost instantly a beautiful small craft appeared to be drifting through a saddle between two of the mountain peaks and settling silently into one of the coves about half a mile from me. It did not lower itself entirely below the crest of the mountain. Only the lower portion settled below the crest, while the upper, or dome section, remained above the crest and in full sight of the rest of my party who were back there watching. Yet it was in such a position that I could see the entire ship as it hovered in the cove ahead of me. At the same time, many miles of the highway and surrounding terrain were in full view of the crew within the saucer.[44]

Adamski quickly moved to snap a photograph of the saucer, "just as a couple more of our planes roared overhead"[45] and as the craft—now described as a "saucer"—flashed away and disappeared over "the same saddle through which it had first come."[46]

While musing on this close "contact" and wishing that he had been able to make actual personal contact with its occupant or occupants, Adamski's wish is fulfilled:

> Suddenly my reverie was broken as my attention was called to a man standing at the entrance of a ravine between two low hills, about a quarter of a mile away. He was motioning to me to come to him, and I wondered who he was and where he had come from. I was sure he had not been there before. Nor had he walked past me from the road.
>
> ....
>
> As I approached him a strange feeling came upon me and I became cautious. At the same time I looked round to reassure myself that we were both in full sight of my companions. Outwardly there was no reason for this feeling, for the man

---

[43] Ibid.,pp. 29-30.
[44] Adamski, *Flying Saucers Have Landed*, pp. 30-31.
[45] Ibid., p. 31.
[46] Ibid.

looked like any other man, and I could see he was somewhat smaller than I and considerably younger.[47]

This man was, of course, Adamski's "extraterrestrial." Note that, thus far, there is nothing at all distinguishing this encounter from the ordinary other than Adamski's "feeling." Indeed, Adamski himself mentions the possibility that the man might even have been a prospector.[48]

But before we continue with this encounter, the issue of one of Adamski's companions, who by Adamski's own account is watching this whole transaction unfold a mile away, must be addressed.

a. George Hunt Williamson and the Baileys

George Hunt Williamson (1926-1986) and his wife, along with the Baileys, was one of the group of four who met Adamski that day. But it is worth noting Williamson's background, and some of *his* connections. According to the biographical note in *Wikipedia,*

> Williamson, born in Chicago, Illinois... was mystically inclined as a teenager, but transferred some of his occult enthusiasm to flying saucers in the late 1940s. In early 1951 Williamson was expelled on academic grounds from the University of Arizona. Having read William Dudley Pelley's book *Star Guests* (1950), Williamson worked for a while for Pelley's cult organization, helping to put out its monthly publication *Valor.* Pelley had generated huge quantities of communications with "advanced intelligences" via automatic writing, and very clearly was an immediate inspiration to Williamson, who combined his fascination with the occult and with flying saucers by trying to contact flying saucer crews with a home-made Ouija board. After hearing about the flying-saucer-based religious cult of George Adamski, perhaps through Pelley, Williamson and his wife, and fellow saucer believers Alfred and Betty Bailey, became regular visitors to Adamski's commune at Palomar Gardens and eventually members of Adamski's Theosophy-spinoff cult. They witnessed Adamski "telepathically"

---

[47] Ibid., p. 32.
[48] Ibid.

channeling and tape-recording messages from the friendly humanoid Space Brothers who inhabited every solar planet.[49]

The article goes on to mention that Williamson was, along with the Baileys, the "witnesses" to Adamksi's "contact," (which the article mistakenly dates to November 18, 1952), but that in fact they experienced "nothing more than Adamski telling them to wait and stay put while he walked over a hill, then came back into view an hour later, with a preliminary story of his experiences—a story subsequently greatly changed for book publication in *Flying Saucers Have Landed* (1953), as Williamson himself later pointed out."[50]

And what of Williamson's contact with William Pelley? It is here that the plot takes a decidedly darker turn.

b. William Pelley and the American Fascists

William Dudley Pelley (1890-1965) claimed to have undergone a near-death experience in 1928, during which he met with God and Christ, who "instructed him to undertake the spiritual transformation of America."[51] Once the Great Depression hit America a year later, Pelley's "spiritual transformation" of America began in earnest when he became politically active. By the time Adolf Hitler had come to power in January 1933 in Germany, "Pelley, an admirer of Hitler, was inspired to form a political movement and on that same day founded the Silver Legion, an extremist and anti-semitic organization whose followers (known as the Silver Shirts and 'Christian Patriots') wore Nazi-like silver uniforms."[52] Having founded branches of the Silver Legion "in almost every state in the country" Pelley soon had a sizeable following.[53]

---

[49] "George Hunt Williamson," *Wikipedia*
http://en.wikipedia.org/wiki/ George_Hunt_Williamson, p. 1.
[50] Ibid.
[51] "William Dudley Pelley, *Wikipedia*,
http://en.wikipedia.org/wiki/William
_Dudley_Pelley, p. 1.
[52] Ibid., p. 2.
[53] Ibid.

By 1940, Pelley's organization and its hatred for President Franklin Delano Roosevelt had earned the ire of the Roosevelt Administration, and in 1940 his North Carolina headquarters in Asheville was shut down by Federal marshals. His followers at the headquarters were arrested and Pelley's property was seized. Pelley himself was summoned to testify before the House Un-American Activities Committee.[54]

Things went from bad to worse. After the Japanese attack on Pearl Harbor, Pelley was forced to disband his Fascist organization, but Pelley himself continued to attack the administration until he was finally charged with sedition and high treason in April 1942. While the sedition charge was dropped, Pelley was "convicted on other charges and sentenced to 15 years imprisonment," being paroled in 1952.[55]

2. The Messages from "E.T."

With Williamson's occult and Pelley's Fascist connections lurking in the background, let us now return to Adamski's record of his "contacts." With respect to this first contact—which Williamson subsequently admitted had been elaborated for Adamski's book—Adamski himself wrote:

1. His trousers were not like mine. They were in style, much like ski trousers and with a passing thought I wondered why he wore such out here in the desert.

2. His hair was long, reaching to his shoulders, and was blowing in the wind as was mine....

Although I did not understand the strange feeling that persisted, it was however a friendly feeling toward the smiling young man standing there waiting for me to reach him. And I continued walking toward him without the slightest fear.

Suddenly, as though a veil was removed from my mind, the feeling of caution left me so completely that I was no longer aware of my friends or whether they were observing me as they had been told to do. By this time we were quite close. He took four steps toward me, bringing us within arm's length of each other.

---

54 Ibid.
55 Ibid.

Now, for the first time I fully realised that I was in the presence of a man from space—A HUMAN BEING FROM ANOTHER WORLD! I had not seen his ship as I was walking toward him, nor did I look around for it now. I did not even think of his ship, and I was so stunned by this sudden realisation that I was speechless. My mind seemed to temporarily stop functioning.

The beauty of his form surpassed anything I had ever seen. And the pleasantness of his face freed me of all thought of my personal self...[56]

Adamski goes on to describe the man as being approximately five feet six inches tall, and about 28 years old, with a round face, high forehead, and grey-green eyes, with sandy hair and a skin color like a "medium-coloured suntan".[57]

As the men approached, the man extended his hand, as if to shake hands, and Adamski "responded in our customary manner."[58] But this was rejected "with a smile and a slight shake of his head. Instead of grasping hands as we on Earth do, he placed the palm of his hand against the palm of my hand, just touching it but not too firmly."[59] Later, in his subsequent contacts with the "extraterrestrials," Adamski elaborated on this "secret handshake":

I jumped to my feet with what probably could be described only as a broad grin. Firkon (the extraterrestrial with whom Adamski is conversing, ed) too wore a wide smile, and we exchanged the customary greeting. Then he said a certain word, stressing it in a way which clearly gave to it some particular significance.

As we left the hotel together...\
(That's right; they're in a *hotel!*)

...he said, 'The handclasp has been described to a certain extent and we thought it best to add the word you have just heard as a further identification between you and those of our worlds who are contacting you here. This will be particularly useful in

---

[56] Adamski, *Flying Saucers Have Landed*, pp. 32-33.
[57] Ibid., p. 33.
[58] Ibid.
[59] Ibid.

case you are approached by someone strange to you, as will sometimes be the case.[60]

In other words, the Space Brothers are quite literally members of a celestial Lodge, exchanging crypto-Masonic greetings with their erstwhile earthman contact by means of a secret handshake and typically Masonic exchanges of code words!

But let us return to the *initial* contact. The "secret handshake" thus exchanged, the two men got down to business. "I am a firm believer," Adamski says, as he is detailing the first communications between himself and the extraterrestrial subject of his first contact,

> that people who desire to convey messages to one another can do so, even though they neither speak nor understand the other's language. This can be done through feelings, signs, and above all, by means of telepathy.

(Remote viewers, eat your hearts out!)

> I had been teaching this as fact for 30 years and now I concluded I would have to use this method if information of any kind was to pass between us. And there were a lot of things I wanted to know, if only I could think of them.
>
> So, to convey the meaning of my first question to him, I began forming, to the best of my ability, a picture of a planet in my mind. At the same time I pointed to the sun, high in the sky.
>
> He understood this, and his expression so indicated.
>
> Then I circled the sun with my finger, indicating the orbit of the planet closest to the sun, and said, 'Mercury'. I circled it again for the second orbit, and said, 'Venus'. The third circle I said, 'Earth,' and indicated the earth upon which we were standing.
>
> I repeated this procedure a second time, all the while keeping as clear a picture of a planet in my mind as I was able to perceive, and this time pointing to myself as belonging to the Earth. Then I indicated him, with a question in my eyes and mind.
>
> Now he understood perfectly, and smiling broadly he point to the sun; made one orbit, made the second, then touching himself with his left hand, he gestured several times with his right index finger toward the second orbit.

---

[60] Adamski, *Inside the Spaceships*, p. 161.

I took this to mean that the second planet was his home, so I asked, 'You mean you came from Venus?' This was the third time I had spoken the word 'Venus' in relation to the second planet, and he nodded his head in the affirmative. Then, he, too, spoke the word 'Venus'.[61]

A Venusian had come to the much cooler climate of the California desert to talk personally to George Adamski!

a. The Venusian and "The Bomb"

From these simple beginnings, Adamski and his Venusian visitor moved quickly to a discussion of interplanetary politics and the "bomb," the first of many "messages" given to Adamski, and the first of many "memes" implanted within the UFO community:

He made me understand that their coming was friendly. Also, as he gestured, that they were concerned with radiations going out from the Earth.

This I got clearly since there was a considerable amount of radiation of heat waves rising from the desert, as if often the case. Such as the waves that are often seen rising from pavements, and highways on hot days.

He pointed to them and then gestured through space.

I asked if this concern was due to the explosions of our bombs with their resultant vast radio-active clouds?

He understood this readily and nodded his head in the affirmative.

....

I wanted to know if this was affecting outer space?

Again a nod of affirmation.[62]

To my knowledge, this is one of the first times in UFO literature that the idea of atomic testing as a cause for "extraterrestrial reconnoitering" was put forward, being subsequently picked up by Frank Edwards, and later by Stanton Friedman. In Adamski's case, however, the idea has gone far beyond extraterrestrial

---

[61] Adamski, *Flying Saucers Have Landed*, pp. 35-36.
[62] Adamsky *Flying Saucers Have Landed,*, p. 36.

"reconnaissance," and was now supplemented by a political message that humanity was on a course of ignorance and error.[63]

b. Adamski's E.T.s, and Religion:
The Interplanetary Federation of Brotherhood and the
"Übermensch ET"

Having established the concerns of the inhabitants of the planet Venus over terrestrial nuclear testing, Adamski then managed to ask the Venusian if he believed in God. Receiving an affirmative answer, Adamski quickly amended this:

> But he made me understand, by elaborating a little longer with his gestures and mental pictures, that we on Earth really know very little about this Creator. In other words, our understanding is shallow. Theirs is much broader, and they adhere to the Laws of the Creator instead of laws of materialism as Earth men do.[64]

Note what we have here: if, on the one hand, one is inclined to take Adamski at his word, and in spite of the abundant evidence not to do so, then whoever it is he is having contact with is subtly conveying the notion that extraterrestrials are not only *technologically*, but *morally and spiritually* superior to human beings. And if one does *not* take Adamski at his word, but rather admits that the whole contact scenario is one gigantic fantasy, then the end result is still the same, only in this case it is *Adamski* who is promulgating the idea of the technological and moral superiority of extraterrestrials.

This idea or meme of the "*Übermensch ET*" is found again in the series of alleged contacts elaborated in Adamski's *Inside the Spaceships*, where Adamski attributes almost angelic and supernatural powers to his "Space Brothers" when he confesses his "deep conviction that these men could answer all questions and solve all problems concerning our world: even to performing feats impossible to Earth men if they deemed such necessary and in keeping with the mission they had come to perform."[65]

---

[63] Ibid.
[64] Ibid.,p. 39.
[65] Adamski, *Inside the Spaceships*, p. 98.

The message being implied by the sum total of Adamski's writing thus far is both subtle and disturbing, for what he is really doing is remaking and refashioning conventional religion, with its angels and messianic expectations and even its "apostolic mission" that the ETs "had come to perform", into a revelation of superior beings in possession of superior technologies with which they could perform miracles, "feats impossible to Earth men". Even the appearance of Adamski's "extraterrestrials" as human beings is all too reminiscent of the appearances of "angels" at various stages of the "disclosure" of the biblical revelations to Abraham, to Moses, and eventually, to the Virgin Mary. Just as in the biblical pattern, Adamski's "angels" or "messengers" appear as humans, bearing a message.[66]

Adamski, in other words, and despite the disregard and even bemused disdain in which he is held by contemporary ufology, is nonetheless implanting all the religious memes into ufology that will later become such subtle and dogmatic foundations in the extraterrestrial faith.

Thus, his initial and subsequent contacts even disclose the attempt to "catholicize" this extraterrestrial faith, for Adamski's Venusian "made me understand that people are coming Earth-ward from other planets in our system, and from planets of other systems beyond ours."[67] Among the specific planets that Adamski mentions as "parishes" in this extraterrestrial catholic religion, besides Venus, are Mars and Saturn.[68]

Earlier we noted the quasi-Masonic nature of the actual "contacts" themselves, with the exchanges of "secret handshakes" and coded words. But the resemblance is more than superficial, for in *Inside the Spaceships*, one of Adamski's extraterrestrial contacts delivers yet another short sermonette containing themes near and dear the teachings of fraternal secret societies: universal brotherhood and reincarnation:

> Never cease to point out to them, my son, that all are brothers and sisters regardless of where they have been born, or have chosen to live. Nationality or the colour of one's skin are but incidental since the body is no more than a temporary

---

[66] Q.v. the foreword to Adamski, *Inside the Spaceships,* p. 86.
[67] Adamski, *Flying Saucers Have Landed*, p. 39.
[68] Adamski, *Inside the Spaceships*, p. 95.

dwelling. These change in the eternity of time. In the infinite progress of all life, each eventually will know all states.[69]

This message of brotherhood and fraternity in the context of reincarnation is coupled elsewhere with another message, one with subtle undertones of its own. "Your school system on Earth," another extraterrestrial tells Adamski,

> is, in a sense, patterned after the universal progress of life. For in your schools you progress from grade to grade, and from school to school, toward a higher and fuller education. In the same war, man progresses from planet to planet, and from system to system towards an ever higher understanding and evolvement in universal growth and service.[70]

Note the extraordinary subtlety with which the idea of degrees of initiation into higher consciousness states —itself a theme of the secret societies - is outlined in this brief passage, and coupled to a very ancient religious idea, that of reincarnation *coupled with an association to celestial bodies.* But there is a darker undercurrent here, and that is the idea of "universal growth and service," which could equally be restated as "perpetual reincarnation and *servitude.*" In other words, behind the seemingly friendly and fraternal messages of Adamski's visitors lies a much more occult agenda, an agenda hinted at, perhaps, by his associate George Hunt Williamson's connection to William Pelley.

Elsewhere, all these religious memes are given yet another twist, this time by a "Martian" who informs Adamski that:

> We live and work here...We have lived on your planet now for several years. At first we did have a slight accent. But that has been overcome and, as you can see, we are unrecognized as other than Earth men.
> At our work and in our leisure time we mingle with people here on Earth, never betraying the secret that we are inhabitants of other worlds. That would be dangerous, as you well know. We understand you people better than most of you

---

[69] Ibid., p. 207.
[70] Adamski, *Inside the Spaceships*, p. 139.

know yourselves and can plainly see the reasons for many of the unhappy conditions that surround you.[71]

As has been seen, Adamski ascribes almost angelic and supernatural capabilities to his extraterrestrials, by dint both of their extraordinary technology as well as by dint of their moral and spiritual superiority. Now, he has added a new dimension, namely, that they constitute a *hidden elite*, a kind of extraterrestrial priesthood, living and moving among us and, presumably, spreading their messages and thus manipulating - socially engineering -mankind.

This twist, coupled with the meme of "universal growth and service," subtly suggests that mankind is meant to *serve* these extraterrestrial overlords.

c. The Revelation of the "Revelation", or "Disclosure", Meme

One of the most peculiar, and intriguing, things that Adamski mentions as a component of his initial contact with the Venusian is the idea of "the revelation of the possibility of revelation":

> Remembering a question that had often been asked of me by people with whom I had talked, I asked why they never land in populated places?
>
> To this he made me understand that there would be a tremendous amount of fear on the part of the people, and probably the visitors would be torn to pieces by the Earth people, if such public landings were attempted.
>
> I understood how right he was, and within my mind wondered if there ever would be a time when such a landing would be safe. I was wondering too, if such a time ever arrived, would they then attempt public landings.
>
> He read my thoughts as they were passing through my mind, and assured me that such a time would arrive. And when it did, they would make landings in populated territories. But he made me understand clearly that it would not be soon.[72]

Again, to my knowledge, this is one of the first times, if not *the* first time, that the idea of a future "disclosure" or "revelation" of

---

[71] Ibid., p. 96.

[72] Adamski, *Flying Saucers Have Landed*, p. 40.

the extraterrestrial presence is broached in UFO literature. It requires little imagination to see how widespread, and diversified, this "meme" has become within ufology in recent years, for it now encompasses not only the original idea of disclosure by the ETs themselves (acting in the place traditionally taken by God in conventional religion), but also disclosure by the various governments (taking the place of the teaching magisterium in conventional religions) presumably suppressing their presence, to disclosure of the hidden technologies presumably gained from extraterrestrial contacts.

d. The End of the Contact

Toward the end of his initial contact, Adamski's Venusian finally speaks in his native tongue (we can only presume that it is Old High Venusian), which, to Adamski, "sounded like a mixture of Chinese with a tongue that I felt could have sounded like one of the ancient languages spoken here on Earth."[73] With this, we have yet *another* meme that is being very carefully, and discretely, introduced for one of the first times, that of the connection of extraterrestrials (of human form) to human antiquity itself. Again, to my knowledge, Adamski was one of the first people writing in ufology to make this connection.[74]

3. The Memes of Adamski's Extraterrestrial Faith Summarized

At this juncture it is worth pausing to take stock of all the memes that have been enunciated by Adamski (or by his visitors, depending on one's point of view), and that will play such significant roles in subsequent ufology and in the wider cultural *perception of the subject* of UFOs. We may catalog these memes as follows:

---

[73] Adamski, *Flying Saucers Have Landed*, p. 43.
[74] The other one to do so, three years later though much more explicitly, was Dr. Morris K. Jessup, who connected UFOs to other "Fortean" phenomena, in *The Case for the UFO: Unidentified Flying Objects* (New York: The Citadel Press, 1955), p. 23.

1) Extraterrestrials are concerned with the human development of nuclear weapons, and view it as a threat to humanity and as an implied threat to themselves, and have thus been visiting Earth and even working among humans to reconnoiter the situation;

2) Extraterrestrials are a technologically and morally superior race of mankind (or in later ufology, an altogether different *species*);

3) The extraterrestrial meme is coupled with those of universal brotherhood, reincarnation, and planetary initiations;

4) Within this extraterrestrial Adamskian faith, all the patterns of conventional religion are stripped of their traditional religious vestments and updated with new technological and extraterrestrial trappings; old concepts have been dressed up in a new context;

5) Extraterrestrials—with all their superhuman technology and morality—constitute a hidden elite living and working amongst humanity (thus discretely inculcating a culture of *suspicion*);

6) Extraterrestrials constitute a "catholic" interplanetary federation, a kind of interplanetary Masonic "brotherhood" in which one's role is to be involved in "universal growth and service," a message implying *servitude to* the technologically and morally superior extraterrestrials, who, let it be noted, *can be identified solely by their possession of superior technology*, a technology which they use *to emphasize their superior morality* and to subtly imply mankind's subservience;

7) Finally, it is revealed that eventually there will be a revelation, i.e., the meme of "disclosure" is discretely planted in and through the Adamski material.

When the Adamski "catalog of ufological memes" is viewed in this way, it is clear that while contemporary ufology has long ago foresworn any connection to or credence in Adamski's wild mythologies, it nonetheless remains true that the major *themes* of his mythology, many of which he enunciated for nearly the first time within ufology, have remained to take deep roots, and to spread wide branches, not only within the field of ufology, but within the wider culture perception of UFOs that it influences.

For these reasons alone, Adamski may not be so glibly dismissed as an embarassment to the subject. But there are also *other* reasons that he may not be so casually dismissed.

4. Adamski's Technological Descriptions and Another E.T. Message:
The Danger of Weaponized Gravity

Adamski is, of course, best known for his wild tales of extraterrestrial contact and visitation, but what many people do *not* realize is that Adamski also gave some descriptions of the technology of his alleged extraterrestrials. Here the plot, once again, is about to take yet another very unexpected turn, for during his first contact with the "Venusian," Adamski asked him how his ship operated and by what power it obtained its energy. When reading Adamski's description in the following exchange, bear in mind that the entire contact itself is deeply and seriously disputed by almost all respected voices within ufology:

> He made me understand that it was being operated by the law of attraction and repulsion, by picking up a little pebble or rock and dropping it; then picking it up again and then showing motion.
>
> I in turn, to make sure I understood, picked up two pebbles and placed them close to each other as though one was magnetic, pulling on the other, illustrating it that way as I spoke the word 'magnetic'. After a short time of doing this, he answered me; even repeating the word 'magnetic' which I had already spoken a number of times.
>
> Then he replied, 'yes'.[75]

Being finally allowed near to the saucer as it began to depart, Adamski "noticed two rings under the flange around the centre disk. This inner ring and the outer one appeared to be revolving clockwise, while the ring between these two moved in a counter clockwise motion."[76] This, by now, should ring a bell—pun

---

[75] Adamski, *Flying Saucers Have Landed*, p. 38.
[76] Adamksi, *Flying Saucers Have Landed*, pp. 47-48.

intended[77]—for as I detail elsewhere in my books, the principle of counter-rotation was a primary conceptual component of the Nazi Bell project, though in the latter case the counter-rotating elements were not nested one inside the other, but were stacked one on top of the other.[78]

The important point to notice here, whether or not Adamski's whole contact scenario actually occurred, or whether he made up the whole thing, or whether the truth lies somewhere between the two, is that Adamski somehow managed to hit upon the concept of rotation and counter-rotation as being central to the configuration of anti-gravity propulsion systems, points that would not be raised in the scientific literature until some three decades later.[79] This is not

---

[77] It should also remind the reader of the disks of British inventor John Searl.

[78] Joseph P. Farrell, *The SS Brotherhood of the Bell*, pp. 171-185; and *Secrets of the Unified Field*, pp. 270-286.

[79] Joseph P. Farrell, *The Giza Death Star Destroyed*, pp. 163-166; and *The Philosophers' Stone*, pp. 99-101, 313-329. It should be pointed out that the German physicist Burkhardt Heim had begun to elaborate his theory at about the same time as Adamski was writing *Flying Saucers Have Landed,* in which rotation is an element. However, it is unlikely that Adamski knew of Heim *or* his theory. The question thus remains, where was Adamski getting his knowledge?

In his Foreword to *Inside the Spaceships*, Desmond Leslie, yet another famous contactee, and notable occultist, of the 1950s, maintained that some UFO witnesses who had had close encounters with the technology, described a forcefield emanating from them that would "flatten the grass" and set the witness "back on his heels." (Adamski, *Inside the Spaceships*, p. 87). Similar effects were reported by some of the first responders on the ground in New York City during 9/11; moreover, as Dr. Paul LaViolette has demonstrated in his recent book *Secrets of Antigravity Propulsion: Tesla, UFOs, and Classified Aerospace Technology* (Bear & Co., 2008), microwaves were being explored as a means of advanced propulsion (q.v. pp. 195-200, 203, 206-209, 235, 284-285, 445). Some of these ideas were being discussed in the 1950s, more or less contemporaneously with Leslie's witnesses who described such forcefields. Use of such intense microwaves might indeed be experienced as something pushing a witness away, but are more likely to be experienced as intense *heat* (if the person encountering them actually survived).

the only case where Adamski displays an unusual and highly anachronistic knowledge, as we shall see shortly.

However, to return for the moment to Adamski's descriptions of the technologies he allegedly saw, it was during his encounters recounted in *Inside the Spaceships* that he details more aspects of the "technology of the saucers". Once inside one of the ships, Adamski

> ...was aware of a very slight hum that seemed to come equally from beneath the floor and from a heavy coil that appeared to be built into the top of the circular wall. The moment the hum started, this coil began to glow bright red but emitted no heat.[80]

Note that the description of the technology here is anything but unusual, since he is describing a wholly conventional, terrestrial *coil.*

Nor was this all. Shortly after this coil began to glow, Adamski describes hearing a sound like "the soft hum as of a swarm of bees."[81] Again, this is a very curious statement, since one of the nicknames the Germans had for their Bell project was *der Bienenstock,* the Beehive, so nicknamed because of the buzzing sound it made, like a swarm of bees![82] Yet, the Bell story would not emerge until decades later, in the 1990s, after the collapse of Communism and the German reunification.

A pole two feet in diameter ran from the top of the ship through the center of the floor, which Adamski was told was the "magnetic pole" of the craft. He was also told that the poles could be reversed.[83] This "rod of power" was anchored at each end by two structures that resembled "great lenses." [84] Here too one is confronted with an odd resemblance to the Nazi Bell device, which had on its central axis a pole, which could function as one pole of an electrical circuit, while the outer counter-rotating components acted as the other.[85] Elsewhere, a "Martian" tells

---

[80] Adamski, *Inside the Spaceships*, p. 101.
[81] Ibid., p. 102.
[82] Farrell, *The SS Brotherhood of the Bell*, p. 177.
[83] Adamski, *Inside the Spaceships*, p. 102.
[84] Ibid., p. 167.
[85] Farrell, *Secrets of the Unified Field*, pp. 262-288.

Adamski that the "magnetic" power of all this technology acts in concert with the Earth's natural magnetic field.[86]

Putting all this together, Adamski's "space brothers" are describing the action of *rotating* fields within *static* ones, a description that sounds suspiciously like another celebrated but wholly *terrestrial* and conventional technology in the lore of "strange technology": the Philadelphia Experiment.[87]

Finally, to round out all these extraterrestrial explanations, one of Adamski's later visitors informs him that the "Space Brothers" would gladly reveal the secrets of gravity control, but that they do not do so for fear that humans will weaponize it and go on a mad spree of interplanetary conquest![88]

What emerges from this is not so much the bizarre nature of the technology described, but the fact that Adamski is describing it in a detail that has so many parallels with *later* actual formal papers and investigations,[89] and with the basic conceptual principles involved in a secret Nazi project that would only come to light four decades later, after German reunification. What is unusual therefore is the highly anachronistic nature of Adamski's descriptions, coupled with his earlier allusions to the Nazi "enemy".

How would one therefore account for this extraordinary accuracy in the midst of an otherwise goofy fantasy involving extraterrestrial contact, a fantasy that few—this author included—take at face value or as genuine?

5. A Doozie of an Anachronistic Revelation

Before one can begin to answer that question, there is a final anachronism that Adamski's *Inside the Spaceships* contains, and it's a doozie. While on his outing to the enormous mothership in orbit above the Earth, Adamski noticed a picture of an even larger ship, several miles long. He is told that "many such ships have been built," specifically, on Mars and Saturn![90]

---

[86] Adamski, *Inside the Spaceships*, pp. 107-108.
[87] Farrell, *Secrets of the Unified Field*, pp. 73, 165-190.
[88] Adamski, *Inside the Spaceships*, p. 140.
[89] We shall examine some of these papers an technologies subsequently.
[90] Adamski, op. cit., p. 121.

What makes this so anachronistic is that the NASA Cassini probe—fifty years in the future from Adamski's bizarre statements!—would send back pictures of Saturn's moon Iapetus in the 21st century, pictures that strongly suggested the entire moon was an artificial object.[91] Additionally, recent European Space Agency photos of Mars' moon Phobos has suggested to Richard Hoagland that this moon, too, might be an artificial object, and Soviet scientists proposed the same idea before Hoagland.[92]

If this is merely a coincidence, then it is the latest, and largest, in a long line of "coincidences" that Adamski racked up. How would one account for this?

Clearly, Adamski is getting information from somewhere, and since it is very unlikely that his contact stories are anything else other than fantasy, then where is the information coming from?

We have already seen his second-hand connection to the American Fascist William Pelley via George Hunt Williamson, suggesting that in part he may have been getting information directly from that quarter connected to esoteric and occult tradition. We have also seen Adamski's own suspicious connections to the American military, a connection initiated not by Adamski, but by the military. But why would the military share any such technological information, much less information about gigantic artificial spaceships from Saturn and Mars? One reason, perhaps, is to render such information *ridiculous* by embedding it in a context of contact lunacy, and doing so while implanting memes to manipulate the perception of that technology.

If, in other words, Adamski is part of some wider covert psychological operation, then *whose* operation is it, and what are its goals?

The answer to that question might be revealed in the final "Adamski Anomaly"...

---

[91] Q.v. Joseph P. Farrell, *The Cosmic War: Interplanetary Warfare, Modern Physics, and Ancient Texts* (Adventures Unlimited Press, 2007), pp. 385-398.

[92] Richard C. Hoagland, "For the World is Hollow and I Have Touched the Sky," www.enterprisemission.com.

Saucers, Swastikas, and Psyops

B. Adamski's Retro-Looking Saucers, and the Nazi Saucer Myth

A picture is indeed worth a thousand words, but in this case, several pictures are worth millions of words. Adamski's pictures of his alleged saucers are now well-known, if not infamous:

Adamski's Decidedly Retro-Looking Flying Saucer

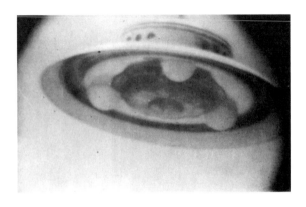

Underview of Adamski's Retro-Flying Saucer

Adamski's Cigar-Shaped Mother-Ship

As is now maintained in some quarters, Adamski apparently fabricated these photos by taking picture of a heater for a chicken coup!

But the problem of Adamski's "flying saucers" is further compounded with the appearance in the 1960s of an alleged SS document showing three purported Nazi flying saucer designs called the Hannebu or Haunebu flying saucers, all of which, especially the first two "marks", looking distinctly like Adamski's saucer.

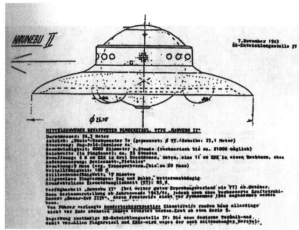

The Alleged SS Document, Showing the Purported Hannebu II

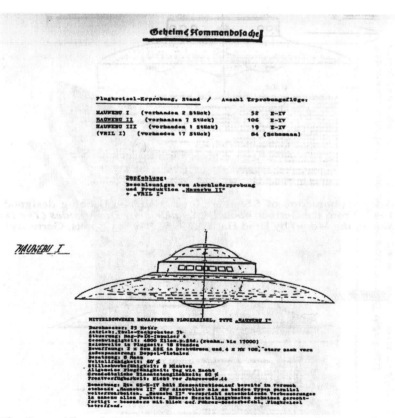

The Same Alleged SS Document Purporting to Show the Hannebu I Flying Saucer

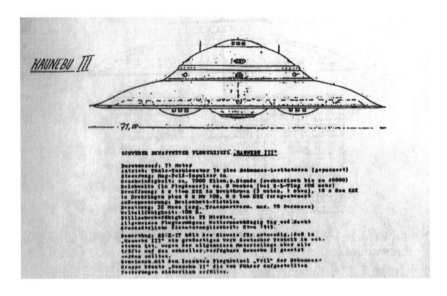

From the Same Alleged SS Document, Showing the Purported Hannebu III Flying Saucer

The question is why would anyone circulate, several years after Adamski's faked photographs, documents that not only depict curiously similar "saucer" designs, but also that have such a dubious provenance? There are no other supporting documents, only postwar stories.

More importantly, how did the Nazis themselves react to these reports when queried? The answer is simple: "ET made us do it."

One of the Alleged Photos of the Hannebu Saucer that Purports to be "Proof" of their existence.

PART TWO:
SWASTIKAS AND PSYOPS:
A PATTERN OF MAGICAL DECEPTION

"If you tell a big enough lie and tell it frequently enough, it will be believed."

"What luck for rulers that men do not think."

"Great liars are also great magicians."
Adolf Hitler

"The man who does not think for himself, does not think at all."
Oscar Wilde

SS Obersturmbannführer (Lieutenant Colonel) Otto Skorzeny

3

"E.T. MADE US DO IT":
THE POSTWAR STATEMENTS OF NAZIS

"Call him a Nazi,
He won't even frown;
'Ha! Nazi schmazi!'
Says Wernher Von Braun."
Tom Lehrer[1]

T here can be no doubt that within the thankfully short twelve years of its proclaimed millennial existence that technology exploded in the Third Reich to a depth and breadth that was never seen before or since. As Nazi armies rolled over Europe expanding the boundaries of the Greater German Reich, Nazi scientists and engineers were rolling back the frontiers of the technological imagination. Major accomplishments and breakthroughs were made in the field of electronics miniaturization, computers, semi-conductors, infrared night-vision, fuel-air explosives, jets, rockets, electromagnetic weapons, lasers and associated technologies, atomic, thermonuclear, and plasma physics and engineering, ballistic missiles and field propulsion, and a whole host of other things that boggle the imagination.

The most breathtaking visible displays of this scientific and engineering prowess were those projects that took conventional technologies to the extreme: the ballistic missiles and rockets raining destruction down on London and other western European cities, the advanced aerodynes, including designs which, though conceived and in some cases built in the 1930s and 1940s, look breathtakingly modern to this day.

How did one *account* for all this sudden and rapid explosion of technology? Even more importantly, how did the German scientists *themselves* account for it? And what, if anything, does it have to do with the odd, anomalous anachronisms that seem to turn up in Adamski's writing at almost every turn?

---

[1] "Wernher Von Braun," song and lyrics by Tom Lehrer, *That Was the Year That Was*, Reprise Records (Time Warner, 1965).

The answer to those questions brings us, inevitably, to the postwar statements of the Nazis themselves, and in particular to...

A. The Strange Case of Dr. Hermann Oberth:
A Benign Biography

If one were to consult only the bibliographies of Dr. Oberth publicly available and and online, *Wikipedia*, for example, one would not have a full appreciation of the measure of the man, for those biographies are, for the most part, benign. One is even tempted to say, sanitized. We would learn, for example, the usual commonplaces: he was born in 1894 at Nagszeben in the Austro-Hungarian empire, died at the age of 95 in December of 1989. Reading the science fiction of Jules Verne, he began to experiment with rockets when he was only 14; began to study medicine in Munich but was drafted into the Kaiser's army when World War One broke out; served on the Eastern front, married in 1918 and had four children.[2]

In the 1920s, Oberth published two works on the use of rocketry in space exploration, *Die Rakete zu den Planetenraumen* (1922—*By Rocket into Planetary Space),* and an expanded version in 1929, *Wege zum Raumschiffahrt* (*Ways to Spaceflight*). Awarded his doctorate in physics in 1923 by the University of Cluj, Romania, Oberth also worked in Berlin during 1928 and 1929 as a consultant for the first science fiction feature film, designing the moon rocket for *Frau im Mond*(*The Woman in the Moon*), the famous science fiction film director Fritz Lang's futuristic vision set in space.[3]

In 1929 Oberth also designed and test fired a rocket with the young Wenher Von Braun, thus beginning a lifelong friendship between the two men based on their mutual designs and obsession with space exploration. Indeed, Von Braun's own praise and indications of Oberth's vast influence was effusive:

> Hermannn Oberth was the first, who when thinking about the possibility of spaceships grabbed a slide-rule and presented mathematically analyzed concepts and designs... I, myself, owe to him not only the guiding star of my life, but also my first contact

---

[2] "Hermann Oberth," *Wikipedia*, en.wikipedia.org/wiki/Hermann_Oberth.

[3] Ibid.

with the theoretical and practical aspects of rocketry and space travel. A place of honor should be reserved in the history of science and technology for his ground-breaking contributions in the field of astronautics. [4]

By 1938 Oberth had moved his family from Romania to Austria and then to Nazi Germany, eventually becoming a member of Von Braun's secret rocket team at Peenemünde in 1941. In 1955 Oberth was personally sought and brought by his former friend in Nazi Germany, Wernher Von Braun, to Huntsville, Alabama, where he remained for three years, contributing to the study *The Development of Space Technology in the Next Ten Years*, returning to West Germany in 1958, where "he published his ideas on a lunar exploration vehicle, a 'lunar catapult,' and on 'muffled' helicopters and airplanes."[5] In 1960 he returned to work as a consultant for the Convair Corporation which was engaged in producing the U.S.A.'s first strategic intercontinental ballistic missile, the Atlas, the very same vehicle that would become the booster for America's first manned space flights in Project Mercury.

But as the *Wikipedia* article hints, there is more to Dr. Oberth than meets the eye:

> The science-fiction movie *Star Trek III: The Search for Spock* mentions the *Oberth*-class of starships hypothetically to be in his honor. Later on, this same class of starships is mentioned in several episodes of the American TV series *Star Trek: the Next Generation.*
>
> *Fullmetal Alchemist the Movie: Conqueror of Shamballa* features Hermann Oberth as the "teacher" of the movie's protagonist, Edward Elric. Oberth is also mentioned in the last episode of the TV series *Fullmetal Alchemist*. In this episode, Elric has heard of a great scientist, named "Oberth", with curious theories.[6]

Just how curious these theories really are we shall now see, for they are a bizarre amalgam of extra-terrestrials, advanced technologies... and the occult.

---

[4] Ibid., citing http://oberth-museum.org/index_e.html.

[5] "Hermann Oberth," *Wikipedia*, en.wikipedia.org/wiki/Hermann_ Oberth.

[6] Ibid.

B. Dr. Oberth's and Dr. Von Braun's Statements on UFOs and Extraterrestrials

By the mid-1950s, various American leaders had already gone on record with their belief that UFOs were the products of an advanced extraterrestrial technology. The well-known Ufologist Timothy Good, for example, mentions a famous statement by U.S. General of the Armies, Douglas MacArthur, who was involved in the establishment of an early UFO study group called the Interplanetary Phenomenon Unit, a division of the U.S. Army's counterintelligence. Speaking in 1955, General MacArthur made a rather astonishing statement:

> The nations of the world will have to unite, for the next war will be an interplanetary war. The nations of the earth must someday make a common front against attack by people from other planets.[7]

What is unusual here is that MacArthur's public statement clearly contradicts the findings of the CIA's 1953 Robertson Panel on UFOs, which had concluded that UFOs were not a national security threat.[8]

Four years later, after General MacArthur had made his celebrated farewell—and—"oh-by-the-way-we're-facing-an-inter-planetary-war"—speech to the cadets of West Point, U.S. Project Paperclip Nazi rocket scientist Wernher Von Braun made yet another curious statement on January 1, 1959,[9] alluding to some sort of "difficulty"—if not outright conflict—in outer space after an American *Juno 2* rocket had been deflected from orbit:

---

[7] Cited in Timothy Good, *Above Top Secret: The Worldwide UFO Cover-up* (New York: Quill Books, William Morrow, 1988), p. 267, citing MacArthur's speech in October 1955 to the graduating cadets of West Point. There may be another connection between the American elite and extreme right wing Fascism, for MacArthur was the first choice to lead the coup against Franklin Roosevelt that ultimately was disclosed to General Smedley Butler. Butler implicated MacArthur himself in the plot. See Charles Higham, *Trading with the Enemy* (Authors Guild Backinprint.com, 2007), p. 164.

[8] See Richard M. Dolan, *Ufos and the National Security State: Chronology of a Cover-Up, 1941-1973* (Hampton Roads, 2000), p. 125.

[9] Richard M. Dolan, *UFOs and the National Security State: Vol 1: Chronology of a Cover-up 1941-1973* (Hampton Roads Publishing Company, 2002), p. 225.

We find ourselves faced by powers which are far stronger *than we had hitherto assumed*, and whose base is at present unknown to us. More I cannot say at present. **We are now engaged in entering into closer contact with those powers**, and in six or nine months' time it may be possible to speak with more precision on the matter.[10]

Notably Von Braun, like MacArthur, did not refer in so many words to "extraterrestrials" but simply to "powers which are far stronger than we had hitherto assumed," leaving open the possibility that he meant something concerning *physical* forces. He alludes to an "unknown base" however, and indicates that "contact" is being attempted.

Into this MacArthurian mix of "people"—the *general's* word, not mine—attacking the earth, and Von Braun's "unknown base" and "powers far stronger than we had hitherto assumed," stepped Von Braun's mentor, Dr. Hermann Oberth, with even more curious

---

[10] Good, *Above Top Secret*, p. 370, citing *Neues Europa*, 1 January 1959, italicized emphasis added, boldface emphasis added by Good. See also Richard M. Dolan, *UFOs and the National Security State: Vol 1: Chronology of a Cover-up 1941-1973*, p. 225. Dolan gives more information about Oberth's statements in the first volume of his excellent two volume study of UFOs:

"Around 1952 or 1954, according to Frank Edwards, the West German government hired him to head a commission studying UFOs. *As a result of this study, Oberth had made a statement, during the summer of 1954, that UFOs were 'conceived and directed by intelligent beings of a very high order. They probably do not originate in our solar system, perhaps not even in our galaxy.'* Like William Lear, Townsend Brown, and Wilbert Smith, Oberth decided that UFOs were 'propelled by distorting the gravitational field, converting gravity into useable energy.'

"In a letter to Keyhoe, Oberth explained his electromagnetic propulsion theory which he believed as the true explanation for UFO propulsion. With the ability to create their own gravitational fields, UFOs would be able to do all the things witesses had attributed to them: hover motionless above the earth, accelerate at tremendous speed, and make violent turns that would cause ordinary aircraft to disintegrate."(Richard M. Dolan, *UFOs and the National Security State, Vol 1: Chronology of a Cover-up 1941-1973*, p. 176, emphasis added)

statements. Answering questions in 1968 about the UFO phenomenon, Dr. Oberth stated the following:

> *...today we cannot produce machines that fly as UFOs do.* They are flying by means of artificial fields of gravity. This would explain the sudden changes of directions... This hypothesis would also explain the piling up of these disks into a cylindrical or cigar-shaped mothership upon leaving the earth, because in this fashion only one field of gravity would be required for all disks.
> *They produce high-tension electric charges in order to push the air out of their path... and strong magnetic fields to influence the ionised air at higher altitudes...* This would explain their luminosity... Secondly, it would explain the noiselessness of UFO flight. Finally, this assumption also explains the strong electrical and magnetic effects sometimes, but not always, observed in the vicinity of UFOs.[11]

There are a number of disturbing things about these statements, if one reads them closely, not the least of these is Dr. Oberth's statements regarding using high-tension (i.e., high voltage) electric charges to ionize the air and decrease drag.

This is significant because this *very idea* had already been proposed by American physicist Thomas Townsend Brown in the mid-1950s in a patent utilizing "electro-gravitic" effects to decrease drag, improve fuel efficiency, and thereby the range, of conventional aircraft, and patented in 1960:

---

[11] Good, *Above Top Secret*, p. 370, emphasis added, citing, Sigma Rho, "Dr. Hermann Oberth Looks at UFOs," *Fate*, December 1968, pp. 45-47, emphasis added by me.

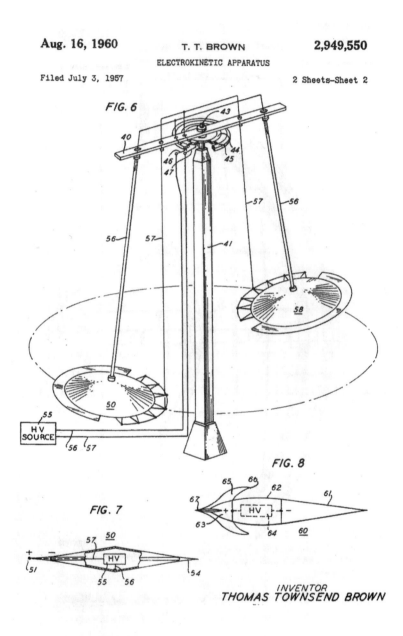

Thomas Townsend Brown, U.S. Patent # 2,949,550

Note the diagram, Figure 8, in the lower right hand corner:

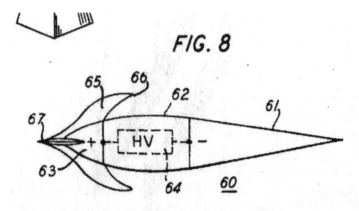

Close-up of Figure 8, Thomas Townsend Brown U.S. Patent 2,949,550

Note on the left hand side of the disk-shaped capacitor, the leading edge is positively-charged, with the trailing edge negatively charged, setting up a charge differential which accounts for the motivation of this "electro-kinetic apparatus." And note on the previous page that this is hooked up to a "H.V. Source," a high voltage, or, in Dr. Oberth's terms, a high tension source.   While the connection to Thomas Townsend Brown is fascinating, we must reserve comment on it to a later chapter, for as we shall discover, there is yet another odd connection to Adamski

For the moment, however, our attention remains focused on Dr. Oberth, for he is describing a wholly terrestrial technology in his UFO remarks, one already patented in 1960, and this suggests in turn that the beginning of his remarks—*"...today we cannot produce machines that fly as UFOs do. They are flying by means of artificial fields of gravity..."*—he has seen the connection to anti-gravity. At the minimum, then, the possibility arises that Dr. Oberth was being deliberately disingenuous in his remarks.

But is there anything *more direct* that would conclusively demonstrate that he *was* being disingenuous?

There is another remark Dr. Oberth allegedly made shortly after his first period in the USA that is reported by Ufologist Fred Steckling. Though I have not been able to verify this quotation, it is worth mentioning here as it is consonant with his later verified remarks concerning his belief that UFOs were extraterrestrial in origin. According to Steckling, upon his retirement from Bell Laboratories, Dr Obert stated to the press, "Gentlemen, we cannot take all the credit for our civilization's rapid technological development over the past decade. We have had help." When he was asked just who had helped us, Dr Oberth reportedly responded, "Those guys out there from the other planets."[12]

Steckling noted the anomaly apparent in these remarks: "This statement quickly earned the good professor the honorable title of 'crack-pot.' However, the people responsible for his promotion never explained exactly how it is possible for a top scientist to turn crack-pot overnight."[13] But perhaps Oberth was not being a "crack pot."

We have already noted his curious description of technologies first advanced by the physicist Thomas Townsend Brown. Additionally, his former student, Dr. Wernher Von Braun, responsible for bringing Oberth to this country in the first place, was himself involved at some point in high level, and very classified, anti-gravity research, for as I pointed out in *Secrets of the Unified Field*, he was very likely one of those who received a copy of the annotated Varo edition of Dr. Morris Jessup's book on UFOs, the edition that outlined a connection to the Philadelphia Experiment.[14]

Before proceeding with a closer look at Dr. Oberth, it is also worth comparing his, with Von Braun's, remarks. In Von Braun's case, it is worth noting that they are very carefully phrased. Nowhere does he allude to extraterrestrials, but simply to "powers" far "stronger" than "us," and operating from some unknown base. It is thus possible to construe his remarks as referring to some unknown *human power*, and to construe that power has possessing a secret base of operations either on, or off, this world. It is equally possible to construe Von Braun's remarks is indicating an *extraterrestrial*

---

[12] Fred Steckling, *We Found Alien Bases on the Moon: II* (George Adamski Foundation, 1981), p. 144. While Steckling is to be questioned for many of his more bizarre ideas about the Moon, it should be noted that Steckling was one of the first and earliest people to point out anomalies in NASA photographs of the Moon that might indicate artificial structures.

[13] Ibid.

[14] See my *Secrets of the Unified Field: The Philadelphia Experiment, the Nazi Bell, and the Discarded Theory* (Adventures Unlimited Press, 2008), pp. 292-296.

power, again, with a secret base of operations either on or off this world.

But Dr. Oberth's remarks contain no such ambiguity, for he clearly attributes UFO activity to extraterrestrials, albeit in a context that leads not to extraterrestrial technology but to terrestrial ones. Nonetheless, for anyone following the story, and the connections between the two men dating back to their work on Hitler's rockets, the meaning was clear: *Dr Oberth's remarks were the "context" in which Von Braun's remarks were to be interpreted.* In short, we may be looking at a psychological warfare operation. That this is the probable case is revealed when one recalls just exactly what projects Dr. Oberth was associated with in Nazi Germany.

C. Dr. Oberth's Background in Nazi Germany

This context strongly suggests that Dr. Oberth, if not deliberately lying, was at least misdirecting attention to extraterrestrials in the face of scientific principles that were already being investigated—quietly to be sure—in American aerospace projects. But there is another context in which his remarks must be viewed: his known involvement in occult belief, and his known connection to the Nazi Bell project and its reported anti-gravity effects. This is where the story begins to get very murky.

Igor Witkowski observed that Dr. Oberth was somehow involved in two curious activities in Nazi Germany: the super-secret Bell project, and occultism:

> In the files of the "Paperclip" project I also found the personal files of several other interesting scientists, but there was no information of any particular value. I began from Professor Hermann Oberth... Immediately after the war a document was discovered in some buildings in Sroda Slaska, on which his name appeared. It referred to a delegation of several scientists, who had arrived from Prague, stopped on the way in Wroclaw/Breslau and Sroda Slaska/ Neumarkt (3 days) and then made their way to Torgau. The business trip took place between 15.IX-25.IX.1944 and consisted of the following individuals: Professor Hermann Oberth, Herbert Jensen, Dr. Edward Tholen, Dr. Elizabeth Adler, and two others, whose names are illegible. The importance of this information lies in the fact that Hermann Oberth was the most outstanding specialist in the world engaged in space flight theory, with a far

superior authority than that of the young von Braun (at that time 32). In short he represented a potential, which is undoubtedly not wasted, particularly when a rocket programme was being put into effect, projecting several decades into the future. ...(This) information reveals to us a certain unusual and significant fact— significant for the work being carried out. *Namely that in principle it is unknown what Prof. Oberth was engaged in during the war.* One could have the impression that this is some kind of light at the end of the tunnel, which until now has been cloaked in the darkness of night. *After all it is known for sure that Oberth was not connected with the centre in Peenemünde since in this case he would have undoubtedly held at least one of the positions of command*, in other words the fact of his engagement would have been known (thousands of specialists employed there worked after the war in other countries, from the USA and USSR to even Egypt and so is out of the question that a possible secret of this kind could not be kept hidden*). So it seems that some kind of alternative program had existed, being carried out for a long time, and quite a serious one at that. This is indicated even by (the) fact alone of there being a lack of information on the wartime work of Oberth.... A certain curiosity is represented by the fact that he was interested in... occultism...* It seems that the Americans were not interested in Oberth due to his purely theoretical pre-war analyses, but for altogether more specific reasons. It looks after all like it had been attempted to recreate the former (Bell) research team—the information about Jensen probably came from Oberth, since it was found in his personal file.[15]

Notice now, what we have:

1) Dr. Oberth was indeed connected to Von Braun in Nazi Germany;
2) But Dr. Oberth's connections to its wartime research are more directly tied to the super-secret Bell project—*a project with obvious antigravity implications*—than to the more "public" rocket program of Von Braun;

---

[15] Igor Witkowski, *The Truth About the Wunderwaffe*, pp. 258-260, emphases added.

3) Dr. Oberth also has an interest in the occult, a fact that may have had something to do with the Bell project's codenames reflecting, in part, an occult influence.[16]

What this quite plainly means, is that *long before Oberth came to the U.S.A. and made his "Extraterrestrial diagnosis" of the UFO phenomenon, he was clearly involved in a very terrestrial project with explicit ant-gravity capability and potentials.*

In other words, when Dr. Oberth was waxing lyrical about intelligences from beyond the solar system, he was *obfuscating at best, or lying at worst.*

If this is so, then this implies in turn that he was under some sort of orders as part of a larger psychological operation.

The question now becomes, *why* was he lying, and under whose orders was he doing so? Or to put it differently, *when, where, how, and for what reasons, did the idea of coupling antigravity technology to psychological operations first begin?* Thus far, all the evidence points to Nazi Germany, but we still need more solid proof.

For that, we shall have to consider, in the next chapter, the actual Nazi flying saucer mythology, and some curious statements of Hitler's favorite commando in chapter four.

---

[16] See my *SS Brotherhood of the Bell*, pp. 166-167.

Dr Hermann Oberth

Dr. Wernher Von Braun

4

THE NAZI UFO MYTHOS:
HANNEBU, VRIL,
AND THE SUCTION SAUCERS

"Prior to 1950, no claim was made of any successful flight by high performance circular or spherical aircraft in Germany during the war."
Andy Roberts Brigantia[1]

W e have seen the traces of a possible psychological operation at work in George Adamski, and clear indications that Drs. Von Braun and Oberth were not being entirely truthful with respect to their opinions that UFOs were extraterrestrial craft, especially given Oberth's status as a member of the Bell project. However, there is another suggestion—perhaps the strongest of them all—of a psychological operation at work with respect to the Nazis, and that is the Nazi UFO mythos itself, and its incredible persistence notwithstanding a paucity of "evidence" in favor of it.

This difficulty is compounded by the fact that, within that mythos, we are dealing with two very different claims, namely, that

1) the Nazis developed circular, disk-shaped craft that were essentially advanced forms of jet aircraft, with vectored exhausts; and,

2) the Nazis developed advanced field propulsion saucers—the infamous Hannebu and Vril craft, or the so-called *Jehnseitsflugzeug*,[2]—that far eclipsed Allied and Soviet technology for decades to come. Within this component of the Nazi mythos, no mention was ever made of anything remotely resembling the Nazi Bell Project, which, as I have

---

[1] Andy Roberts Brigantia, "Secrets of Lies? Investigating the Nazi UFO Legends," http://www.ufoinfo.com/news/secrets.shtml.
[2] See my *SS Brotherhood of the Bell* (Adventures Unlimited Press, 2006), pp. 109-114.

stated elsewhere, I believe to be the kernel or core truth to this component of the mythos.[3]

We are confronted by yet another difficulty as well, and that is the fact that there is an historical "gap" between the end of the Second World War in Europe, and the first appearance of the allegations of Nazi flying saucers in the early 1950s. In this, as we shall argue in this chapter, there is a profound clue that we are dealing with a psychological operation designed both to obfuscate the actual core truth—the Bell project—and to confuse the enemy, the Soviet Union, with claims of advanced technology that fell into Allied hands.

A. The Problematic of the Historical Gap
1. The Basic Elements of the Mythos
a. The Belluzo Allegations

Researcher Kevin McClure has been one of the foremost, and most capable, researchers to challenge the two components of the Nazi UFO mythos, in an excellent online article entitled "The Nazi UFO Mythos: An Investigation."[4] Indeed, for its concision and for the rich details it provides, it is also the best introduction to the subject. McClure notes that

The earliest claim by an individual of the construction of a wartime flying disk was made by Guiseppe Belluzzo on or around March 27 1950, at a time when there had been a number of flying saucer reports in the Italian media, and European interest in the subject was high. On that date the Italian newspaper 'Il Mattino dell'Italia Centrale' published, with a vague and uninformative line-drawing as illustration, Belluzzo's apparent claim that circular aircraft had been developed since 1942, first in Italy, and then in Germany. The Italian idea was, supposedly, developed by the Germans in North-East Norway. The story also appeared in 'Il Corriere della Sera', 'La Nazione', and 'La Gazzetta del Popolo', and, in 'Il Corriere d'Informazione' of March 29-30 1950, with a comment by a General Ranza of the Italian Air Force dismissing Belluzzo's claims. It seems that Belluzzo did not claim that the disc flew during the war but that, by 1950, it had been sufficiently developed to deliver an atom

---

[3] Farrell, *The SS Brotherhood of the Bell*, p. 142.

[4] Kevin McClure, "The Nazi UFO Mythos: An Investigation," http://magonia.haaan.com/2009/nazi-ufo-00-intro/

bomb. This development was said to be some 10 metres wide, constructed with very light materials, and unmanned.

We know something of Belluzzo's background and competence. Verga notes that he lived from November 25 1876 to May 21 1952, and was a turbine expert who published nearly fifty technical books. He was elected to the pre-war Fascist parliament, and from 1925 to 1928 served as Minister of the National Economy. I have traced a listing for a book of his – on turbines – full of technical drawings and translated into English in 1926. It is quite feasible that he could have contributed to a range of technological projects, but it seems that he never claimed to have built a flying disc, nor to have named those who worked with the Germans in Norway. *As in all such reports, no viable propulsion, launch, lift, flight, control or landing data is provided,* and the criteria for publication seems to have been that the object should resemble the flying saucers which, as ever, had caught the media's attention.

It is quite possible that a former Fascist minister would be happy to seek a little belated glory for his nation and his regime, but for all of the later interpretations of his role in the history of Nazi UFOs his claims were very limited, and *so far as the assertion of a design for a reasonably-sized, unmanned flying disc was concerned, they are neither unique nor implausible. Belluzzo may, in part at least, have been telling the truth.*[5]

Note the highlighted points, for they bear both on McClure's skeptical assessment of the mythos, and upon our own critique of the skeptics, and our hypothesis that the mythos may represent a psyop:

1) The first claim for the development of a Nazi flying saucer is made in 1950;
2) The claim comes, not from an Nazi, neo-Nazi, or German source, but from a former member of Mussolini's Fascist government in Italy;
3) Belluzo—whose name is altered in subsequent reports to Bellonzo—was indeed a turbine expert, and thus, a logical candidate to be involved in the development of jet powereed saucers;

---

[5] Kevin McClure, "The Nazi UFO Mythos 03: Major Lusar, The Saucer Builders and the Test Flight," http://magonia.haaan.com/2009/nazi-ufo-3/, emphasis added.

4) Belluzo provides no significant details regarding the technological aspects of the alleged research, beyond providing enough information to satisfy even skeptic McClure that the design "for a reasonably-sized, unmanned flying disc" was "neither unique nor implausible," and that thus "Belluzo may, in part at least, have been telling the truth."

This last point is an astonishing admission, for the core of the Nazi saucer mythos is that, in fact, the first prototypical developments were not of field propulsion craft, but of suction turbine—jet—craft with vectored exhausts.

b. The Schriever Allegations in Der Spiegel*(The Mirror)*

Belluzo made his statements in Italy on March 27, 1950, and these statements were followed a mere three days later, on March 30, 1950, with the first claims for the Nazi development of such a craft coming from a German source, *Flugkapitän* Rudolf Schriever. Schriever in effect made similar claims to Belluzo, claiming "only that he had developed blueprints,"[6] but again, the article "lacked any technical meaningful technical information"[7] to allow one to assess their veracity by "reverse engineering" the concepts involved.

c. Dr Richard Miethe

After these initial reports, claims of Nazi flying saucers died down until 1952, when once again the claims surfaced, this time by a "Dr. Richard Miethe", which appeared on June 7, 1952, in *France-Soir*.[8] According to this article, Miethe stated that he was 40 years old, "and claims that he built a flying saucer—the V7 which he built in 1944, the motors of which the Russians found at Breslau."[9] This is a crucial point that we shall return to subsequently, namely, that the Russians recovered some of the actual technical components, and in

---

[6] McClure, "The Nazi UFO Mythos 03: Major Lusar, The Saucer Builders and the Test Flight," http://magonia.haaan.com/2009/nazi-ufo-3/, emphasis added.

[7] Ibid.

[8] Ibid.

[9] Ibid.

some versions of the mythos, some of the documentation and technicians involved.

More importantly, Schriever explicitly mentioned that he had been a member of the team of former German military and SS officers and engineers sent to Egypt after the overthrow of King Farouk, where he claimed "he had been working with others to reconstruct the engine with which his earlier flying disc had been powered. The trigger for the expulsion may have been a breakdown in diplomatic relations between (West) Germany and Egypt."[10] These assertions pose some problems, partially because they have the ring of truth, and partially because the overthrow of King Farouk that brought in the former German Wehrmacht and SS officers and engineers occurred on July 23, 1952, and yet Miethe's interview occurred the previous month, prior to the coup, and, as far as we know, prior to the injection of German military personnel and scientists into Egypt in the wake of the coup! Miethe's statements, in other words, suggest that this injection was secretly underway prior to the coup and that, in fact, there was on-the-ground Nazi presence in Egypt prior to the coup, which was used in the coup itself.

Yet, the first component of Miethe's interview with *France-Soir* rings true, for as I have documented elsewhere, the West German government, under the auspices of the CIA-sponsored coup, brought in military advisors and engineers precisely to work on missiles for Egypt for use against the newly-established state of Israel.[11] Even here, however, there is a problem, for why would Miethe, who—if one is to take the article at face value—had been working for Egypt, subsequently make his way to Israel, the hated enemy of the Nazis? The only explanation that seems plausible is that the Israelis "made him an offer that he could not refuse."

---

[10] McClure, "The Nazi UFO Mythos 03: Major Lusar, The Saucer Builders and the Test Flight," http://magonia.haaan.com/2009/nazi-ufo-3/

[11] See my *Nazi International: The Nazis' Postwar Plan to Control Finance, Conflict, Physics, and Space* (Adventures Unlimited Press, 2008), pp. 191-199.

d. George Klein and Habermohl

Besides Miethe, the only alleged eyewitness to the Nazi flying saucers was one Georg Klein, who supposedly saw the test flight of the disk Schriever claimed to have built. There is, in fact, a CIA report of May 27, 1954, that states:

A German newspaper (not further identified) recently published an interview with George Klein, famous German engineer and aircraft expert, describing the experimental construction of 'flying saucers' carried out by him from 1941 to 1945. Klein stated that he was present when, in 1945, the first piloted 'flying saucer' took off and reached a speed of 1,3000 miles per hour within 3 minutes. The experiments resulted in three designs: one designed by Miethe was a disc-shaped aircraft, 135 feet in diameter, which did not rotate; another designed by Habermohl and Schriever, consisted of a large rotating ring, in the centre of which was a round, stationary cabin for the crew. When the Soviets occupied Prague, the Germans destroyed every trace of the 'flying saucer' project and nothing more was heard of Habermohl and his assistants.[12]

McClure goes on to observe that "The German newspaper appears to have been *Welt am Sonntag* for (different dates are given) April 25 or 26 1953. The article is titled "Erste 'Flugscheibe' flog 1945 in Prag", and there is a photo of 'George Klein' pointing at the same vague diagram that Lusar reprints."[13] As McClure also notes, this is the first, and only verifiable, mention of the name of Habermohl in connection with the alleged development of Nazi flying saucers.[14]

-----

[12] McClure, "The Nazi UFO Mythos 03: Major Lusar, The Saucer Builders and the Test Flight," http://magonia.haaan.com/2009/nazi-ufo-3/
[13] Ibid.
[14] Ibid.

Saucers, Swastikas, and Psyops

e. Major Rudolf Lusar

We come at last to the name that did so much to spread the Nazi UFO mythos: Luftwaffe Major Rudolf Lusar, and his book, first published in 1959 in the United Kingdom. Here all the elements of the Nazi UFO mythos were gathered and summarized, and we italicize the portions of Lusar's text—cited in full by McClure—that shall concern us here:

Flying saucers have been whirling round the world since 1947, suddenly turning up here and there, *soaring in and darting off again at unprecedented speed with flames encircling the rim of the saucer's disc.* They have been located by radar, pursued by fighters and yet nobody has so far succeeded in establishing the existence of such a 'flying saucer' or managed to ram or shoot one down. The public, even the experts, are perplexed by an ostensible mystery or a technical miracle. But *slowly the truth is coming out that even during the war German research workers and scientists made the first moves in the direction of these "flying saucers". They built and tested such near-miraculous contraptions.* Experts and collaborators in this work confirm that the first projects, called "flying discs", were undertaken in 1941. *The designs for these "flying discs" were drawn up by the German experts Schriever, Habermohl and Miethe, and the Italian Bellonzo. Habermohl and Schriever chose a wide-surface ring which rotated round a fixed, cupola-shaped cockpit. The ring consisted of adjustable wing-discs which could be brought into appropriate position for the take-off or horizontal flight.* respectively. Miethe developed a discus-shaped plate of a diameter of 42m in which adjustable jets were inserted. Schriever and Habermohl, who worked in Prague, took off with the first "flying disc" on February 14. 1945. Within three minutes they climbed to an altitude of I2,400m and reached a speed of 2,000 km/h in horizontal flight (!) It was intended ultimately to achieve speeds of 4,000 km/h.
Extensive preliminary tests and research were necessary before construction could be started. Because of the great speed and the extraordinary heat stress, special heat-resisting materials had to be found. The development, which cost millions, was almost completed at the end of the war. *The then existing models were destroyed but the plant in Breslau where Miethe worked fell into the hands of the Russians who took all the material and the experts to Siberia, where work on these "flying saucers" is being successfully continued.*

Schriever escaped from Prague in time; *Habermohl, however, is probably in the Soviet Union, as nothing is known of his fate. The former designer Miethe is in the United States and, as far as is known, is building "flying saucers" for the United States and Canada at the A. V. Roe works.* Years ago, the U.S. Air Force received orders not to fire at "flying saucers". This is an indication of the existence of American "flying saucers" which must not be endangered. The flying shapes so far observed are stated to have diameters of 16, 42, 45 and 75 m respectively and to reach speeds of up to 7,000 km/h. (?). In 1952 "flying saucers" were definitely established over Korea and Press reports said they were seen also during the NATO maneuvres in Alsace in the autumn of 1954. It can no longer be disputed that "flying saucers" exist. But the fact that their existence is still being denied, particularly in America, because United States developments have not progressed far enough to match the Soviet Union's, gives food for thought. There also seems some hesitation to recognise that these novel "flying saucers" are far superior to conventional aircraft – including modern turbo-jet machines – that they surpass their flying performance, load capacity and maneouvrability and thereby make them obsolete.[15]

The Nazi UFO mythos has, with Lusar, reached its penultimate form, encompassing the following elements:

1) Incredible performance characteristics and clearly a craft that is jet propelled: *"soaring in and darting off again at unprecedented speed with flames encircling the rim of the saucer's disc..."*
2) The claim that Nazi scientists were the first to attempt to construct such "Near-miraculous" craft: *"slowly the truth is coming out that even during the war German research workers and scientists made the first moves in the direction of these "flying saucers". They built and tested such near-miraculous contraptions."*
3) The crucial element that some of the technology and technicians were captured by the Soviets who continued the research: *"The then existing models were destroyed but the*

---

[15] McClure, "The Nazi UFO Mythos 03: Major Lusar, The Saucer Builders and the Test Flight," http://magonia.haaan.com/2009/nazi-ufo-3/, citing Lusar, Rudolf (1959) Trans Heller, R P and Schindler, M German Secret Weapons of the Second World War Philosophical Library New York.

plant in Breslau where Miethe worked fell into the hands of the Russians who took all the material and the experts to Siberia, where work on these "flying saucers" is being successfully continued," and finally,

4) The claim that the other center of postwar research into flying saucer type craft was continued in the U.S.A. and Canada: *"Habermohl, however, is probably in the Soviet Union, as nothing is known of his fate. The former designer Miethe is in the United States and, as far as is known, is building "flying saucers" for the United States and Canada at the A. V. Roe works."*

However, there is another component of the Nazi UFO mythos, one much more sensational as we have seen: the claim to have built actual functional field propulsion craft, the so-called Hannebu and Vril series and other miscellaneous claims of a similar nature.

f. The Field Propulsion Saucer Myth

Researcher Henry Stevens, over a lifetime of research, has assembled what is perhaps the clearest exposition of the development of Nazi field propulsion saucer claims under one cover, in his *Hitler's Flying Saucers*. Stevens comes right to the point in stating what the problem is:

The existence of World War Two German field propulsion flying saucers is a topic which is denied by virtually every reputable authority in aviation history. It is also denied by many researchers studying German saucers. The problem is that in the years immediately following the Second World War the earth's skies suddenly began to be populated by flying craft which did some remarkable things. They flew at unheard of speeds. They made very sharp turns, seemingly non-aerodynamic turns, even at this extreme speed. They lacked the glowing tail of jets or rockets but they glowed or gave off light at night from their periphery or from the whole craft. They were silent or almost silent. Sometimes they gave off sounds that an electric generator or motor might make. Sometimes vehicles with electrically based ignition systems ceased to operate in the presence of these saucers. No government claimed these flying craft, yet they were seen all over the world.[16]

---

[16] Henry Stevens, *Hitler's Flying Saucers*, p. 139.

Indeed, this is the problem posed by the Nazi flying saucer mythos, for the only terrestrial government claiming them publicly was *a government supposedly defunct*, and it was doing so through a few lone voices in scattered newspaper and magazine articles, voices that claimed to have been associated with their development. Moreover, the earliest claims did not involve field propulsion at all.

The claims to field propulsion saucer achievements were advanced much later, and by a narrow circle with its own dubious connections to postwar Nazis.[17] And here, as Stevens notes, the claims and the people advancing them get very murky indeed, for the claim being advanced in these circles is that the field propulsion saucers were developments from an understanding of the physics basis of obscure occult teachings:

> Mention of the "occult" brings us to another line of evidence concerning field propulsion, that put forth by Norbert Juergen-Ratthoder and Ralf Ettl. Mr. Ettl became involved while doing research for a film project on Dr. Wernher von Braun. A film company was paying for this research. A package or several packages of information were obtained by the production company which had more to do with UFOs than rocketry. This information was laid aside by Mr. Ettl but he returned to it after enlisting the help of Norbert Juergen-Ratthofer who had a special interest in that subject.
>
> The package contained breathtakingly clear photographs of German saucers in flight. Some of these pictures may be just models but some look authentic and are posed against a landscape. Nowadays, pictures can be generated via computer and these pictures surfaced within modern times...
>
> Besides the pictures, these writers provide an entire historical and cultural context for these saucers within the Third Reich. This context involves secret organizations with the SS. Further, the context provided by these writers (involves) the occult, channeling, and extraterrestrials. This is the weak point of their presentation since the case for these latter connections is really not strong enough to be in evidence.[18]

---

[17] See my *Nazi International* (Adventures Unlimited Press, 2008), pp. 16-43,

[18] Stevens, *Hitler's Flying Saucers*, p. 159.

Indeed, it is this same group that promulgated the idea, through another researcher, Jan Van Helsing, that the Germans, through the use of mediums, "channeled" technical information—in Sumerian!—for the construction of the alleged saucers, having contacted extraterrestrials by this means.[19] Shades of Adamski once again.

We note that we are confronted with a kind of "Nazi version" of the infamous Cooper-Cantwheel Majic-12 documents: packages that allegedly arrive *at a film production company* from some anonymous source, in this case, containing photographs and diagrams of alleged German field propulsion saucers. It goes without saying that a film production company could indeed hoax photographs of "Nazi flying saucers."

It is here, with the Juergen-Raffhofer group and this package of pictures and alleged "plans," that the now infamous Hannebu and Vril saucers made their first major appearance, spawning further elaborations of the mythos that the Nazis actually mounted manned Moon missions, and even a "suicidal" one way mission to Mars!

> Mr. Juergen-Ratthofer, Mr. Ettle and allied writers offer two different systems for field propulsion. the smaller saucer-type, which they designate "Vril" was powered by three moving magnetic fields. The larger type, designated "Haunebu" was powered by a series of devices according to these writers. In this arrangement, the output of smaller of the Hans Coler "free energy" devices, the "Magnetapparat", was used to supply input for the larger Coler device, the "Stromerzueger". The output of this second device was used to turn a Van de Graaf generator. This energy was directed into something called a Marconi ball dynamo (which) supplied lift to the saucer.
>
> All that seems to have been said about the latter device is that it is mentioned in the same sentence with special saucer condensers developed by (Thomas Townsend) Brown and Professor Paul Biefeld in the nineteen wtenties and that "such" ("solche") with a rotor system was done by Professor Marconi, in Italy, in the nineteen thirties. Mr. Juergen-Ratthofer goes on to say that this device is to be considered, in principle, a forerunner to the Searl system.[20]

---

[19] See my *SS Brotherhood of the Bell* (Adventures Unlimited Press, 2006), pp. 104-115

[20] John Searl is a British engineer and inventor who during the late 1960s and throughout the 1970s built a number of levitating disks using

The Haunebu pictures strongly resemble the Adamski saucer pictures of the early 1950s... Mr. Ettle and Mr. Juergen-Ratthofer maintain that these "Adamski saucers" are really the German-designed Haunebu type saucers. Since they were flown after the war, certain questions as to their origin arise.[21]

Leaving aside for a moment any commentary on the dubious technological and historical claims—claims no doubt made to provide an aura of "veracity" to the story—we note that two memes have now been joined in the Nazi saucer mythos, that of Nazi technological prowess, with Adamski's "extraterrestrial contact." Why this has occurred will be explored more fully in the next chapter.

This fusion of the memes of extraterrestrial contact, occult influences and practice, and Nazi technology reached the zenith with the claims of Jan Van Helsing, who maintained that in the interwar period, mediums made contact with an extraterrestrial civilization, which civilization communicated technological information allowing the Germans to build a flying saucer.[22]

The reader will have noticed an immediate problem, and this is the historical *gap* between the earliest appearances of German suction saucer stories in the early 1950s, Adamski's contact stories from the same period, and the much later claims—with little substantiation—of field propulsion saucers.

2. The Gap and the Critics of the Mythos

We may now gain an appreciation of the problematic posed by the historical gap in these reports of jet-propelled and field propulsion saucers by pointing out the observations of researcher Andy Roberts Brigantia:

> 1. Prior to 1950, no claim was made of any successful flight by high performance circular or spherical aircraft in Germany during the war.

---

roller magnets. These disks were seen by several observers to levitate and simply fly off into space.

[21] Henry Stevens, *Hitler's Flying Saucers,* p. 161, emphasis added.
[22] See my *SS Brotherhood of the Bell*, pp. 104-115.

2. No contemporary documentary evidence (from before 1946) has been produced regarding any successful flight by high performance circular or spherical aircraft in Germany during the war.

3. The only sources of original information and evidence for the wide, circular 'Schriever, Habermohl, Miethe and Bellonzo Flying Disc' come from a brief news agency report quoted in Der Spiegel in 1950, under the name of a "Captain Rudolph Schriever" (also possibly appearing at the same time in the Italian press), and from *German Secret Weapons of the Second World War* by Major Rudolf Lusar, published in Germany in 1957, and in London and New York in 1959. Schriever seems to suggest that the craft did not progress beyond blueprint stage, but Lusar appears to have taken the 'Schriever' account, turned the planned speed and height figures into ones that had actually been achieved, changed some of the technical details, and added the vague, non-technical drawing of this supposed craft which has been reprinted in various contexts since.

I am not aware that Schreiver's existence has ever been confirmed, and no proof has been produced to show that Lusar would have had direct access—denied to conventional historians—to any source of information about such a 'flying disc', which he claims "climbed to an altitude of 12,400m" "within three minutes", "and reached a speed of 2,000 kmh", on 14 February 1945. There is no independent evidence which suggests that these claims have any basis in fact. An extensive search of conventional literature on the war, together with German encyclopedias, has found no mention of Lusar, or of any 'Flying Disc' with such a performance record.

4. The only source of original information and evidence for the spherical craft described as *Feuerball* and *Kugelblitz* is the writer Renato Vesco, author of (the English title) *Intercept— But Don't Shoot*, published in Italy in 1968 and in the USA in 1971, and of two other books in Italian. He was also the first to make the link between those alleged craft and various reports of light anomalies during the war, suggesting that they were the cause of the 'foo fighter' phenomenon. No proof has been produced to show how or why Vesco would have had access— denied to conventional historians—to any source of information about these flying spheres, and there is no independent evidence which suggests that these claims for *Feuerball* and *Kugelblitz* have any basis in fact. An extensive search of conventional literature on the war together with

Italian encyclopedias, has found no mention of Vesco, or the *Feuerball* and *Kugelblitz*.

5. There is no contemporary (pre-1946), or other documentary proof of any kind for the existence or flight, during the war, or at any other time, of the unconventional 'flying saucer' craft known as Vril and Haunebu. The material suggesting that these craft, and the related methods of propulsion, existed appears to have made its first appearance some 40 years after the war. An extensive search of conventional literature on the war has found no mention of Vril or Haunebu.

6. Schriever and Lusar make no mention of the *Feuerball* and *Kugelblitz*. Vesco makes no mention of the 'Schriever, Habermohl, Miethe and Bellonzo Flying Disc'. Neither Lusar nor Vesco mention the Vril or Haunebu craft.[23]

Without prejudice to the main arguments advanced by Brigantia, it should be noted with respect to the last point that *if* there was any truth to the claims of Schriever, Lusar, and Vesco, it is unlikely that in the highly compartmentalized secret weapons projects of the Third Reich, that any of them were *likely* to have known of the projects the others were working on.

3. A Critique of the Critics: The Suction Saucers

In my book *Roswell and the Reich* I noted that there is at least *some* evidence for the existence of German suction saucers, in that during the 1950s, the German engineer Heinrich Fleissner attempted to take out a patent on such a craft in the United States—patent number 2,939,648—based on work he claimed to have done earlier in the Third Reich at the secret Peenemünde rocket facility.[24] As I noted there, this craft looks suspiciously like the declassified plans for the American "Project Silverbug" flying saucer of the same period, and indeed, the delay in awarding Fleissner his patent when he filed in 1955, to its final award, was an unheard of five-plus years, ample time for the Air Force to copy and modify his designs.

Additionally, it is incontestable that the suction saucer designs of Viktor Schauberger, who unquestionably also worked for the SS on

---

[23] Andy Roberts Brigantia, "Secrets of Lies? Investigating the Nazi UFO Legends," http://www.ufoinfo.com/news/secrets.shtml.

[24] Joseph P. Farrell, *Roswell and the Reich* (Adventures Unlimited Press, 2010), pp. 494-499.

similar designs, was of interest to postwar American corporations and engineers.[25] Thus, one must assume that the Americans had *some* knowledge of German saucer research, however sketchy, and that they were also involved in psychological operations obfuscating their existence.

B. The Historical Gap, the Gehlen Organization, and Psychological Warfare

So how does one rationalize the sudden appearance of these reports concerning Nazi flying saucer accomplishments in the early 1950s, along with the claims of Adamski? There is one important clue overlooked by most advocates—and opponents—of the Nazi UFO mythos, and that is the possibility of psychological operations within the wider context of the postwar intelligence arrangements between the CIA and Nazi military intelligence.

As I have repeatedly pointed out in my books on Nazi secret weapons, the Bell project, and the continuation of Nazism after the war, one of the crucial interfaces between the western elite, its agencies of power, and the postwar Nazi "International" was Nazi general Reinhard Gehlen's military intelligence unit, *Fremde Heere Ost*, or Foreign Armies East, a vast network of spies within the Soviet Union and Eastern Europe. Gehlen undertook negotiations with OSS station chief in Zurich, Allen Dulles, to turn this network over to American intelligence at the conclusion of the war, provided that he, General Gehlen, remain in day-to-day operational control of this network. As I observed in *The SS Brotherhood of the Bell*, this meant effectively that when the ink was dry on the National Security Act of 1947, the CIA's civilian character was already compromised, for the CIA's on-the-ground Soviet intelligence and analysis division was, virtually in its entirety, General Gehlen's Nazi military intelligence group, otherwise known at the time as the Gehlen Organization, or simply, the "Gehlenorg." This organization often worked in close conjunction with other postwar Nazi organizations such as ODESSA and The Spider, the *Kameradenwerk* and the *Bruderschaft*.

This is a crucial point, for it means that in the postwar period and well into the 1950s, the CIA's on-the-ground intelligence network,

[25] Joseph P. Farrell, *Reich of the Black Sun* (Adventures Unlimited Press, 2004), pp. 206-221.

not only in Eastern Europe and the Soviet Union, but also in Western Europe, was largely a Nazi organization under nominal American command.

Within this context, the CIA sponsored covert operations from 1949-1950 to prevent Italy from electing a Communist government, and, as I have detailed elsewhere, also was in nominal control to overthrow Egyptian King Farouk.[26] The Gehlenorg, during this same time period, had given its American cousins in the CIA an analysis of Soviet military capabilities and intentions, an estimate that so deliberately over-estimated these capabilities and intentions that it was one of the crucial factors in driving the postwar American arms race and doctrine of "containment."

We now propose that the sudden appearance of Nazi suction-saucer stories during this crucial period of Cold War tensions was not accidental, but an intentional psychological operation of this CIA-Gehlenorg nexus, designed to do two things:

1) On the American side, to convince the Soviets that the alleged Nazi technology fell into American hands, and thus, that America had a preponderant technological advantage in air power over the Soviets;

2) On the Nazi side, the purpose was, as I shall argue below, two-fold yet again:

    a) To obfuscate the real story of suction saucer development; and,

    b) To obfuscate the development of genuine field propulsion technology, namely, the Bell.

1. The Bell Story and the Nazi UFO Mythos: Core Elements

The last point may not be entirely clear until we compare it, on the one hand, to the wild claims for Nazi field propulsion saucers, claims which are, in themselves, baseless and unfounded, and on the other hand, to the story of the Bell itself. As we have seen, there are two core components of the Nazi Saucer mythos:

---

[26] See my *Nazi International* (Adventures Unlimited Press, 2008), pp.

1) The suction saucers were developed in Nazi Germany and some were actually flown in test flights shortly before the end of the war, and,

2) *Some* of this technology and the technicians and documentation associated with it fell into Soviet hands and continued to be secretly developed by them after the war.

As has been seen, there is at least *some* threadbare evidence that something like a suction saucer project was underway in Nazi Germany, both at Peenemünde (Fleissner), and within the SS (Schauberger), but these projects have nothing to do with the claims of Schriever, Belluzo, and others.

But what of the field propulsion component of the mythos?

Here, there is no evidence of anything like the "Hannebu" and "Vril" saucers, other than the wild contactee fantasies of Adamski—whose technological descriptions we have noted in a previous chapter are suspiciously like the Bell project—and the even wilder fantasias of Jürgen-Ratthofer, Ettl, and Van Helsing. With respect to the Bell project, this device gave off such deadly field effects that, reports of its ability to levitate notwithstanding, it is unquestionable that any human inside the device would have been exposed to fatal and deadly forces.[27] Its use in practice as a manned field propulsion craft would have been nil. Additionally, there are *no* reports of the Bell exhibiting the performance capabilities of UFOs, though certainly the implications of its reported levitation open up such potentialities.[28]

In the version of the Bell story recounted by Igor Witkowski, Nick Cook, and myself, the evidence for the project is based upon a tapestry of bits of evidence that, taken together, allow one to "reverse engineer" the parameters of the project:

1) the Polish war crimes trial affidavit of SS general Jakob Sporrenberg, who was sentenced to death in Poland for the murder of some 60 scientists and technicians involved with the project. It should now be noted that Witkoski holds open the possibility that, during Sporrenberg's execution, a last minute substitution of a double was made, and Sporrenberg

---

[27] Joseph P. Farrell, *The SS Brotherhood of the Bell*, pp. 171-179.
[28] Ibid.

himself was spirited out of Poland by the Soviet N.K.V.D., forerunner of the KGB,[29] thus, there *is* a Soviet connection to the only *known* Nazi field propulsion project, exactly as was seen in the Nazi UFO mythos;

2) The Bell project was known to have been developed in lower Silesia, and there are installations in the region that would be commensurate with such a project. Similarly, the Nazi UFO mythos consistently locates the base of operations in lower Silesia, in the provincial capital of Breslau (modern day Wroclaw, Poland); and, finally

3) It is possible to "reverse engineer" the physics conceptions of the Bell based on descriptions of the device, and other data.[30] By following the clues of these conceptions, it is clear that the Nazis continued to research this project independently in Juan Perón's Argentina in the early 1950s in Dr. Ronald

---

[29] Igor Witkowski, *The Truth About the Wunderwaffe* (European History Press, 2003), p. 243. Witkowski states: "In December 1952 the death sentence was announced, which was officially soon carried out. In reality however the day before the planned execution, by the so-called 'operational measures' all persons obliged to be present during the execution have been changed, and instead of Sporrenberg a prisoner foreman (Kapo) from Stutthof concentration camp was executed, while Sporrenberg himself was flown to the USSR. In all probability he did not live there for very long—if only for the reason that the possibility of escape had to be excluded with 100% certainty. Sporrenberg however must have expected the deception and informed his family through his lawyer, since even in the 1960s petitions were sent for his release (to KC PZPR—(the) central committee of the main party.

"In 1947 Rudolf Schuster died suddenly in obscure circumstances (if he really died). Col Szymanski, who had interrogated him was killed in an air crash along with a group of witnesses, soon after completing the investigation. His superior and chief of the Polish Military Mission in Berlin—General Jakub Prawin died in 1950(as far as I remember—he capsized his boat and drowned). Major Walczak was killed in a car crash....

"The Soviets took over the whole affair and cut off all links, in Poland only traces remained... in Poland nobody was able to define either 'the bell's' principle of operation, or why this device was considered so state-of-the-art."

[30] See my books *SS Brotherhood of the Bell*, pp. 171-271; *Secrets of the Unified Field*, pp. 227-288; *The Philosophers' Stone: Alchemy and the Secret Research for Exotic Matter* (Feral House, 2009), pp. 247-329.

Richter's "controlled fusion" project.[31] These conceptions involved:

a) high speed mechanical and electrical counter-rotation of a plasma inducing substance composed most likely of mercury and thorium 229 isomer oxide, to achieve magnetic fields separation and a quasi-super-conductive state; and,

b) high voltage direct current stressing of that plasma, to create momentary fusion reactions in the substance.

The basic goal of all of this, as I have argued elsewhere, is to create a "torsion shear" effect in the fabric of space time, a kind of "gravity bubble" around the device, which would account for its ionizing radiation and reported levitation.

Interestingly enough, a patent, filed on May 17, 1988, exists for an electromagnetic plasma reactor that sounds suspiciously like the concepts of Dr. Ronald Richter some three decades previously, concepts for which he was roundly denounced. The claims for this patent read as follows:

> What is claimed is:
> 1. A plasma arc reactor for refining raw materials comprising: spaced electrode means including at least one anode electrode defining a reaction chamber and at least one cathode electrode mounted within said reaction chamber and variably spaced from said anode electrode; electrical circuit means connected to said anode and cathode electrodes for creating a plasma arc within said reaction chamber; and an induction coil means externally mounted circumferentially about said reaction chamber for producing a magnetic field therein.
> 2. The plasma arc reactor of claim 1, wherein said anode electrode comprises a hollow elongated cylinder having a central vertical longitudinal axis and opposed first and second closed ends.
> 3. The plasma reactor of claim 2, wherein said anode electrode defines a reaction chamber comprising a frusto-conical interior cavity.
> 4. The plasma reactor of claim 2, wherein said reaction chamber comprises a frusto-conical interior cavity which tapers from a small

---

[31] Joseph P. Farrell, *The Nazi International*(Adventures Unlimited Press, 2008), pp. 249-350.

interior diameter at said first end to a larger interior diameter at said second end.

5. The plasma reactor of claim 4, wherein said reactor includes support means secured to said anode electrode, said support means operating to move said anode electrode along the longitudinal axis thereof relative to the cathode.

6. The plasma arc reactor of claim 1, wherein said induction coil means operates to impose a magnetic field within said reaction chamber to rotate said plasma arc.

7. The plasma arc reactor of claim 3, wherein said induction coil means operates to impose a magnetic field within said reaction chamber to rotate said plasma arc produced between said anode electrode and said cathode electrode.

8. The plasma arc reactor of claim 7, wherein said cathode electrode comprises a spherical, cathode ball electrode spaced from said anode electrode within said reaction chamber.

9. The plasma arc reactor of claim 8, wherein said reactor incudes support means secured to said anode electrode, said support means operating to move said anode electrode along the longitudinal axis thereof relative to said cathode ball electrode.

10. The plasma arc reactor of claim 9, wherein said cathode ball electrode is mounted within said reaction chamber, on a cathode stem, said cathode stem extending out said first closed end of said reaction chamber.

11. The plasma arc reactor of claim 10, wherein said cathode stem is rotatably mounted to allow rotation of said cathode ball electrode within said reaction chamber.

12. The plasma arc reactor of claim 1, wherein said plasma sustaining gas is an inert gas.

13. The plasma arc reactor of claim 12, wherein said reactor includes means for admitting said gas to said reaction chamber in a flow counter to the force of gravity. [32]

This patent indicates something quite profound about the Bell and Richter story, namely, *that with the Bell project, unlike for the alleged Nazi field propulsion UFOs, the physics conceptions involved are* **real***, and* **consistent over time and with notions and inventions that emerge much later in the public record.** *It is thus reasonable to locate the core of the Nazi UFO story with the Bell project, and to view*

---

[32] The full text of the patent is available for viewing at http://www.freepatentsonline.com/4745338.html.

that project as being decades in advance of Allied or Soviet technology of the era.

But what, ultimately, was the origin of the idea of coupling such advanced technology with a psychological operation? And what was the *purpose* of this psychological operation? We have alluded to some of these purposes already. The origin, as we have suggested in this chapter, was the Nazis themselves. But the dark purposes for which they conceived of this elaborate operation remain to be explored in the next two chapters. But the real origin, and real purpose, was perhaps hinted at in the other component of the Nazi UFO mythos: the esoteric, and the religious and social engineering themes first enunciated in George Adamski's contactee stories.

The real story, as we shall now see, is very murky indeed, and it all begins with a strange remark of Nazi Propaganda Minister Dr. Josef Göbbels...

Nazi Propaganda Minister Dr. Josef Göbbels

5

THE *SONDERKAMPF* OF THE *WELTANSCHAUUNGSKRIEG*:

THE ORIGIN OF THE ALCHEMY OF SOCIAL ENGINEERING AND PSYCHOLOGICAL OPERATIONS

"Imagine in 1960 you discover a radar blip. This radar blip appears to be a satellite orbiting the Earth... but this satellite isn't listed along side Sputnik or Explorer, in fact no-one (or any country) knows of its origin. Not only that, but this satellite, named 'Black Knight'— has a polar orbit!... Neither the USA nor the USSR/Soviets have accomplished a polar orbit. Black Knight was found to be many, many times larger than any current satellite orbiting our planet."
Stephen Williams[1]

Reich Propaganda Minister Dr. Josef Göbbels' wife, Magda, sometime around Christmas of 1944, told her sister-in-law that her husband had seen a secret weapon "so visionary" that it would ensure a wonderful victory.[2] The problem here, of course, for traditional or conventional interpretation is that Germany's V-1s and V-2s were already raining destruction down on London and other Western European cities, and Germany's jets had already taken to the skies, and Germany's various anti-aircraft missiles were already being fired at Allied bombers. In other words, whatever it was that the Propaganda Minister had seen, it was not any of these things. It was, nonetheless, something that, as Igor Witkowski observes, must have "physically existed at the end of that year," and which created an astounding, "'visionary' impression through its appearance alone—therefore it must have been something completely different to the weapons known up until then."[3]

To make matters very much worse, apparently Hitler's favorite commando, SS Colonel Otto Skorzeny, had seen

---

[1] Stephen Williams, "The Black Knight Satellite Revisited," http://paranormal-mysteries.co.uk/?p=630

[2] Igor Witwkoski, *The Truth About the Wunderwaffe*, p. 231.

[3] Ibid.

something very similar, and proposed utilizing it in a novel fashion. And among all the Third Reich's weird and wonderful arsenal, there is nothing as visionary as its alleged suction saucers, and the more promising Bell project.

A. The *Sonderkampf* of the *Weltanschauungskrieg:* The Nazi Bell and the Beginning of the Coupling of Advanced Technology and Psychological Operations

The idea of using such advanced technologies as represented by UFOs in conjunction with psychological operations thus begins – once again – in World War Two, and once again, it is the Nazis who came up with the idea. I mention this first in *The SS Brotherhood of the Bell*,[4] but its importance for our discussion here is too crucial, so I will expand upon it here. The idea of using advanced technology with "special operations" or "special warfare" was first noticed, predictably enough, by Polish researcher Igor Witkowski, who mentions it in his superb study of Nazi secret weapons projects, *The Truth About the Wunderwaffe*:

> Later, in documents brought over from the American NARA archive at College Park near Washington, I found among other things a report referring to the interrogation of one of Otto Skorzeny's commandos. He was Skorzeny's aide-de-camp, SS-Sturmbannführer Karl Radl, at the same time Chief of the VI-S/2 Division at the General Office for Reich's Security (RSHA – Reichs-sicherheithauptamt). Radl stated —would you believe it —that *since the beginning of 1944 Skorzeny simply had no head to organize acts of sabotage on the enemy's rear areas, since he had come into contact with the "wonder weapon" and as a result had "been possessed" by the idea of "Sonderkampf" ("Special Warfare"), regarding the use of this weapon, to such an extent, that he considered it the only sure way to win the war.*[5]

But what exactly did Skorzeny mean by a *Sonderkampf* or special warfare being conducted by his SS commando "Black Knights"?

---

[4] Joseph P. Farrell, *The SS Brotherhood of the Bell*, p. 172.

[5] Igor Witkowski, *The Truth About the Wunderwaffe*, trans Bruce Wenham (Farmborough, Hampshire: Books International, 2003), pp. 231-232, emphasis added.

Generally speaking, the term meant precisely commando-style actions such as sabotage in enemy rear areas, but it also meant, in the Nazis' case, anti-partisan actions. But clearly, given the context of Witkowski's observations, Skorzeny was *already* commanding such actions, so clearly he had something quite different in mind entirely.

One answer might lie in the Nazis' conception of *Weltanschauungskrieg*, or "World View Warfare," their term for what we would call "psychological warfare," though the German term is, as is evident, much deeper and more comprehensive. But how does *Weltanschauungskrieg* differ from standard psychological operations? To answer this question, we must delve deeply into its American counterpart—psychological warfare—for as we shall see in future chapters, clear indications emerge of a Nazi nexus with American corporations and foundations, a nexus forged prior to the war. What we propose to do in this and the next chapter, in other words, is to "reverse engineer" not a technology, but a psychological operation *deliberately conceived in connection with* that technology.

1. The Components of Psyops

In early 1948, the U.S. Army circulated a top-secret definition of psychological warfare. This definition was the distilled experience of waging psychological warfare against an equally talented opposition when it came to propaganda: Nazi Germany. In the U.S. Army's case,

> Psychological warfare employs all moral and physical means, other than orthodox military operations, which tend to:
>   a. destroy the will and ability of the enemy to fight.
>   b. deprive him of the support of his allies and neutrals.
>   c. increase in our own troops and allies the will to victory.
> Psychological warfare employs *any* weapon to influence the mind of the enemy. **The weapons are psychological only in the *effect* they produce and not because of the nature of the weapons themselves**. In this light, overt (white), covert (black), and gray propaganda; subversion; sabotage; special operations,; guerilla warfare; espionage; political, cultural, economic, and racial pressures are all effective weapons. **They are effective because they produce dissension, distrust,**

fear and hopelessness in the minds of the enemy, not because they originated in the psyche of the propaganda or psychological warfare agencies.[6]

Note carefully the implication of these statements, for clearly the U.S. Army is coupling the idea of technologies—"the weapons themselves"—with a *matrix or context with which they are to be interpreted to "produce dissention, distrust, fear and hopelessness"* in a target population.

While those technologies are not specified in the document, clearly they must be of such an advanced nature that they lend themselves to use in psychological operations; in other words, we are looking at the conceptual matrix of a psychological warfare operation tailor made to exploit the properties of UFOs—whether they are terrestrial or extraterrestrial in origin—in order to confuse and demoralize a target population.

In respect to the distinction between black and white propaganda, communications researcher Christopher Simpson— whom we have quoted above—notes that black propaganda

> "...stresses *trouble, confusion...* and *terror.*"[7]
> A variation of black propaganda tactics involves forging enemy documents and distributing them to target audiences as a means of discrediting rival powers. The U.S. government officially denies that it employs black propaganda, but in fact it has long been an integral aspect of U.S. foreign **and domestic policy.**[8]

Ponder that last line carefully...

...for those familiar with the role of *documents* within UFOlogy will immediately recall two infamous cases when

---

[6] Christopher SImpson, *Science of Coercion: Communication Research and Psychological Warfare* (New York: Oxford University Press, 1996), p. 12, italicized emphasis in the original, boldface emphasis added.

[7] Ibid., citing U.S. Department of the Army, Joint Strategic Plans Committee, *JSPC 862/3*, August 2, 1948, Appendix "C," P&O 332 TS (section 1, case 1), RG 319, U.S. national Archives, Washington, D.C. Simpson notes that this was "originally top secret, now declassified."(p, 137, n. 26)

[8] Ibid., pp. 12-13, boldface emphasis added.

documents purporting to deal with the subject of UFOs were mailed to various recipients from anonymous or pseudonymous sources, from the Majic-12 documents to the "SS Hannebu and Vril" documents.

And this has a profound implication for our purposes. Given the indications already explored that both the SS and the U.S. Army conceived of psychological operations *in conjunction with the use or display of advanced technology, and given the pre- and post-war links to be explored later in this book, the possibility emerges that we are dealing with two components of one psychological operation, one component of which stresses the extraterrestrial origins of this technology, and another which stresses its Nazi origin.* Additionally, each component—the American one and the Nazi one—while coordinated, might also represent underlying *factions* or "vested interests" within our "breakaway civilization."

One purpose of this seemingly implausible coordination, according to Simpson, is to "manage empire" and to function "as an instrument for maintaining grossly abusive social structures, notably in global North/South relations."[9] In the case of our "breakaway civilization," this function would be redefined to maintain the abusive and parasitic relationship between it and its "host" societies.

Furthermore, in the maintenance of such a hidden empire, the breakaway civilization will, like its more conventional counterparts, utilize all the components of psychological operations, from "techniques of persuasion, opinion measurement", i.e., polling, "interrogation, political and military mobilization, propagation of ideology,"[10] to "social psychology, communication effect studies, anthropological studies of foreign communication systems,"[11] and so on. It is my contention that given the necessarily small population base of any such breakaway civilization, plus the fact that it is coupled to a matrix of advanced infrastructure to conduct and deploy its advanced technologies, that its *primary method of military operations will*

---

[9] Simpson, *Science of Coercion*, p. 8.
[10] Ibid., p. 4.
[11] Ibid., p. 9.

be precisely via psychological warfare operations to compensate for its much smaller population base.

2. Managing Perceptions: The Engineering of a Scientific Consensus

Given that one principal goal of psychological warfare is to manage perceptions of a target group or population, and thus to inhibit or otherwise influence that group's decision-making and world-interpreting processes, and given that there is a clear and explicit coupling of advanced technologies with psychological warfare operations both in the conceptions of the U.S. Army and of SS Colonel Otto Skorzeny, it is worth noting that one of the principal targets of such "perception management" is the scientific community itself. As Simpson notes, the very study of psychological warfare, of communications science, "became something like a Rorschach test through which favored academics spoke about the world as they believed it to be, and thereby helped institutionalize that vision at the expense of its rivals."[12] This is, in strictest terms, already something beyond "psychological warfare" in the traditional sense, and approaches what the Nazis meant by *Weltanschauungs-krieg* or "World View Warfare," for the effect of the promotion of certain views and scientists who hold them, is to create a "matrix of interpretation" or "matrix of perception", which matrix in turn opens up only certain avenues of decision and action.

What came of this activity—at least in the case of the United States—was a transformation of the scientific method and community itself, with the creation of a "publicly received and officially sanctioned 'science'," and a hidden science privy only to those in the black community itself (about which we shall have more to say subsequently):

> U.S. psychological warfare programs between 1945 and 1960 provide *a case study of how the priorities and values of powerful social groups can be transformed into the "received knowledge" of the scientific community, and, to a certain extent, of society as a whole.* It is a twofold story, first of the successes and failures of the government's effort *to achieve the engineering of consent*

---

[12] Simpson, *Science of Coercion*, p. 5.

of targeted populations at home and abroad, and, contained within that, the story of the mechanisms by which consent was achieved among the scientists who had been hired to help with the job.[13]

Obviously, Simpson means his remarks to apply not to our breakaway civilization, but to the efforts of U.S. psychological warfare operations during the Cold War, to buttress its own ideological position in the targeted populations of the West and the Third World, in opposition to the supposed expansionist aims of the Communist bloc and its ideology.

But it takes little imagination to see how such operations would be used by a breakaway civilization to create a false scientific consensus in all scientific disciplines—from physics to genetics to sociology—that related to its own secret research, to prevent the widespread dissemination of ideas or concepts that formed the basis of its research when possible, and to direct the mis-interpretation of them when it could not. This leads us directly to...

3. The Techniques of Obfuscation

Within the American conception of psychological operations, various techniques of obfuscation have emerged, techniques designed to inhibit the interpretive and decision-making faculties of target groups directly. The two most salient components of these techniques are "the use of 'plausible deniability' to permit the government to deny responsibility for 'black' operations that were in truth originated by the United States;'" and "a conscious policy of polarizing neutral nations into either 'pro-' or 'anti-U.S.' camps."[14] In the case of the breakaway civilization, these two techniques are quite the crucial points, for on the one hand, such a civilization must seek both to cloak the technologies it is utilizing, and to cloak or deny its own very existence, and on the other hand, must obfuscate the interpretation of its technologies in case they are discovered.

With respect to the last point, in a previous book, *Roswell and the Reich*, I noted the creation of what I called "the Roswell

---

[13] Ibid., p. 10, emphasis added.
[14] Simpson, *Science of Coercion*, p. 13.

dialectic," a creation I noted that was linked to the U.S. military which was seeking to control *the interpretation*, to *manage the perceptions*, of the Roswell event, by casting the interpretation into one of two alternatives: either it had to be extraterrestrial, or it was a purely mundane event that had been misinterpreted; it was, in short, either a crashed extraterrestrial craft, or merely a mistaken balloon of some sort. In other words, Roswell— *whatever* the reality of the event underlying the interpretations—showed all the classic hallmarks of a psychological warfare operation.[15] This dialectic is a classic case of the employment of the "polarization" technique, only in this case, is it *not a pro-US or anti-US posture that the target group is being urged to take, but rather, a pro-ET or an anti-ET posture with respect to the alleged recovered technology.*

4. American Private Foundation Funding of Psyops Studies

None of this, however, establishes that one is dealing with a breakaway civilization in the sense that Mr. Dolan hypothesized, and that we reviewed in chapter one. For such a case to begin to gain some *prima facie* credence, one would have to show that forces, powers, and/or "instruments"— in Quigley's sense—that were more or less private and independent of the government were involved in the formulation and deployment of psychological warfare operations.

Fortunately, we *do* have evidence, highly *suggestive* evidence, that this indeed is the case, for during World War Two, not only did the U.S. government allocate "between $7 million and $13 million annually for university and think-tank studies of communications-related social psychology, communication effect studies" and "anthropological studies of foreign communication systems,"[16] but major foundations, including the Carnegie, Ford, and Rockefeller Foundations also privately funded this research,[17] thus gaining access to the results of these studies. As we shall discover in the last section of this book, the

---

[15] See my *Roswell and the Reich: The Nazi Connection* (Adventures Unlimited Press, 2010), pp. 315-318.

[16] Simpson, *Science of Coercion*, p. 9.

[17] Ibid., pp. 9, 13, 60-61.

nexus between the Ford and Rockefeller interests on the one hand, and Nazism on the other, predate the war, and form a vital component of the matrix in which the crystal of the breakaway civilization, and its conception of its relationship to its host societies, is grown. For the moment, however, we note that there is a direct and established relationship between powerful private groups and financial interests, and the rise of psychological warfare as a component of "managing empire," in this case, the private empires represented by those interests.

5. Back to the Nazi Component: The Implications of **Weltanschauungskrieg**

It is important to understand that psychological warfare operations developed during World War Two *largely as a response* to the totalitarian state of Nazi Germany, and its ideological understanding that psychological warfare was a "World View Warfare:"

> The phrase 'psychological warfare' is reported to have first entered English in 1941 as a translated mutation of the Nazi term *Weltanschauungskrieg* (literally, worldview warfare), meaning the purportedly scientific application of propaganda, terror, and state pressure as a means of securing an ideological victory over one's enemies. William "Wild Bill" Donovan, then director of the newly established U.S. intelligence agency Office of Strategic Services (OSS), viewed an understanding of Nazi psychological tactics as a vital sources of ideas for "Americanized" versions of many of the same strategems.[18]

Of course, this raises the philosophical question of just how much of this essentially Nazi conception can be "borrowed" and "Americanized" before the Nazi ideology itself comes to dominate the process, transforming the society adopting it. How can such processes of "scientific manipulations" via propaganda, terror, and state pressure via mass communication, of targeted populations cohabitate with the ideal of a free and independent people?

---

[18] Simpson, *Science of Coercion*, p. 24, see also p. 11.

The answer, of course, is that it cannot. Thus, the process of the "Nazification" of the West began before the war was even over. Peter Levenda summarizes the effect of this "psychological total war" that *Weltanschauungskreig* implies with chillingly apt accuracy:

> "World-view warfare" says it all: a battle between our perceptions and those of an enemy population. After all, one could say, isn't that what war is really about anyway?... Even the most crazed suicide bomber is acting from a belief that what he is doing is right, morally justified, and has the sanction of the people that matter, the people that count: God's people. "The best," says the poem, "lack all conviction," but rob the worst of *their* conviction and the war is over. It is tantamount to waking up and finding a voodoo doll in your bed, studded with pins... or a horse's head, á la Mario Puzo's *The Godfather*. You've been cursed; you will die. And your mind does the rest. That is the value of psychological warfare, or "world-view warfare," and it works... at least, just as well as the voodoo doll or the dead horse. In the right hands, one can kill (or influence) without firing a shot.
>
> Psy-war was never perceived as a substitute for the real thing, but only as a complement to an existing arsenal of weapons. The basic psy-war techniques are only useful insofar as they make the enemy soldiers lose faith in the ability of their army, and their country, to win. One can shake that faith in may ways: by ridicule, by fake prophecies of doom, by appeals to reason or emotion. Another way is through fear.
>
> When we speak of "psychological warfare" we are often speaking of ways to make the enemy feel afraid, and in order to do this we must understand an enemy's psyche: what makes him love, hate, fight, run. We must understand how an enemy will react under stress: will he fight harder, or simply surrender? Or will he start making errors in judgment, winning the war for us, in a manner of speaking? The costliest mistakes of psychological warfare operations are always those made in ignorance of an enemy's mindset. The psychological warfare officer must be able to play an enemy's mind like a violin. This implies a deep knowledge of human psychology, which is itself a kind of black art. And since this is a war of perceptions, of "world views," it is important that the psychological warfare officer understand the impact of art, music, literature, theater and other cultural modes of expression and how world-views

are represented by them, even changed or modified by them. What plays in Peoria may not—very assuredly *will* not—play in Phnom Penh...

...And eventually, the temptation will arise to test some of these principles on the domestic population. After all, with whose mindset are we the most familiar but our own? What better place to test new theories of psychological warfare than among our native populace? And how better to control our population politically than through the judicious use of propaganda, using the robust media of the most turned-on, tuned-in, mentally-massaged nation on earth: the United States of America?[19]

Weltanschauungskrieg is thus a kind of psychological warfare version of "full spectrum dominance" of all aspects of a target population's interpretive and decision making faculties by the employment of all of the techniques of mass communication, propaganda, and the all-important component, the calculated application of terror. Indeed, the idea of such total psychological "full spectrum dominance" owes its origin to the "total totalitarian" *Weltanschauung* of Nazism.

But there are crucial differences between "psychological warfare" as the American component of this breakaway civilization practiced it, and the Nazi one, and they are revealed in the ideological principles of each.

In this respect, it is to be stressed that Nazism *arose* as a fully-formed breakaway civilization, being midwifed into existence by a variety of occult and secret societies, eventually capturing an entire great power, and wrenching that power away from its roots within Western civilization, and orienting it along entirely new ideological lines, the components of which included:

1) the belief that *it* was racially superior to other races both genetically, culturally, and technologically, and, more importantly,

2) within the "state within a state" that was the SS, the further belief that this race, the Aryans, descended from

---

[19] Peter Levenda, *Sinister Forces: A Grimoire of American Political Witchcraft*, Book One: *The Nine* (Walterville, Oregon: TrineDay, 2005), pp. 125-126.

an "extraterrestrial" race; and that it was this descent that gave it its alleged racial, genetic, and intellectual superiority over others; and finally,

3) that no conventional moral inhibitions or restraints were permissible—and indeed had to be jettisoned—to return this "master race" to its "rightful position" within world affairs.

In short, the ideological commitments of Nazism were at variance with the broader foundations of Western civilization, and thus, Nazi Germany itself may be viewed as an attempt of the breakaway civilization to "go public." As we shall encounter later, the elitism implied in this view squared quite well with similar views in the corporate elites of the USA, forming a perfect nexus for the postwar re-emergence of the breakaway civilization.

For the moment, however, we now return to SS Colonel Otto Skorzeny and his calls for a "special warfare" or *Sonderkampf* and to a consideration of their implications within this wider context of *Weltanschauungskrieg* and the above ideological components of Nazism. Let us recall Witkowski's summary:

> Later, in documents brought over from the American NARA archive at College Park near Washington, I found among other things a report referring to the interrogation of one of Otto Skorzeny's commandos. He was Skorzeny's aide-de-camp, SS-Sturmbannführer Karl Radl, at the same time Chief of the VI-S/2 Division at the General Office for Reich's Security (RSHA – Reichs-sicherheitshauptamt). Radl stated —would you believe it – that *since the beginning of 1944 Skorzeny simply had no head to organize acts of sabotage on the enemy's rear areas, since he had come into contact with the "wonder weapon" and as a result had "been possessed" by the idea of "Sonderkampf" ("Special Warfare"), regarding the use of this weapon, to such an extent, that he considered it the only sure way to win the war.*[20]

Under ordinary circumstances, *Sonderkampf* meant precisely "special battle" or "special operations", comprising guerilla

---

[20] Igor Witkowski, *The Truth About the Wunderwaffe*, trans Bruce Wenham (Farmborough, Hampshire: Books International, 2003), pp. 231-232, emphasis added.

warfare, sabotage, assassination, and other operations behind enemy lines.[21]

But clearly, Skorzeny had seen a technology of some sort that had to be something *other* than the V-1s, V-2s, and jet airplanes, for none of these would easily lend themselves to "guerilla operations" behind enemy lines. In other words, *some other technology entirely* was involved.

Additionally, Skorzeny, as Witkowski notes, no longer believed in the effectiveness of special warfare behind enemy lines, or, to put it differenly, Skorzeny, like many Nazi officers, realized the war was lost, and that there was no reason to do so. So what did Skorzeny mean by a *Sonderkampf*, a special guerilla warfare in this case?

I believe there can be only one reasonable answer. Since the war was lost, the "enemy lines" meant, quite literally, a new kind of special guerilla warfare was to be waged from a postwar Nazi underground, quite literally "behind enemy lines" which would in the aftermath of the war, cover the entire globe, and that warfare was deliberately conceived in conjunction with an advanced technology that, in the hands of *Weltanschauungskrieg* experts, would be used to spread fear, terror, confusion, and thereby to demoralize the enemy, short circuit his world-interpretation and decision making processes.

But what, precisely, *was* that technology?

Here we are in the fortunate position of not having to guess, nor to argue, the case that it was some version of the German suction saucers, or perhaps even some scaled down version of the Bell itself:

---

[21] See also Simpson, *Science of Creation*, p. 12.

Spies Bid for Franco's Weapons

◇　◇　◇　◇　◇

Agents Ascribe 'Flying Saucers' to New Rocket

By LIONEL SHAPIRO.

GENEVA.—Three German scientists working under the personal sponsorship of Generalissimo Francisco Franco have developed two highly advanced weapons of war, according to specifications and blueprints smuggled out of Spain by the agent of an independent European spy organization.

The first weapon is an electromagnetic rocket which, it is claimed, is responsible for the "flying saucers" seen over the North American continent last summer and for at least one and perhaps two hitherto unexplained accidents to transport aircraft.

The second weapon is an artillery warhead employing the principle of nuclear energy and described as having a startling disintegrating power.

Blueprints of the weapons have been offered for sale to at least three of the great powers. The degree of credence placed in them by the military intelligence sections of these powers is indicated by the fact that two of them—of whom this correspondent has certain knowledge—have made strenuous and, indeed, dramatic efforts to acquire the blueprints.

Big Sums Offered

The disclosure that these plans were available has touched off the most intense activity among secret agents in European capitals since the end of the war. Huge sums of money and even threats of death have been involved in negotiations.

The nation which coupled a threat of death to its bid is Soviet Russia.

I came upon the story three weeks ago by accidental interception of a document cataloging the weapons. This was being circularized through Europe's intricate n e t w o r k of secret a g e n t s. Since then, careful checking among agents and military intelligence organizations in several countries has disclosed:

That the principal powers fully believe Franco has been developing new weapons.

That the weapons (particularly the electro-magnetic rocket) do actually exist and are now being manufactured in Spain.

According to the information available, the weapons were developed in secret laboratories located near Marbella on the south coast of Spain just east of Gibraltar. They were tested in Franco's presence early last summer. The rocket, known as KM2 after its inventors, Professors Knoh and Mueller—was tested off Malaga while Franco watched from the deck of his yacht.

The rocket is described as having a range of 16,000 kilometers (9,942 miles) traveling in a given direction. Its flight can be controlled by radio for at least the first 5,000 kilometers (3,107 miles) and when the control is removed the rocket is attracted by electric vibrations of flying planes or the magnetism of the nearest mass of metal. It explodes when it reaches the attracting element.

The agent who smuggled the blueprints out of Spain, and who presumably was present at the tests, claims that the rockets were directed over North America and that they were responsible for at least one and probably two transport-plane accidents which, for want of better explanation, were attributed to structural defects.

The nuclear-energy projectile is credited to a Professor Haikmann. It is described as twenty-two centimeters (8.7 inches) long and is used as a warhead for artillery shells. The agent claims that Franco is already mass-producing automatic guns to fire these new shells and that the first tests of the projectiles show them to have unprecedented explosive qualities.

Denver Post, November 9, 1947 Article About Spanish Nationalist Leader General Francisco Franco's Alleged Flying Saucer[22]

The article reads as follows:

Spies Bid for Franco's Weapons
Agents Ascribe 'Flying Saucers' to New Rocket
By Lionel Shapiro.
GENEVA- Three German scientists working under the personal sponsorship of Generalissimo Francisco Franco have developed two highly advanced weapons of war, according to

---

[22] Henry Stevens, *Hitler's Flying Saucers*, p. 131.

specifications and blueprints smuggled out of Spain by the agent of an independent European spy organization.

The first weapon is an electromagnetic rocket which, it is claimed, is responsible for the "flying saucers" seen over the North American continent last summer and for at least one and perhaps two hitherto unexplained accidents to transport aircraft.

The second weapon is an artillery warhead employing the principles of nuclear energy and described as having a startling disintegrating power.

Blueprints of the weapons have been offered for sale to at least three of the great powers. The degree of credence placed in them by the military intelligence sections of these powers is indicated by the fact that two of them—of whom this correspondent has certain knowledge—have made strenuous efforts to acquire the blueprints.

Big Sums Offered

The disclosure that these plans were available has touched off the most intense activity among secret agents in European capitals since the end of the war. Huge sums of money and even threats of death have been involved in the negotiations.

The nation which coupled a threat of death to its bid is Soviet Russia.

I came upon the story three weeks ago by accidental interception of a document cataloguing the weapons. This was being circulated through Europe's intricate network of secret agents. Since then, careful military intelligence organizations in several countries has disclosed:

That the principal powers fully believe Franco has been developing new weapons.

That the weapons (particularly the electro-magnetic rocket) do actually exist and are now being manufactured in Spain.

According to the information available, the weapons were located near Marbella on the south coast of Spain just east of Gibraltar. They were tested in Franco's presence early last summer. The rocket, known as KM2 after its inventors, Professors Knoh and Mueller—was tested of Malaga while Franco watched from the deck of his yacht.

The agent who smuggled the blueprints out of Spain, and who presumably was present at the tests, claims that the rockets were directed over North America and that they were responsible for at least one and probably two transport-plane accidents which, for want of better explanation, were attributed to structural defects.

The nuclear-energy projectile is credited to a Professor Halkmann. It is described as twenty-two centimeters (8.7 inches) long and is used as a warhead for artillery shells. The agent claims that Franco is already mass-producing guns to fire these new shells and that the first tests of the projectiles show them to have unprecedented explosive qualities.[23]

The article makes a number of specific assertions, and there are two basic approaches by which to interpret them within the assumption that the article represents a psychological operation of some sort.

The first is that the article contains some kernels of truth, i.e., that some sort of advanced technology was being worked on by German scientists in postwar Nationalist Spain. The second is to assume that the article contains no kernels of truth, but is part of a psychological operation to convince the Soviets that postwar Nazi scientists were in possession of advanced technologies, and by implication, that their allied and neutral hosts were as well.

There would seem to be some substance to both possibilities, and this brings us back to SS Colonel Otto Skorzeny, for as I and other researchers have pointed out, Skorzeny's postwar headquarters, as for so many other Nazis, was Franco's Nationalist Spain, and in Skorzeny's case, it was Spain's capital, Madrid itself.[24] Skorzeny's presence raises considerably the possibility that we are dealing at the minimum with a psychological warfare operation, one conceived and executed by the Nazis, and at the maximum, with a psychological warfare operation conceived and executed by the Nazis *in conjunction with certain technologies they brought with them to Spain and were perhaps researching and manufacturing there. We have, in*

---

[23] *Denver Post*, November 9, 1947, cited in Henry Stevens, *Hitler's Flying Saucers*, p. 131.

[24] Joseph P. Farrell, *Nazi International*, pp. 199-200. See also "Exposing the Nazi International,"pp. 271-309, in *Secret and Suppressed: Banned Ideas and Hidden History,* Jim Kieth, ed., (Feral House, 1993). Skorzeny's headquarters was in the same building as the Madrid office of the later CIA. See also my extended essay, "Exposing the Nazi International: An Analysis," pp 218-229, in *Secret and SuppressedII: Banned Ideas and Hidden History into the 21st Century*, ed. Adam Parfrey and Kenn Thomas (Feral House, 2008).

*other words, clear indication that a **Sonderkampf** was being waged after the war, "behind enemy lines."*

But did the Nazis in *fact* plan for postwar psychological operations in conjunction with their plans to form a "Nazi International" extra-territorial state?

This is where the story becomes *very* intriguing!

B. The Nazis' Post-War Plan for Psyops

There can be no doubt whatsoever that the Nazis not only had a "come back" plan, but that this plan was intimately tied to their economic and "strategic evacuation" plans and their schemes to form a postwar extra-territorial "state," a "Nazi International". Psychological warfare, or *Weltanschauungskrieg* became the actual *military* operations performed by this "state":

> Captured Nazi documents reveal they had a comeback plan. Their plan to regain power after the war revolved around using their friends and fascist sympathizers in other countries— *particularly in the United States*— to do their bidding while rebuilding Germany. The documents note that, as late as 1944, the Nazis were hoping for a Republican victory in the presidential election because they would get an easier peace. The second part of their plan aimed at provoking a war between the U.S. and the Soviet Union which would allow the Nazis to retake power in Germany without U.S. intervention.[25]

Part of the matrix in which the Nazis hoped to accomplish this campaign is revealed by the detailed connections between postwar German and Nazi leaders on the one hand, and high-ranking members of American society and government on the other.

For example, John J. McCloy, the pre-war American attorney for I.G. Farben, and who had once shared Hitler's box during the Berlin Olympics, and postwar American High Commissioner for Germany(and, let it be noted, subsequently a member of the Warren Commission on the assassination of President John F.

---

[25] Glen Yeadon and John Hawkins, *The Nazi Hydra in America: Suppressed History of a Century* (Joshua Tree, California: Progressive Press, 2008), p. 23.

Kennedy), was brother-in-law to American General Draper, and the first West German Chancellor, Konrad Adenauer, for all three men had married daughters of John Zinsser, a partner in the JP Morgan interests![26]

Similar connections were forged between Hjalmar Schacht, Hitler's one-time Reichsbank president, and Greek shipping magnate Aristotle Onassis. And of course, the notorious Bilderberger meetings themselves were the brainchildren of David and Laurence Rockefeller and the London Rothschilds on the one hand, and Nazi SS officer former I.G. Farben manager Prince Bernhard of the Netherlands, with early meetings in the 1950s featuring the regular presence of Dr. Herman Josef Abs, head of Deutschebank and at one time, the banker who actually paid Hitler's salary. And of course, let it be remembered that Colonel Skorzeny had married Hjalmar Schacht's daughter.[27] As we shall see in the next section of the book, this is but the tip of a very large American-Nazi iceberg.

However it is precisely the existence of such networks and personal connections that the Nazis were counting on, as is revealed by their documents outlining the long range plan for extended *Weltanschauungskrieg.* For example, in a 1944 edition of the French version of the German magaszine *Combat(Angriff),* a German propaganda sheet designed to win the French over to the Nazi cause, an article by German General Von Stulpnagel admitted not only that the current war was lost, but outlined the long range objective of an extended psy-op:

> In the next war, which should take place within 25 years, the same mistake must not be made. The principal adversary will be the United States, and the entire effort must be concentrated against this country from the beginning... Our defeat in the present war need not be considered except as an incident in the triumphant march of Germany towards the conquest of the world, and from now on we must give a defeated Germany the spirit of a future conqueror. What does a

[26] Glen Yeadon and John Hawkins, *The Nazi Hydra in America: Suppressed History of a Century,* pp. 23-24.

[27] Farrell, *The Nazi International,* pp. 193-197, 241-246 , *Babylon's Banksters,* pp. 64-70, *LBJ and the Conspiracy to Kill Kennedy,* pp. 139-142,

temporary defeat matter if, through the destruction of people and material wealth in enemy countries, we are able to secure a margin of economic and demographic superiority even greater than before 1939? If we can succeed in doing this, this war will have been useful, since it will enable us, within the next 25 years, to wage another war under better conditions... Our enemies will grow weary before we do. We shall have to organize a campaign of pity designed to induce them to send us needed supplies at the earliest possible moment. Above all we must hold on to the assets we have deposited in neutral countries. The present war will thus have been a march forward towards our supremacy. We have not to fear conditions of peace analogous to those we have imposed, because our adversaries will always be divided and disunited.[28]

But Von Stulpnagel was being evasive, though clearly hinting at (West) Germany's postwar "Blackmail" diplomacy,[29] i.e., the diplomacy whereby (West) Germany threatened that it would be absorbed into the Communist bloc if not allowed to re-industrialize and re-arm.

This "Blackmail" diplomacy was conceived during the end of WW2, even as Bormann was formulating his economic "strategic evacuation" plans. A document from Admiral Canaris' *Abwehrabteilung* dated March 15, 1944, and classified *Geheime Reichssache* (Secret State Matter), calls upon strong psychological warfare measures "to the fullest extent possible" and utilizing "all available possibilities in neutral and enemy countries in order to support our military efforts with political and propaganda campaigns" with the goal to eventually thwart the Allies, whose goal "it is to destroy forever the German Reich militarily, economically and culturally."[30]

The handwriting was, however, on the wall, as I have noted elsewhere, in early 1943, after the German defeat at Stalingrad.[31] It was during this period that the first strategic evacuation plans

---

[28] Glen Yeadon and John Hawkins, *The Nazi Hydra in America: Suppressed History of a Century*, p. 345.

[29] Ibid., p. 344.

[30] Ibid., 628.

[31] Farrell, *The Nazi International*, pp. 63-64.

were first being formed, and as well, that the first plans for postwar psychological operations were also being formed:

On July 27, 1943,[32] the German Foreign Office expert on the U.S., the geopolitician Colin Ross, suggested in a 15-page memorandum a "Plan for an Ideological Campaign in the United States."

Recognizing Germany's inability to bring the war to a victorious end, Ross proposed the immediate implementation of carefully planned psychological warfare to undermine the anticipated U.S. military victory. Ross regarded American public opinion as the weakest link because the American people seemed especially susceptible to scare propaganda hinting that a defeated Germany would join the ranks of Bolshevism. The memorandum, which was addressed to the German Secretary of State in the Foreign Office, von Steengracht, became the guidepost for Germany's highly successful blackmail diplomacy in post-war America. Here follow some significant parts of the memorandum.

PLAN FOR AN IDEOLOGICAL CAMPAIGN IN THE UNITED STATES
The prerequisites for psychological warfare:
1. Analyze the spiritual temper of world public opinion.
2. Evaluate correctly the ideological weapons available.
3. Put before the eyes of the world a strategic concept which will impress not only our own people, but also the neutrals and our enemies.
4. Select the most effective tactical methods for the accomplishment of the above.
5. Co-ordinate the ideological campaign in support of our military and economic warfare.

The more the prospects for outright military victory diminish, the more urgent becomes the necessity for all-out psychological warfare....
...Therefore, it is necessary to set up a far-flung organization in every country which, under enemy

---

[32] Note the date! This would place the following memorandum *after* the defeat of the last large German offensive on the Eastern Front, the Battle of Kursk, and after the final loss, for about one year, of its ability to launch any major offensive.

occupation, must carry on the task from the underground.
We must do everything possible to impress upon American public
opinion that after the liberation of Europe they will become
involved in an endless maze of insoluble contradictions.[33]

Note that this document explicitly states that Nazism would have
to go underground, and create a vast international network—
requiring perforce a vast warchest—to conduct such an all-out
Weltanschauungskrieg. Note also that part of this operation
involved the use of the technique of *polarization*, i.e., of creating
mutually contradictory sets or contexts of interpretation by
which the American public opinion was to be paralyzed.

The U.S. Department of State was not oblivious to these
plans, for on March 30, 1945, it published a document indicating
that the U.S.A. was aware of both aspects—the economic and
psychological warfare components—of the postwar plan:

> Nazi Party members, German industrialists, and the German
> military, realizing that victory can no longer be attained, are
> now developing post-war commercial projects, *are*
> *endeavoring to renew and cement friendships in foreign*
> *commercial circles and are planning for renewals of pre-war*
> *cartel agreements.* An appeal to the courts of various countries
> will be made early in the post-war period through dummies for
> "unlawful" seizure of industrial plants and other properties
> taken over by Allied governments at the outbreak of war. In
> cases where this method fails German repurchase will be
> attempted through "cloaks" who meet the necessary
> citizenship requirements...
>
> ...German capital and plans for the construction of ultra-
> modern technical schools and research laboratories will be
> offered at extremely favorable terms since they will afford the
> Germans an excellent opportunity to design and perfect new
> weapons. This Government is now in possession of photostatic
> copies of several volumes of German plans on this subject. The
> German propaganda program is to be an integral part of the
> over-all post-war program.[34]

---

[33] Glen Yeadon and John Hawkins, *The Nazi Hydra in America:*
Suppressed History of a Century, p. 630, all emphases added.

[34] Glen Yeadon and John Hawkins, *The Nazi Hydra in America:*
Suppressed History of a Century, p. 631, emphasis added.

Note the very significant point that part of this plan revolves upon re-establishing *the corporate and personal relationships that existed prior to the war between Germany, and Nazism on the one hand, and American corporate elites on the other.*

In other words, the Nazis were counting on the American components of those pre-war relationships to wage the *Weltanschauungskrieg* for and with them to some extent.

Before we can examine the American and Nazi components of this postwar *Weltanschuungskrieg*, however, we must turn to that aspect of it that couples the display of technology with its magical interpretation...

Admiral Wilhelm Canaris, Head of Germany's Abwehrabteilung, or Military Intelligence

6
THE ALCHEMY OF UFOS:
SOCIAL ENGINEERING, PSYOPS, AND ALCHEMICAL TECHNOLOGY

"I think UFOs are perpetrating a deception by presenting their so-called 'occupants' as being messengers from outer space, and I suspect there are groups of people on Earth exploiting this deception.
"I have written this book because I am concerned with the changes which would be triggered by the belief in an outer space invasion, real or simulated."
Dr. Jacques Vallee[1]

"What if the deception operations of World War Two extended beyond the end of hostilities with Germany?"
Dr. Jacques Vallee[2]

F lying saucers, whether they originate on or off planet, present unique opportunities for the conduct of *Weltanschauungskrieg* and social engineering. Viewed in this way, the UFO represents both an alchemical *technology* and *technique*, for one of the goals of alchemy has always been the transformation of man and his consciousness, and no one can doubt that the UFO has done just that.

And no one has better appreciated this fact than the famous French scientist and ufologist, Dr. Jacques Vallee. In this chapter, we will review his work with a purpose to extract those principles indicative of the use of psychological operations and to detect, if possible, the ideology motivating the breakaway civilization. Indeed, Vallee hints at some of this vast potential for social engineering near the beginning of his book *Messengers of Deception:*

> Visitors from outer space would be a convenient interlude. They would offer the space effort—and all its attendant industrial technology—a new purpose in life. They would

---

[1] Jacques Vallee, *Messengers of Deception: UFO Contacts and Cults* (Daily Grail Publishing, 2008), p. 68.
[2] Ibid., p. 223.

115

rescue Western civilization from its acute spiritual malaise. They would help transcend political emotions and pave the way to the unification of that enormous economic marketplace: Planet Earth. Take these possibilities into consideration, and you will begin to understand why the idea of life in space is no longer a simple scientific speculation but a social and political issue as well. Sensing this, the military authorities have tried to stay away from it as long as possible. So has the scientific community.[3]

But we have already established that two prominent Nazi scientists—Oberth and Von Braun—spoke out in provocative terms about the "extraterrestrial presence" in the postwar period when it is clear that a case can be made that some of the advanced "flying saucer" technology that UFOs represented already existed in Nazi Germany. Moreover, we have pointed out that Dr. Oberth was clearly involved in the Bell project.

In short, in the Nazis' case at least, these scientists were *lying*, and lying it would appear to a purpose, the purpose being to promote the idea of extraterrestrial life—and to imply an extraterrestrial threat—while simultaneously protecting advanced technology by managing the public perception of it. This is a classic *Sonderkampf* of a *Weltanschauungskrieg.*

Moreover, as we shall discover in the next section of this book, the postwar Nazis are working hand-in-hand with the American corporate elite after the war, which elite helped place the Nazis into power before the war. As we discovered in the previous chapter, the postwar Nazi scheme to survive and eventually regain power focused precisely on re-forging these relationships. As most readers of this book are probably aware, one of the consistent goals of this Anglo-American corporate and banking elite has been to forge a global new world order, a global corporate fascist state, and thus, *this elite would have strong incentive to pursue, or acquiesce in, such a Weltanschauungskrieg itself.* Moreover, as we observed in the previous chapter, this elite had already established funding of psychological warfare studies in the United States through the mechanisms of the Ford, Carnegie, and Rockefeller foundations,

---

[3] Jacques Vallee, *Messengers of Deception: UFO Contacts and Cults* (Daily Grail Publishing, 2008), p. 53.

and thus, had access to all the techniques that research discovered.

Vallee, in pondering similar questions, comes to a somewhat startling conclusion, namely, that from the standpoint of social engineering,

> *it doesn't matter any more whether flying saucers are real or not.* It still matters to me, of course, as an individual scientist. I have often stated, and I still believe today, that UFOs are real and technological. When I say it doesn't matter whether they are real or not, I am speaking **of their social impact.**
>
> You can find scholars whole will "prove" to you that the supernatural powers of Jesus Christ never existed. You can also find scholars who will "prove" to you that they did exist. Does it matter? Of course not! It only matters to the experts, who have staked their academic reputations on either side of the argument. *The effects of the belief in Jesus, the impact of the doctrine* based on the story of his life and death, are real enough. *Socially, historically, the consequences are beyond question.* I claim that the same now applies to flying saucers because *enough people believe in them, enough people believe that contact with them is possible, and enough people even believe that they have secretly achieved such contact.*[4]

Note the resemblance, in terms of the alchemical architecture of social engineering, between UFOs and religion, a parallelism we have already encountered with George Adamski and the other early contactees. Indeed, the fact that the later alleged Nazi "field propulsion saucers" of the Hannebu type so closely resemble Adamski's, and the fact that there are clear parallels between Adamski's "messages from ET" and Nazi doctrine, indicates the profound possibility that the whole Adamski affair was one large psychological operation, a possibility that increases dramatically when one recalls that Adamski's initial contacts were from the American military.

In short, what UFOs represent from the social engineering standpoint is a "veritable mass conversion" of "the public and media elite,"[5] for "the phenomenon serves as a vehicle for images

---

[4] Vallee, *Messengers of Deception*, pp. 54-55, italicized emphasis in the original, boldface emphasis added.

[5] Ibid., p. v.

that can be manipulated to promote belief systems tending to the long-term transformation of human society."[6] To put it succinctly, UFOs represent, for the psychological warfare specialist, an alchemical technology to transmute mankind himself into a philosophers' stone.

A. UFOs and the Social Engineering of a New Religion

We noted in chapter two the close resemblance of Adamski's alleged "messages" from extraterrestrials to the components of religion: an expectation of revelation, a "magisterium" appointed to deliver the message, and an implicit technological threat of impending apocalyptic judgment if humanity did not mend its ways and acquiesce to ET's "advice."

But according to Dr. Vallee, there is more to this parallel to religion than meets the eye, for the specific parallels between the UFO phenomenon and religion and myth are quite detailed, suggesting, again, that the phenomenon is being manipulated precisely for the purpose of a transformation of the human psyche, both individual and social; it is being manipulated as a conditioning process:

> The most clear result was that the phenomenon behaved like a conditioning process. *The logic of conditioning uses absurdity and confusion to achieve its goal*, while hiding its mechanism. There is a similar structure in the UFO stories.
>
> I am beginning to perceive a coherent picture of the "flying saucer" phenomenon for the first time, now that I am pursuing the idea that UFOs may be a control system, and now that I am aware of their link to human consciousness. I still think there is a genuine technology at work here, causing the effects witnesses are describing. But I am not ready to jump to the conclusion that it is the technology of some kind of "spacemen."[7]

It is worth pausing to consider the implications of these remarks in some detail.

---

[6] Ibid., p. vi.
[7] Vallee, *Messengers of Deception*, p. 7, emphasis added.

Notably, Vallee is alluding to the technique of *polarization*, of the deliberate obfuscation of data by the creation of two mutually opposed contexts by which to perceive and interpret it, thus conditioning a population. In this case, it is worth considering the stories of ET-human contact *in toto*. As we saw with Adamski and the early contactees, the "ETs" were essentially human, and the contacts themselves— notwithstanding the darker implications of their "message"— were fairly benign. But during the 1970s and 1980s, the ETs had morphed into robotic "grays" and reptilians, kidnapping their hapless victims, and subjecting them to a variety of invasive procedures that can only be described, from the human point of view, as a form of physical if not psychological torture. In both cases, however, a subtle "meme" is shared, namely, that humanity is helpless, its technology outclassed, and it must submit to the guidance of an elite. In the case of the later abduction stories, it is even said on many occasions that the behavior of the "ETs" is not quite rationalizable from a human perspective, and *ipso facto*, their intellect and moral understanding must be as superior to us as we to the animals. In any case, the meme remains the same. But throughout both types of contact it is important to recall *that polarization itself is a purely human technique of psychological operations.*

Vallee states this point about the aggregate effect over time of UFO contact stories with his customary directness:

> The social, political, and religious consequences of the experience are enormous if they are considered, not in the days or weeks following the sighting, but over the time span of a generation. Could it be that such effects are actually intended, through some process of social conditioning? Could it be that both the believers and the skeptics are being manipulated? Is the public being deceived and led to false conclusions by someone who is using the UFO witnesses to propagate revolutionary new ideas?[8]

---

[8] Vallee, *Messengers of Deception*, p. 9. See also Vallee's remarks in *Passport to Magonia:*

"What does it all mean? Is it reasonable to draw a parallel between religious apparitions, the fairy-faith, the reports of dwarf-like beings

A little further on, Vallee answers these questions in no uncertain terms:

I believe there is a machinery of mass manipulation behind the UFO phenomenon. It aims at social and political goals by diverting attention from some human problems and by

---

with supernatural powers, the airship tales in the United States in the last century, and the present stories of UFO landings?

"I would strongly argue that it is—for one simple reason: *the mechanisms that have generated these various beliefs are identical.* Their human context and their effect on humans are constant. And it is my conclusion that the observation of this very deep mechanism is a crucial one. *It has little to do with the problem of knowing whether UFO's are physical objects or not.* Attempting to understand the meaning, the purpose of the so-called flying saucers, as many people are doing today, is just as futile as was the pursuit of the fairies, if one makes the mistake of confusing appearance and reality. The phenomenon has stable, invariant features, some of which we have tried to identify and label clearly. But we have also had to note carefully the chameleon-like character of the secondary attributes of the sightings: the shapes of the objects, the appearances of their occupants, their reported statements, vary as a function of the cultural environment into which they are projected."(Jacques Vallee, *Passport to Magonia*, [Chicago: Contemporary Books, 1993), pp. 148-149.

Obviously, this would imply that the historical roots of such social engineering pre-date the Nazis, but such would require a book on its own to explore adequately, as the roots would be locked deep within esoteric societies and rare manuscripts. Here our focus remains on the modern manifestation of the phenomenon of the use of advanced technology for social engineering, represented by the Anglo-American elite and the Nazis.

One aspect of this story, again beyond the pale of this book, is the fact that the social engineering aspects of the story *change with the type of technology that accompanies it:* "The entire mystery we are discussing contains all the elements of a myth that could be utilized to serve political or sociological purposes, a fact illustrated by the curious link between the contents of the reports themselves and the progress of *human* technology, from aerial ships to dirigibles to ghost rockets to flying saucers—a link that has never received a satisfactory interpretation in a sociological framework." (Vallee, *Passport to Magonia*, p. 162, emphasis added).

120

providing a potential release for tensions caused by others. The contactees are a part of that machinery. *They are helping to create a new form of belief:* an expectation of actual contact among large parts of the public. In turn this expectation makes millions of people hope for the imminent realization of that age-old dream: salvation from above, surrender to the greater power of some wise navigators of the cosmos.

With the release of popular UFO movies, many people who previously were skeptics have begun to jump on this bandwagon from outer space. I wish them *bon voyage.* However, if you take the trouble to join me in the analysis of the modern UFO myths, you will see that human beings under the control of of a strange force that is bending them in absurd ways, forcing them to play in a bizarre game of deception. This role may be very important if changing social conditions make it desirable to focus the attention of the public on the distant stars while obsolete human institutions are wiped out and rebuilt in new ways. Are the manipulators, in the final analysis, nothing more than a group of humans who have mastered a very advanced form of power?

Let me summarize my conclusions thus far. UFOs are real. They are physical devices used to affect human consciousness. They may not be from outer space. Their purpose may be to achieve social changes on this planet, through a belief system that uses systematic manipulation of witnesses and contactees; covert use of various sects and cults; control of the channels through which the alleged "space messages" can make an impact on the public.[9]

With these conclusions I wholeheartedly concur, for throughout my books on Nazi secret weapons, I have been at pains to show the terrestrial origins of the fantastic technology represented by their Bell project, at pains to "reverse engineer" the possible physics basis for it, and to show that they survived the war in a position secure and strong enough to continue that research independently of the victories Allied powers. In short, the ET hypothesis is simply not necessary as an interpretive template by which to rationalize Nazi achievements.

---

[9] Vallee, *Messengers of Deception*, pp. 20-21, all emphases in the original.

As I showed in the previous chapter, the Nazis before the war's end conceived and planned a vast psychological operation, a tactical *Sonderkampf* of a long range strategic *Weltanschauungskrieg* designed to restore Nazism to power, if the testimony of Otto Skorzeny is to be believed. I have also shown that, given Dr. Oberth's presence on the Bell project itself, his pronouncements regarding the extraterrestrial origins of UFOs should be greeted with some skepticism. These psychological operations, moreover, were conceived within the context of a *wider* operation to restore pre-war links between Nazism and the Anglo-American corporate and banking elite, an elite which, as we saw, itself privately funded much war-time psychological warfare research. Vallee's remarks thus testify to yet another aspect of this stratagem, and also strongly suggest that there is a *belief system* being put into play, a belief system we saw first enunciated with George Adamski, to whom we shall return in a moment.

For Vallee, the consequences of this social engineering, if left unchecked, are nothing less than global: "To let UFO speculation grow unchecked would only make the public an easy and defenseless prey to charlatans of all kind. It would mean that any organized group bent upon the destruction of our society could undermine it by skillful use of the saucer mythology..."[10]

But what exactly constitutes this mythology, this religion? What are its core beliefs or doctrines?

1. The Resemblance to Myths

In chapter two, I pointed out the parallel between Adamskian-type contactee mythos, and that of western religion itself. Vallee compiles a useful catalogue of contactee beliefs:

> A catalogue of contactee themes, compiled from interviews I have conducted, includes the following:
> *Intellectual abdication.* The widespread belief that human beings are incapable of solving their own problems, and that extraterrestrial intervention is imperative to save us "in spite of ourselves." The danger in such a philosophy is that it makes

---

[10] Jacques Vallee, *Passport to Magonia: On UFOs, Folklore, and Parallel Worlds* (Chicago: Contemporary Books, 1993), p. 132.

its believers dependent on outside forces and discourages personal responsibility: why should we worry about the problems around us, if the Gods from Outer Space are about to solve them?

Racist philosophy. The pernicious suggestion that some of us on the Earth are of extraterrestrial descent and therefore constitute a "higher race." The dangers inherent in this belief should be obvious to anybody who hasn't forgotten the genocides of World War II, executed on the premise that some races were somehow "purer" or better than others. (**Let us note in passing that Adamski's Venusian, the Stranger of the Canigou seen by Bordar, and many other alleged extraterrestrials were all tall Aryan types with long blond hair.**)

Technical Impotence. The statement that the birth of civilization on this planet resulted not from the genius and ability of mankind, but from repeated assistance by higher beings. Archaeologists and anthropologists are constantly aware of the marvelous skill which the "Ancient Engineers" (to use L. Sprague de Camp's phrase) developed the tolls of civilization on all continents. No appeal to superior powers is necessary to explain the achievements of early culture. The belief expressed by the contactees reveals a tragic lack of trust on their part in human ability.

Social utopia. Fantastic economic theories, including the belief that a "world economy" can be created overnight, and that democracy should be abolished in favor of Utopian systems, usually dictatorial in their outlook.[11]

Note that the themes of dictatorship, racial and technical superiority, and an off-planet origin for humanity from higher beings, and a social utopia, would all be memes or ideas well in keeping with the ideology both of Nazism, and, as we shall see in the next section, within certain circles of the American corporate and banking elite, particularly those represented by the Ford and Rockefeller dynasties.

To these we may add the memes we discovered operative in Adamski's case:

1) The meme of *immanent revelation, or "disclosure;"*

---

[11] Vallee, *Messengers of Deception*, pp. 112-113.

2) The meme of "conversion," i.e., the claim of *some* to have
had a special "Damascus road" revelation, ala St. Paul,
with extra-terrestrials, and thus to constitute themselves
part of a magisterium of illumination and truth, whose
statem,ents are to be taken on faith in the authority of
their personal experience, as opposed to the "outside
world" of skepticism and non-belief.

The last point cannot be pondered too long, for it is the standard
technique of "the Three Great Yahwisms" or the three great
monotheisms, which came, by claims of special revelation
coupled with the "judicious application of force and terror"—in
other words, by dint of a *psychological warfare operation*—to
supplant the older *philosophia perrenis* of the cultures around
them. In short, the Three Great Yahwisms *produced the same
precise results of these later contactee revelations*:

1) A *social schism* between "truth" and "error" or "believer
and infidel" or, in the case of contactees, believers and
skeptics;
2) The requirement of a revelation to enforce the status of
the former; and therefore,
3) An incipient introduction of unending *conflict* between the
two groups;[12] and thus,
4) The fulfillment of a utopian or messianic expectation
sometime in the future.[13]

Vallee is alive to the fact that there are parallels between religion
in the proper sense, and contactee-ism, for in his view, the
Mormon religion would be today viewed precisely as a contactee
phenomenon.[14] Succinctly stated, a mere "physics" approach to
the UFO phenomenon is inadequate, for the phenomenon

---

[12] Vallee, *Messengers of Deception*, p. 8: Vallee notes that the "space
messages" created a "counter-culture" within wider society.

[13] For a fuller exposition of the social engineering aspects of the
Three Great Yahwisms, see my and co-author Scott D. de Hart's *Altars,
Alchemy, and the Apocalypse: A Grimoire of the Alchemical Agenda for
the Transformation of Man* (Feral House, in press), chapter two.

[14] Vallee, *Messengers of Deception*, pp. 12-13.

encompasses wider aspects of social, alchemical transformation.[15]

On only one point would I perhaps disagree with Vallee, and that is that the ancient belief in a connection between humanity and extraterrestrials need necessarily represent a connection with something *inhuman*, for as I have argued in other books, the possibility exists that we have "genetic cousins" of the genus *homo* out there, with whom we might be biologically connected.[16]

In any case, it is worth noting that what was yesterday's "contactee-counter-culture" is today's mainstream speculation as evidenced by a recently published NASA-sponsored academic paper entitled "Would Contact with Extraterrestrials Benefit or Harm Humanity?"[17] Papers such as this, plus the statements of prominent military or political leaders should be viewed against the backdrop of the existing psychological warfare operations, for they tend to legitimize the memes implanted in those operations, plus sow an element of confusion and doubt by fueling speculations that "the government knows more than it is telling."

So persistent are the memes of the contactee-abduction faith that it bears little distinction from the "elves, sylphs, and *lutins* of the Middle Ages."[18] Indeed, as Vallee notes, the details of

---

[15] Ibid., p. 27.

[16] See my *The Cosmic War: Interplanetary Warfare, Modern Physics, and Ancient Texts* (Adventures Unlimited Press, 2007), pp. 139-203; *Genes, Giants, Monsters, and Men* (Feral House, 2011).

[17] Seth D. Baum, Jacob D. Haqq-Misra, and Shawn D. Domagal-Goldman, "Would Contact with Extraterrestrials Benefit or Harm Humanity?", *Acta Astronomica*, April 22, 2011.

[18] Vallee, *Passport to Magonia*, p. 57. Vallee's comments occur within a wider context which should be cited here, and its clear implications noted: "Yet in no way am I excluding the possibility that this controlling intelligence (behind the UFO-fairie phenomenon) is human, and I shall elaborate on this idea in later chapters. For the time being, let me simply state again my basic contention: the modern, global belief in flying saucers and their occupants is identical to an earlier belief in the fairy-faith. The entities described as the pilots of the craft are indistinguishable from the elves, sylphs, and *lutins* of the Middle Ages. Through the observations of unidentified flying objects, we are concerned with an agency our ancestors knew well and

abductions are consistent, not merely across several stories, but across the *centuries*, as in the famous case of Betty Hill, who was examined by "extraterrestrials" who inserted a long needle into her abdomen, a detail, he observes, is also found on a fifteenth century French calendar, the *Kalendrier des Bergiers*, which depicts demons "piercing their victims' abdomens with long needles."[19] This "continuum of belief" spans the whole period "from primitive magic, through mystical experience, the fairy-faith, and religion, to modern flying saucers"[20] to such an extent that even the ancient idea of chimerical offspring of humans and ETs is reproduced.[21] Again, the persistence of these themes, particularly in Nazism, strongly suggests that their recurrence in the context of the advanced technology represented by UFOs might be a component of Skorzeny's *Sonderkampf* which he conceived to operate "behind enemy lines" in conjunction with advanced technology.

2. The Three Effects of UFOs

Thus, according to Vallee, there are three components to the UFO phenomenon, each of them fitting, as we have suggested, the

---

regarded with terror: we are prying into the affairs of the Secret Commonwealth."

In other words, Vallee is implying several significant things:(1) that there is a breakaway or secret civilization, and that it is very old, (2) it has been active throughout history, employing a variety of social engineering techniques in conjunction with the technologies and belief systems of a particular age, and (3) that the controlling intelligence behind this activity *may be human*. And that, of course, implies a hidden elite at work throughout human history to engineer mankind's consciousness, a theme I have explored in some of my books (See. *Babylon's Banksters: The Alchemy of Deep Physics, High Finance and Ancient Religion* [Feral House, 2010], pp. 159-205; *Genes, Giants, Monsters, and Men: The Surviving Elites of the Cosmic War and Their Hidden Agenda* [Feral House, 2011]; and, with Scott D. de Hart, *The Grid of the Gods: The Aftermath of the Cosmic War and the Physics of the Pyramid Peoples* [Adventures Unlimited Press, 2011]).

[19] Vallee, *Passport to Magonia*, p. 95.
[20] Ibid., p. 131.
[21] Ibid., p. 127.

component features of a *Sonderkampf,* of a *Weltanschauungskrieg:*

> The first aspect is *physical.* The UFO behaves like a region of space, of small dimensions (about 10 meters), within which a very large amount of energy is stored. This energy is manifested by pulsed light phenomena of intense colors, by other forms of electromagnetic radiation, and by microwaves that create distortions of the witnesses' sense of reality.
>
> The second aspect is *psychological.* It is debatable whether anybody has seen the actual technology that supports the phenomenon. What is seen, and reported, is an *image*; that is, the *perception* of a UFO by a human witness. Reports of UFOs show all kinds of psychophysiological effects on the witnesses: perception distortions, unconscious barriers, and mental blocks. Witnesses also show evidence of suggestion and post-hypnotic effects. Exposure to the phenomenon causes visions, hallucinations, physiological effects, and long-term personality changes.
>
> The third aspect is *social.* Belief in the reality of UFOs is spreading rapidly at all levels of society throughout the world.[22]

I suggest that the SS, of which Skorzeny was an officer—by its investigations of mind control techniques, by its ideological commitments to the idea of a "master race", by its study of occult manuscripts detailing mediaeval accounts of abductions and invasive procedures, by the belief in some of its quarters with an extraterrestrial link[23]—was in the perfect position to appreciate the significance of the technology it possessed for its ability to unite each of these three components in a psychological operation.

But is there a stronger case that can be made to connect psychological operations, UFO contactees, and Nazism? Indeed there is, and once again, it is Dr. Vallee who makes it.

3. The Nazi Connection:

---

[22] Vallee, *Messengers of Deception*, pp. 7-8.

[23] For the belief in the extraterrestrial link, see my *The Philosophers' Stone: Alchemy and the Secret Research for Exotic Matter* (Feral House, 2009), pp. 255-259.

The Alchemy of UFOs

The Fascist Overtones of Adamski's Contactee Messages

Vallee begins by asking a logical question: if, as he suggests, there is a controlling intelligence manipulating the UFO phenomenon for its *social* impact, a group he calls The Manipulators", then could the goal be massive deception?

> I have given this name to the hypothetical agents who might cause the UFO contacts and engineer their effects. Everything now centers on their role, their identity, their designs. Who could they be? Alien beings coming from the end of the galaxy? Psychic entities from the "other side"? Automata controlled by some nonhuman consciousness? Holographic nightmares? But perhaps we are looking far away for something which is right under our nose: *could they simply be human?* Could they be masters of deception so skillful that they plan to counterfeit an invasion from space?[24]

Vallee contacted one of his sources within the American military, a Major Murphy, who then repeated, almost to the exact detail, the components of the Nazi flying saucer mythos!:

> "In 1943," he said, as we sat in his study, "we already had evidence that several countries were working on circular aircraft that they hoped to develop into secret weapons. The Germans were also doing advanced research on controlled electrical discharges and 'controlled lightning,' and tried to combine these things together.[25]

(Recall that in my rationalization of the physics behind the Bell device, that strong high voltage impulses—essentially controlled lightning—were used in the device.)[26]

> When we invaded Germany, a lot of hardware fell into our hands, but the Russians had gotten most of the good stuff. Then people started seeing the modern UFOs in Sweden in 1946.
>
> ...

---

[24] Vallee, *Messengers of Deception*, p. 166.
[25] Vallee, *Messengers of Deception*, p. 166.
[26] Joseph P. Farrell, *The SS Brotherhood of the Bell*, pp. 171-185, and Farrell, *Secrets of the Unified Field*, pp. 270-282.

"And what does that have to do with UFOs or with rockets, or secret weapons? I asked rather brusquely.

He took my outburst with patience. "On the surface, if you just look at a few isolated cases, like scientists arguing about UFOs, well, I agree it doesn't mean anything. *But suppose somebody had obtained a device by the end of the war, which perhaps wasn't a very effective weapon. Perhaps it couldn't fly very effectively, couldn't carry guns and bombs, but had other properties. For instance, it could emit radiation that caused paralysis and hallucinations as it flew over an area, so that witnesses exposed to it would think they saw the phantasms of their own imagination.* Did somebody test that kind of a device in Sweden in 1946, and in the States in 1947, and find it to be ineffective as a flying machine, but very useful as a means of propaganda? Has such a group already understood what UFOs were, and are they confusing the issue by simulating UFO waves? Or is the entire phenomenon under their control?[27]

Note that the Bell, still in the mid-to-late 1940s in a prototypical stage of development, would well fit the requirements of a technology that was not yet perfected as a flying machine or a weapon.

The conversation then quickly comes directly to the point, and the point is the Nazi possibility, as "Major Murphy" then continues:

You need to face all the possibilities. You have to draw the consequences. Someone may have solved the (UFO) problem. perhaps there is an elegant solution to multidimensional travel, and it is being applied. I am not a physicist. You should ask your theoretician friends what they think. I can only tell you that silent, disk-shaped flying machines can be built. If they are equipped with the right devices, they can create astonishing effects and be reported as flying saucers. I wish I still had my files on the German experiments.

Suppositions, I thought. Assumptions. We're going to need more than that to explain the UFO problem. "Major, I can't believe that some Nazi group had managed to survive secretly with this kind of technology in its power."[28]

---

[27] Vallee, *Messengers of Deception*, pp. 167-168, emphasis added.
[28] Vallee, *Messengers of Deception,* p. 168.

But Vallee himself subsequently presents precisely the prospect of a hidden international group doing precisely that!:

> The institutions created to carry them out are still in existence, with their privileged communications channels, their hidden sources of procurement and capital, their recruiting procedures. The answer to the question, "Could such an international group *fake, use, or manipulate* UFO activity?" has to be *YES*. The argument that such a secret could not be kept very long is not tenable.[29]

Ponder this conclusion carefully, for as I have consistently argued in previous books and presented evidence here, the Nazis not only survived the war as an intact extraterritorial state,[30] but they did so with enough capitalization and organization to continue advanced postwar research projects,[31] and, if Skorzeny is to be believed, with a plan for psychological operations in conjunction with that technology.

It is in this connection that Adamski's Fascist and Nazi connections should be viewed, for they raise considerably the possibility that the whole affair was a psychological warfare operation of some sort:

> According to some of my own informants, contactee George Adamksi had prewar connections with American fascist leader William Dudley Pelley, who was interned during the war. Another seminal contactee, George Hunt Williamson (whose real name is Michel d'Obrenovic), was associated with Pelley's organization "Soulcraft," in the early fifties. In fact, Pelley may have put Williamson in touch with Adamski. other associates of Williamson during the great era of the flying saucers were such contactees as John McCoy and the two Stanford brothers, Ray and Rex.
>
> The connections between all these men, who have been influential in shaping the UFO myth in the United States, are

---

[29] Ibid., p. 226, all emphases in the original. It should be noted that the argument that such a secret could not be kept for that period of time was one of the arguments heard in some circles of Roswell research. See my *Roswell and the Reich*, pp. 97-99.

[30] See my *Nazi International*, pp. 1-43,

[31] Ibid., 249-350.

quite intricate. William Dudley Pelley, who died in 1965, was the leader of the *Silver Shirts*, an American Nazi group which began its activities about 1932. Its membership overlapped strongly with Guy Ballard's "I Am" movement. Pelley declined to join the other fascist groups in their support for Congressman Lemke in 1936, standing on his own in Indiana as a "Christian Party" candidate. His opposition to Roosevelt increased until his eight-year internment for sedition in 1942. After the war, he started an occult group, *Soulcraft*, and published a racist magazine called *Valor*. He also wrote the book *Star Guests* in 1950, a compilation of automatic writing reminiscent of the *Seth Material.* [32]

Such Fascist links go a long way to explaining why in so many abduction-contactee circles that there is such a heavy emphasis "on the existence of 'superior races,'[33] of people with chosen missions, their references to Atlantis and ancient astronauts,"[34] and powerful symbols and social images of "universal peace, the exploration of space," and "a single world economy."[35]

But there is, as I suggested in the previous chapter, an *American* component to this global psychological warfare game as well, and Vallee is quite alive to it:

> My guess is that someone deep within the U.S. government structure is using the stories of crashed saucers to hide something else. The Pentagon is clearly in possession of the world's most extensive collection of UFO photographs and films, electromagnetic recordings, and radar reports. *But data is not information.* At some point the public relations arm of the Air Force was tasked with the deliberate spreading of confusion and disinformation about UFOs. It used its own officers and its public relations agencies... to spread the rumors, making a deliberate effort to enlist the UFO amateur

---

[32] Vallee, *Messengers of Deception*, p. 217.

[33] Ibid., p. 211. Vallee connects the racist theme to, among others, Jack Parsons and the founding of the Jet Propulsion Laboratory. Yet another "meme" associated with UFOs and ETs is that of blood sacrifice, this time in the form of the famous animal mutilations also commonly reported in conjunction with UFO activity (see Vallee, op. cit., pp. 202-203, for a connection even to human sacrifice.)

[34] Ibid., p. 59

[35] Ibid., p. 60.

groups in support of various forgeries... They used their assets in Hollywood and in the publishing world to initiate the rumor that the United States had recovered crashed saucers. My ufologist friends should awaken to the fact that in one way or the other all the stories they are happily spreading about MJ-12 and the aliens originate with the Pentagon itself, a clear indication that they may have been planted in the first place.[36]

But that is not the only possibility that Vallee sees as emanating from the American side:

Or there could be a deeply buried renegade group of believers with extreme political and religious beliefs within the American intelligence community itself, piggybacking on classified channels to spread disinformation in support of their own peculiar goals. This hypothesis is not as farfetched as it might appear. In the last two decades federal investigators have uncovered and prosecuted several infiltration groups linked to various cults such as Reverend Moon's sect, Scientology, or the shadowy LaRouche organization. In any case, we must realize that those who claim to *expose* a cover-up may be the very tools of that cover-up, and we must look for the truth in a different direction. [37]

And one of those directions must surely be the fact that U.S. intelligence, in the wake of the "bargain" struck between OSS Station chief in Zurich, and later CIA director Allen Dulles, and the then-head of Nazi military intelligence in the East, General Reinhard Gehlen, resulted in a large segment of the CIA being the home to precisely such a rogue group, with precisely such extreme ideological beliefs.

The end result of these psychological and social engineering operations are, for Vallee, full of dire portent, for "They also suggest that our civilization may be headed for very serious trouble, with irrational forces tearing apart the old structures and replacing them by the blind institutions of inhuman

---

[36] Vallee, *Revelations: Alien Contact and Human Deception* (Ballantine Books, 1991), p. 91.
[37] Ibid., pp. 91-92.

beliefs."[38] Indeed, Vallee notes that the "potential discovery of extraterrestrial life", or even *the manufactured appearance of it,*

> ...Would help in transcending local conflicts and in achieving within a single generation behavioral changes that might otherwise take a hundred years to complete. If this is in fact the contribution of the UFO phenomenon, then we are in fact dealing with one of history's major transitions.[39]

And this, is, in fact, the goal of psychological warfare, namely to achieve a victory over an enemy without firing a single shot.

4. The UFO as an Alchemical, Psychotronic Technology

Before concluding this chapter, we must make final mention of something that must, to the attentive reader, by now become evident: much of the psychological warfare operations that we suspect is performed in conjunction with UFOs is for the purpose of social engineering, and thus, relies for its success by "carefully borrowing its concepts from basic human archetypes in order to force a global behavioral change."[40] It goes without saying that the study of psychological archetypes was the cornerstone of Jungian analysis, and that Carl Gustav Jung was, himself, a supporter of the Nazis. As such, for Vallee, UFOs represent a kind of alchemical psychotronic technology, i.e., a technology designed not only to act physically, but also upon human consciousness.[41] Given all the evidence and data presented thus far, all the conditions are there—from the study of psychological archetypes, to the occult doctrines of extraterrestrial-human origins and descent, to the use of a prototypical technology, to allow both the American and Nazi components of a postwar breakaway civilization to conduct psychological warfare operations to promote its distinctively different ideology and world order.

It remains to be seen, in the final section of this book, if indeed the other prerequisites for such a breakaway civilization

---

[38] Ibid., p. 61.
[39] Vallee, *Messengers of Deception*, p. 61.
[40] Ibid., p. 33, see also p. 48.
[41] Ibid., p. 45.

can be met, but before we can turn to that, we must summarize the results of the first two sections.

Carl Gustav Jung, Founder of the Psychologcial Archetypes Theory of Analysis

French Scientist and Ufologist Dr. Jacques Vallee

7

Patterns in the Fog and Mirrors:
Conclusions to Parts One and Two

"...Just because a message comes from heaven doesn't mean it's not stupid."
Dr. Jacques Vallee[1]

Thus far the principal activity that the breakaway civilization has exhibited has been that of a large psychological warfare operation. But we must now place this operation within the wider context of the requisites for a breakaway civilization itself, to ascertain more precisely what the purposes of the psychological warfare might be. We thus shall review here the requisites and activities of the breakaway civilization before proceeding to outline in the next section its structure, funding, and its other activities.

We noted in chapter one that there were six initial points about this civilization as outlined by Richard M. Dolan:

1) It has "loose connections at various points" to the open civilization(s) of humanity;
2) It possesses "great independence" from them;
3) It is secret, that is to say, its structure, components, and activities are largely hidden from the open civilizations of humanity; and finally and most importantly,
4) It holds a monopoly over certain scientific concepts and the technologies that result from them; thus,
5) It possesses a different, and perhaps even a *radically* different physics than the standard models of "public consumption" physics, and thus, possesses different principles of engineering and technology.
6) A breakaway civilization, having monopolies over advanced technologies and theoretical science, will likely employ that technology in covert activities;
7) It will seek to *cloak* those activities, if discovered, behind stories and fabrications of a different origin for the technologies, lest the knowledge become accessible publicly, and end the monopoly of the breakaway civilization.

---

[1] Vallee, *Messengers of Deception*, p. 57.

I believe enough evidence has been presented thus far to show that the breakaway civilization has been engaging in a psychological operation with respect to at least *some* UFO and contactee activity, and that this operation was likely born in the closing days of World War Two and conceived by the Nazis in conjunction with the technologies represented by the Bell and similar projects, and that this operation was also taken over and controlled by the American component of the breakaway civilization after World War Two. But the concept of *Weltanschauungskrieg* strongly suggests that elements of Nazi ideology formed components of this operation, and indeed, as we have seen, the technology itself was conceived as an alchemical or "psychotronic" technology to effect a social transformation. Adamski's contactee visitations have all the hallmarks of aspects of this ideology, and moreover, Adamski's associates were themselves connected to Fascism.

Adamski's contactee stories also planted the memes of UFOlogy for the first time, which memes have remained well-embedded within the field since that time, notwithstanding the fact that most UFOlogy now shies away from Adamski's claims. These memes may be viewed as a kind of "UFO Yahwism," complete with its own magisterium of "experiencers" who, like St. Paul, have had a "Damascus road experience," but this time with extraterrestrials, and who, due to that experience, can claim the status of prophet or apostle to some extent. Additionally, this "meme" also carries with it two assumptions also implicit within Yahwism, namely, a "social schism" between believers and infidels (or skeptics), and a belief in a future apocalyptic revelation or "disclosure," which, it is to be noted, *is brought to pass by the possessors and wielders of the technology itself, be they ET or humans.* Given the Fascist overtones of Adamski's contactee story, this should give one pause.

The rise of the Nazi UFO mythos at approximately the same time as the alleged Adamski contactes is, in our opinion, not accidental, but rather, both aspects form components of one operation, in that both emerge with the appearance of coordinated efforts after the "historical gap" from the end of the war to the emergence of the mythos. We must also factor into this context the disclosure of Dr. Ronald Richter's "fusion" project in Argentina during the same period,[2] plus the fact that in the case of the Paperclip Nazis' pronouncements on the extraterrestrial origin of UFOs, at least Dr. Herman Oberth was lying, given his connection to the Bell project.

But as we saw in chapter one, according to Dr. Quigley, there are three other requisites for a civilization:

1) A civilization must be so organized as to invent new things or techniques of doing things.
2) A civilization must possess a *means of the accumulation of surplus.* For our purposes, this will mean that we must look for mechanisms or, as Quigley calls them, "instruments" of funding for such inventions that are relatively stable and secure, but, by the nature of the case, that are also relatively secret;
3) Any civilization, including a breakaway civilization, must also be organized so that accumulated surplus is used to pay for, or utilize, the invented technologies or techniques.

These requirements occur within a matrix involving six levels:

1) military,
2) political,
3) economic,
4) social,
5) religious, or as we shall see in this book, ideological,
6) intellectual

Viewed in this fashion, it is clear that the psychological operation outlined in this section evidences the operation of a group—a civilization—at the military, religious (Adamski) and intellectual (Nazism and its doctrines), level.

We must now examine in the next section whether or not evidence exists for a hidden group or groups to fulfill the conditions of (1) invention, (2) accumulation of surplus, and (3) expenditure of the surplus on black projects, including psychological warfare operations.

---

[2] Joseph P. Farrell, *The Nazi International*, p. 249ff.

Here again, Quigley becomes crucial to point the way, for as noted in chapter one, other hallmarks of civilization include the following things:

1) the ability to collect taxes, or tribute;
2) a military that is subject to the "government" of the civilization;
3) the ability to compartmentalize functions of government.

Here it is well worth recalling that Quigley distinguished clearly between *parasitic* and *producing* civilizations. As we shall now discover in the next section, the breakaway civilization is a mixture of both types, and as we shall also discover, it has yet two other factions besides the Nazi faction, for there is a strong Anglo-American corporate elite faction, and also a strong international criminal syndicate...

PART THREE:
THE HISTORICAL, GEOGRAPHIC, AND FINANCIAL MATRICES OF THE BREAKAWAY CIVILIZATION

"I.G. Farben's joint chairman Hermann Schmitz was crucial to the activities of The Fraternity... He became a close friend of Hjalmar Horace Greeley Schacht, who introduced him to the idea of a world community of money that would be independent of wars and empires."
Charles Higham,
Trading with the Enemy, p. 130.

"There exists a shadowy government with its own Air Force, its own Navy, its own fundraising mechanism, and the ability to pursue its own ideas of the national interest, free from all checks and balances, and free from the law itself."
Senator Daniel K. Inouye (D-HW),
during the Iran-Contra scandal,
cited in Webster Tarpley, *9/11 Synthetic Terror: Made in USA*, p. 5.

8

THE FINANCIAL MATRIX:
CORPORATIONS, CRIMINAL SYNDICATES, AND THE FINANCING OF THE BREAKAWAY CIVILIZATION

"The keynote speech of America First was delivered by acting chairman General Robert E. Wood on October 4, 1940, before the Chicago Council on Foreign Relations. General Wood contended that totalitarian states could not be destroyed by war and that a German-dominated Europe would not destroy our foreign trade. Intervention in the war must be avoided at all costs. General Wood was chairman of Sears Roebuck, whose president, Donald Nelson, was head of the War Production Board."
Charles Higham[1]

By any standard of analysis, the Third Reich was a breakaway society; it had been mid-wifed into existence by a variety of secret societies with ideological beliefs at variance with, and even counter to the Western Civilization that surrounded it, and the Nazis pursed these beliefs at the point of a gun. It conducted psychological operations—*Weltanschauungskrieg*—with all the components thereof, including terrorism—against its own people in an effort to convert the mass consciousness into compliant servants of those doctrines. It fulfilled one complex requirement of a breakaway civilization by its very existence, for it was both a productive, and parasitic, society.

And the Nazi Reich- along with its American opponent overseas—had invented yet another crucial component of the breakaway civilization, for like America, it had created vast and secret bureaucracies, with their own infrastructures independent of the state itself to conduct secret research into advanced technologies, and to bring those technologies into existence. Indeed, Reich Armamants Minister (*Reichrüstungsminister*) Albert Speer complained of the creation of this vast and hidden "state within a state" in a book published just a few years prior to his death:

---

[1] Charles Higham, *American Swastika: The Shocking Story of Nazi Collaborators in Our Midst from 1933 to the Present Day* (Doubleday & Company, Inc., 1985), p. 13.

In the spring of 1944 Hitler approved of Himmler's proposal to build an SS-owned industrial concern in order to make the SS permanently independent of the state budget..... (Hitler) wanted to secure a position for the SS that would keep it independent of the state *and* the Party. In case a successor should try to use the state budget as an instrument to curtail the power of the SS and Gestapo, *Hitler wanted to create a financial source to provide the SS with its own budget.* [2]

In other words, Hitler wanted to create a *black budget*, doubtless in an effort to mask the vast secret weapons research being conducted within Himmler's SS, and in coordination with the slave labor available in the concentration camps. Of course, by the time Hitler gave his formal approval to this, the process had already been underway for a number of years.

Nonetheless, this creation of a "state within the state" highlights crucial structural components of the breakaway civilization that we will discover being duplicated after the war:

1) A nexus between *intelligence* agencies, in this case the SS's vast array of security agencies: the *Reichsicherheithauptamt*, (RSHA) the *Sicherheitdienst* (SD), the Gestapo, and so on, and the corporations conducting the actual research and production. Here one need only think of how these relationships are encapsulated at Auschwitz, where I.G. Farben maintained an enormous production facility, in direct liaison with the SS-run camp. This facility, I have argued elsewhere, was for the enrichment of uranium and other radioactive isotopes.[3]
2) An instrument of independent finance that is hidden; and
3) Facilities not generally known or accessible to the general public.

----

[2] Albert Speer, *Infiltration: How Heinrich Himmler Schemed to Build an SS Industrial Empire* (New York: MacMillan, 1981), p. 3, emphasis added.
[3] See my *Reich of the Black Sun* (Adventures Unlimited Press, 2004), pp.

In exploring the most crucial component of the breakaway civilization, finance, it is therefore vital to note that this complex story has three broad phases:

1) The pre-war nexus and relationships between large German and American corporations and banking houses, a relationship that we shall call "The Fraternity," following Charles Higham's terminology
2) The wartime creation of vast hidden bureaucracies and infrastructure to conduct its research and production; and,
3) The post-war reeastablishment of the nexus of relationships, and the possibilities of factional infighting within that structure.

In our examination in this chapter, we shall concentrate on the first and third of these points, leaving the second point to a later chapter, for the creation of the infrastructure of this breakaway civilization fulfills—in a very odd fashion—Quigley's distinction of "core" and "peripheral" societies within a civilizaiton. Additionally, as our examination in previous chapters focused on psychological warfare operations, our focus now becomes centered on the other component activities of this breakaway civilization:

1) Its instruments for the generation of surplus, i.e., the instruments of financing its activities. In this respect, we note that there are three basic sources of funding, all interlocked and evident within the above pre-war and post-war patterns of relationships:
   a) Overt funding from state budgets;
   b) Covert, or "black budget" funding that is "off-the-books" of official budgets, or whose items are hidden from scrutiny; and
   c) Criminal, or underground and *completely independent* sources of funding. This will be particularly evident in the post-war period.

2) Its sponsorship of terrorism as a component of its psychological warfare;[4]

3) Its instruments for the *invention* of technology, i.e., the basic bureaucratic structure of its research.

We have already noted in previous chapters that the Nazis deliberately planned to reconstitute the pre-war nexus of relationships with the American corporate world in the post-war period, supplemented by vast intelligence exchanges highlighted by the bargain between Allen Dulles and German General Reinhard Gehlen. Thus, any history or hypothetical reconstruction of a breakaway civilization that does not take into account these Nazi plans is perforce a flawed history and reconstruction.

A. The Pre-War Tapestry
1. The Central Ideological Component: The "Empire of Money"

Before the war, Hitler's Reichsbank President, Dr. Hjalmar Horace Greeley Schacht, moved in the elite circles of American and German corporate and banking power, to such an extent that he was convinced that the power of high finance could lead to "a world community of money that would be independent of wars and empires."[5] Schacht, who had imbibed these ideas from the American financial elite, passed them on to his friends, Carl Krauch and Hermann Schmitz, whom he aided to found the huge I.G. Farben chemicals cartel, a cartel so large and powerful that when one says "Nazi War Machine," one is essentially talking about I.G. Farben.[6] This idea of a "world community" or "empire" of money is already a significant clue and argument that these Tsars of corporate cartels and high finance already viewed themselves as a distinct social entity, as a breakaway "civilization," able, and willing, to influence the rest of the world according to their designs.

For example, Carl Krauch, the founder of I.G. Farben, was encouraged by Schacht to develop

---

[4] Inasmuch as acts of terrorism are complex acts of actual warfare, in addition to psychological operations, we shall comment only in passing on it in this work, leaving a detailed analysis to a future work.

[5] Charles Higham, *Trading With the Enemy: The Nazi-American Money Plot, 1933-1949* (Authors Guild Backinprint, 2007), p. 130.

[6] Ibid.

a series of crucial friendships in England and the United States, always aiming unerringly for the greatest powers. One of his earliest allies was Walter Teagle of Standard Oil, who shared his views on international financial solidarity. Another was Edsel Ford, son of Henry Ford.

In 1929, Schmitz, his nephew, Max Ilgner, Walter Teagle, Edsel Ford, and Charles E. Mitchell of the ever-reliable National City Bank jointly set up the American Farben organization known as American I.G./Chemical Corp. Hermann Schmitz became president, with his brother Dietrich delegated to take over in his absence in Europe....

In 1931, President Herbet Hoover received Schmitz at the White House. Hoover shared Schmitz's attitude toward Russia: that it must be crushed.[7]

Such links between large American corporations and banks and the huge German cartels were a common feature of pre-war financial arrangements.

a. Dr. Quigley Again

Here we must return to Dr. Quigley once again, and to the *purpose* for these arrangements, for in creating them, the German and American factions of this "empire of money" were, in effect, establishing the long-term structure of the breakaway civilization, as the Nazis made it a deliberate component of their plans to survive the war intact as a major though extra-territorial influence in global affairs. In short, *the German and American factions of this empire of money existed before the war. What was new during and after the war, was the injection of Nazism as yet another contending faction within it, with all its ideological and covert operations commitments.* It is therefore crucial to one's understanding of the breakaway civilization to have an understanding of the pre-war structure of these arrangements.

Quigley's views on these matters were expressed in his *opus magnum, Tragedy and Hope: A History of the World in Our Time*, a book that has become something of a "bible" for conspiracy theorists ever since its publication by the MacMillan publishing house—

---

[7] Higham, *Tradining With the Enemy*, pp. 130-131.

related to the British Prime Minister of that name—in 1966. Quigley had no hesitations about revealing his "insider knowledge" of the machinations of the international bankers and corporate cartels:

> There does exist, and has existed for a generation, an international Anglophile network which operates, to some extent, in the way the radical Right believes the Communists act. In fact, this network, which we may identify as the Round Table Groups, has no aversion to cooperating with the Communists, or any other groups, and frequently does so. I know of the operations of this network because I have studied it for twenty years and was permitted for two years, in the early 1960s, to examine its papers and secret records. I have no aversion to it or to most of its aims and have, for much of my life, been close to it and to many of its instruments. I have objected, both in the past and recently, to a few of its policies (notably to its belief that England was an Atlantic rather than a European Power and must be allied, or even federated, with the United States and must remain isolated from Europe), but in general my chief difference of opinion is that it wishes to remain unknown, and I believe its role in history is significant enough to be known. [8]

Heady, powerful words indeed from a tenured professor at Georgetown, for these were not the ravings of some "lunatic fringe" conspiracy theorist, but of a man very much a part of the academic establishment.

The aims of this group—and we shall deal with its American and British components in a moment before turning our attentions to the German one—was, according to Quigley, "largely commendable," namely, "to coordinate the international activities and outlooks of all the English-speaking world into one..."[9] Elsewhere, however, Quigley is less euphemistic:

> In addition to these pragmatic goals, the powers of financial capitalism had another far-reaching aim, nothing less than to create a world system of financial control in private hands able to dominate the political system of each country and the economy of the world as a whole. *This system was to be controlled in a feudalist*

---

[8] Carroll Quigley, *Tragedy and Hope: A History of the World in Our Time* (Macmillan, 1966), p. 950.
[9] Ibid., p. 954.

fashion by the central banks of the world acting in concert, by secret agreements arrived at in frequent meetings and conferences. The apex of the system was to be the Bank for International Settlements in Basle, Switzerland, a private bank owned and controlled by the world's central banks, which were themselves private corporations. Each central bank, in the hands of men like Monague Norman of the Bank of England, Benjamin Strong of the New York Federal Reserve Bank, Chales Rist of the Bank of France, and Hjalmar Schacht of the Reichsbank, sought to dominate its government by its ability to control Treasury loans, to manipulate foreign exchanges, to influence the level of economic activity in the country, and to influence cooperative politicians by subsequent economic rewards in the business world.[10]

Note the mention of feudalism, for this is a crucial component of the longer-term story, one which I hope to address in a future book.

For our purposes of the moment, however, we note the crucial role played by the Bank of International Settlements in Basle, a point to which we shall return shortly. But to understand its central role in the tapestry of pre-World War Two financial arrangements, we need to look closer at the context of those instruments of power that Quigley surveys.

> The chief backbone of this organization grew up along the already existing financial cooperation running from the Morgan Bank in New York to a group of international financiers in London led by Lazard Brothers.[11]

The London branch of this network was headed by Lord Milner, who founded a number of banks that would eventually become one of Britain's largest, the Midland Bank.[12] Milner placed his disciples and associates in key positions throughout Great Britain, including "the editorship of *The Times,* the editorship of *The Observer,*" various banks, and the Universities of Oxford and London.[13]

The end of the First World War necessitated that this system be extended throughout the British Commonwealth, and accordingly,

---

[10] Quigley, *Tragedy and Hope*, p. 324, emphasis added.
[11] Ibid., p. 951.
[12] Ibid.
[13] Ibid.

front groups for this Empire of Money were established in the various Commonwealth nations.[14]

> This front organization, called the Royal Institute of International Affairs, had as its nucleus in each area the existing submerged Round Table Group. In New York it was known as the Council on Foreign Relations, and was a front for J.P. Morgan and Company...
>
> The New York branch was dominated by the associates of the Morgan bank. For example, in 1928 the Council on Foreign Relations had John W. Davis as president, Paul Cravath as vice-president, and a council of thirteen others, which included Owen D. Young, Russell C. Leffingwell, Norman Davis, *Allen Dulles*, George W. Wickersham, Frank L. Polk, Whitney Shepardson, Isaiah Bowman, Stephen P. Duggan, and Otto Kahn...
>
> The academic figures have been those linked to Morgan, such as James T. Shotwell, Charles Seymour, Joseph P. Chamberlain, Philip Jessup, Isaiah Bowman and, more recently, Philip Moseley, Grayson L. Kirk, and Henry M. Wriston. The Wall Street contacts with these were created originally from Morgan's influence in handling large academic endowments. In the case of the largest of these endowments, that at Harvard...
>
> Closely allied with this Morgan influence were a small group of Wall Street law firms, whose chief figures were Elihu Root, John W. Davis, Paul D. Cravath, Russell Leffingwell, *the Dulles brothers* and, more recently, Arthur H. Dean, Philip D. Reed, and *John J. McCloy.*[15]

We shall return to the Dulles brothers, and in particular, to Allen Dulles, in a moment.

It is crucial to note that the "Empire of Money," both in its British and American branches, had after the First World War made deep penetrations into the most prestigious academic institutions in each country, and thus, exercised influence over what Quigley himself would call the "instruments of invention." Effectively, the same system and structural alliances were mirrored in each country. For example, the Morgan faction—and it is important to understand by this time this also meant the Morgan-Rockefeller faction[16]— had set up

---

[14] Ibid.
[15] Quigley, *Tragedy and Hope*, p. 952, emphasis added.
[16] Ibid., p. 531.

in Princeton a reasonable copy of the Round Table Group's chief Oxford headquarters, All Souls College. This copy, called the Institute for Advanced Study, and best known perhaps, as the refuge of Einstein, Oppenheimer, John von Neumann, and George F. Kennan, was organized by Abraham Flexner of the Carnegie Foundation and Rockefeller's General Education Board after he had experienced the delights of All Souls while serving as Rhodes Memorial Lecturer at Oxford.[17]

To put it succinctly, the Empire of Money was founding, in each country, special instruments(to use Quigley's term) for all manner of advanced scientific study of everything from geopolitics and social engineering to physics. By its influence over the media of the time, it could thus also engage directly in propaganda and other psychological operations.

With this context in mind, we turn to the German faction of this "Empire of Money, " and to a brief consideration of how Nazism penetrated and manipulated it for its own ends, and why the British and American factions would have *allowed* such an arrangement to exist in the first place.

2. The Nazi Bank of International Settlements
a. The Problem of German War Reparations, the Dawes and Young Plans, and the Establishment of the BIS

As previously noted, the Bank of International Settlements in Basle, Switzerland, was the keystone in the arch of the Fraternity's attempt to influence international politics and finance. The reason why lies in the Versailles Treaty's imposition of war reparations on post-World War One Germany, an imposition that, in effect, made Germany pay for the entire war effort of the Allies. Germany, in other words, was mortgaged to the bankers who had loaned money to the Allies, and this, in effect, meant that Germany was mortgaged to the *American* faction of this international Empire of Money, for American banks were during the war the only banks with the credit and reserves to loan money, the British and French banks having long exhausted themselves in the war effort.

The result of the war reparations was met with an unusual German response, or rather, an unusual response by the German

---

[17] Ibid., p. 953.

faction of this international empire of money, and here, again, Quigley is a key, requiring the reader to read carefully between the lines:

> Instead of taxing and retrenching, the German government permitted an unbalanced budget to continue year after year, making up the deficits by borrowing from the Reichsbank. The result was an acute inflation. This inflation was not forced on the Germans by the need to pay reparations (as they claimed at the time) but by the method they took to pay reparations (or more accurately, to avoid payment). The inflation was not injurious to the influential groups in German society, although it was generally ruinous to the middle classes, and thus encouraged the extremist elements. Those groups whose property was in real wealth, either in land or in industrial plant, were benefitted by the inflation which increased the value of their properties and wiped away their debts (chiefly mortgages and industrial bonds).[18]

In 1923, the French responded to this provocation of being paid reparations with increasingly worthless Reichsmarks by seizing *real* wealth, and occupied Germany's industrial heart, the Ruhr Valley.

In response to *this*, the Germans simply refused to work, called a general strike, and effectively ruined the purpose for the French occupation in the first place. At this juncture, the Morgan-Rockefeller faction stepped in with the first of many schemes, the Dawes plan:

> The Dawes Plan, which was largely a J.P. Morgan production, was drawn up by an international committee of financial experts presided over by the American banker Charles G. Dawes. It was concerned only with Germany's ability to pay, and decided that this would reach a rate of 2.5 billion marks a year after four years of reconstruction. During the first four years Germany would be given a loan of $800 million and would pay a total of only 5.17 billion marks in reparations. This plan did not supersede the German reparations obligation... Thus Germany paid reparations for five years under the Dawes Plan(1924-1929) and owed more at the end than it had owed at the beginning.
>
> ...
>
> Specifically, Germany was able to borrow abroad beyond her ability to pay, without the normal slump in the value of the mark which would have stopped such loans under normal circumstances.

---

[18] Quigley, *Tragedy and Hope*, pp. 306-307.

It is worthy of note that this system was set up by the international bankers and that the subsequent lending of other people's money to Germany was very profitable to these bankers.

The only things wrong with the system were (a) that it would collapse as soon as the United States ceased to lend, and (b) in the meantime debts were merely being shifted from one account to another and no one was really getting any nearer to solvency... Nothing was settled by all this, but the international bankers sat in heaven, under a rain of fees and commissions.[19]

It is within this context that we may now turn to the Bank of International Settlements, its founding, and how it was subsequently used by the Nazis.

To handle all these shifting, shuffling debts, it was decided to create a "Central Bankers' Bank," the Bank of International Settlements in Basle, Switzerland, owned by "the chief central banks of the world."[20]

> In the final days of the system, these central bankers were able to mobilize resources to assist each other through the B.I.S., where payments between central banks could be made by bookkeeping adjustments between the accounts which the central banks of the world kept there. The B.I.S. as a private institution was owned by the seven chief central banks and was operated by the heads of these, who together formed its governing board. Each of these kept a substantial deposit at the B.I.S., and periodically settled payments among themselves (and thus between the major countries of the world) by bookkeeping in order to avoid shipments of gold.[21]

In other words, the mountain of debt incurred during World War One had far outstripped the ability of the gold standard to keep pace, and thus, under the crush of circumstances, it was abandoned in favor of yet a new central bank.

> As a matter of fact its establishment in 1929 was rather an indication that the centralized world financial system of 1914 was in decline. It was set up rather to remedy the decline of London as

---

[19] Ibid., pp. 308-309.
[20] Quigley, *Tragedy and Hope*, p. 310.
[21] Ibid.,p. 324.

the world's financial center by providing a mechanism by which a world with three chief financial centers in London, New York, and Paris could still operate as one. The B.I.S. was a vain effort to cope with the problems arising from the growth of a number of centers. It was intended to be the world cartel of ever-growing national financial powers by assembling the nominal heads of these financial centers.[22]

Accounts could be handled simply by "shifting credits from one country's account to another on the books of the bank."[23] But here, Quigley is for once not telling the whole story.

b. The German Faction and the B.I.S.

The inspiration for the BIS came from none other than Dr. Hjalmar Schacht, later president of Hitler's Reichsbank.[24] And here the plot thickens, considerably:

Sensing Adolf Hitler's lust for war and conquest, Schacht, even before Hitler rose to power in the Reichstag, pushed for an institution that would retain channels of communication and collusion between the world's financial leaders *even in the event of an international conflict. It was written into the bank's charter, concurred in by the respective governments, that the BIS should be immune from seizure, closure, or censure, whether or not its owners were at war.* [25]

But that was by no means all. For while the bank was originally and ostensibly created to handle the payments and transfers of war reparations between Germany and the former western Allies, "the Bank soon turned out to be the instrument of an opposite function. It was to be a money funnel for American and British funds to flow into Hitler's coffers and to help Hitler build up his war machine."[26]

Thus, by the time World War Two broke out in September 1939, the BIS was almost completely under the control of Hitler via his various proxies, and included among its directors the head of I.G.

---

[22] Quigley, *Tragedy and Hope*, pp. 324-325.
[23] Ibid.
[24] Higham, *Trading With the Enemy*, p. 1.
[25] Ibid., pp. 1-2, emphasis added.
[26] Ibid., p. 2.

Farben(of course), Hermann Schmitz, Baron Kurt von Schröder, "head of the J.H. Stein Bank of Cologne and a leading officer and financier of the Gestapo; Dr. Walther Funk of the Reichsbank" and Emil Puhl.[27] And at the head of this, as president, "was the smooth old Rockefeller banker, Gates W. McGarrah, formerly of the Chase National Bank and the Federal Reserve Bank, who retired in 1933."[28]

As Charles Higham reports, after the Nazi annexation of Austria in 1938, and later its annexation of Bohemian Czechoslovakia in 1939, the gold reserves of those nations fell into Nazi hands. By this time, "the BIS had invested millions in Germany, while Kurt von Schröder and Emil Puhl deposited large sums in looted gold in the Bank."[29] In other words, the nexus for the postwar relationship between the Nazis and the Western banksters of London and New York was being created even before the war, and its principal mechanism was the BIS.

As the plundered gold of the former Czechoslovakia flowed into the BIS's vaults, it received a new president, the American Thomas Harrington McKittrick, "an associate of the Morgans and an able member of the Wall Street establishment."[30] The collusion between the Nazis and the Western capitalists continued under McKittrick, for in 1940, sensing war looming between Germany and the U.S.A., McKittrick went to Berlin "and held a meeting at the Reichsbank with Kurt von Schröder of the BIS and the Gestapo. They discussed doing business with each other's countries if war between them should come."[31] An even more remarkable journey was undertaken by McKittrick in 1943, and with it, we see the beginnings of the outline of the shadowy postwar Nazi International beginning to emerge, and with it, the entrance of the third faction—the Nazis— into the postwar structure of the breakaway civilization:[32]

---

[27] Ibid.

[28] Ibid.

[29] Higham, *Trading With the Enemy*, p. 7.

[30] Ibid.

[31] Ibid.

[32] I have referred to three factions in this international empire of money, and I mean these to be represented by the London-based faction, the New York-based faction, and the pre-war German and post-war Nazi faction. Obviously, this is a gross simplification, since we have not considered the most powerful rival faction in London, the Rothschilds. As we shall see later in this book, there are strong ideological reasons for the

153

In the spring of 1943, McKittrick, ignoring the normal restrictions of war, undertook a remarkable journey. Despite the fact he was neither Italian nor diplomat and that Italy was at war with the United States, he was issued an Italian diplomatic visa to travel by train and auto to Rome. At the border he was met by Himmler's special police, who gave him safe conduct. McKittrick proceeded to Lisbon, whence he traveled with immunity from U-boats by Swedish ship to the United State. In Manhattan in April he had meetings with Leon Fraser, his old friend and BIS predecessor, and with the heads of the Federal Reserve Bank. Then McKittrick traveled to Berlin on a U.S. passport (!) to provide Emil Puhl of the Reichsbank with secret intelligence on financial problems and high-level attitudes in the United States.[33]

But just what was all this unusual travel *for*?

A hint is provided by looking at other pre-war Nazi-American business relationships, at meetings of the BIS in 1944, and at the July 1944 bomb plot against Adolf Hitler. We have already had occasion to mention the Gestapo man and banker Kurt von Schröder, who maintained business relationships with Standard Oil's Walter Teagle, with Winthrop Aldrich of the Rockefeller Chase Bank, and with Colonel Sosthenes Behn, head of the American international communications giant, International Telephone and Telegraph.[34] But von Schröder was not the only Nazi with such links. The head of I.G. Farben, and BIS board member Hermann Schmitz, had before the war cultivated a close relationship with none other than Walter Schellenberg, head of the SS's notorious *Sicherheitdienst*, the SD. And here the plot once again thickens:

> Army Intelligence documents declassified in 1981 show that Schellenerg discussed Schmitz as head of a Council of Twelve. The

---

New York Morgan-Rockefeller interest to be allied with the Nazis against their   (obviously Jewish) rivals, the Rothschilds. The complexities of the internal factional infighting between these groups is beyond the purposes of this book.

[33] Higham, *Trading with the Enemy*, p. 11.

[34] Ibid., p. 132. Higham notes that Schellenberg was actually a prominent shareholder of ITT (p. xvi.) During the war, ITT agents met with Rockefeller and Gestapo representatives in Madrid to find ways to improve the Getsapo's technological surveillance capabilities (see p. 93).

council would place Hitler under the protection and rulership of Himmler while the Führer remained a prisoner of Berchtesgaden. Knowing that Schmitz was dedicated to Himmler and the Gestapo cause, Schellenberg plotted constantly toward this end. However, Himmler vacillated constantly. He could not bring himself to depose the Führer, nor did he expose Schellenberg to the Führer.

The underlying purpose of the Schellenberg plan, revealed in the same recently declassified Army Intelligence report, was clearly to bring about the negotiated peace between Germany and the United States that was the overriding dream of The (banking) Fraternity.[35]

In other words, the Fraternity was manipulating behind the scenes to bring an end to the war between Germany and the Western Allies, leaving the Soviet Union to fend for itself.

But what of the American side of this? Enter McKittrick the BIS, and the Morgan-Rockefeller interests once again. In May of 1944, the board of BIS convened a meeting under McKittrick's oversight "to discuss such important matters as the $378 million in gold that had been sent to the Bank by the Nazi government after Pearl Harbor for use by its leaders after the war."[36] Of course, the Nazis had originally deposited the gold with the view that after they won the war, it would be available for their purposes after its conclusion. But as I wrote elsewhere, after the defeat at Stalingrad in 1943 and the later failure of the German offensive at Kursk in July of 1943,[37] the plans changed, but now it is to be noted, that while the *plans* changed according to the circumstances, the Nazi goal of survival and influence after the war did not, *nor did the structures of the financial arrangements they sought to employ in that purpose.* In short, the Nazis decided deliberately to go underground, to constitute themselves as a breakaway civilization, *and to do so in concert with and connection to the American corporate and banking elite.*

Meanwhile, the American faction of this nexus continued covertly to support the anti-Hitler resistance, in hopes of bringing to power a government in Germany with which it could negotiate a separate peace. The bomb plot against Hitler in July of that year, on

---

[35] Higham, *Trading With the Enemy*, pp. 132-133.
[36] Ibid., p. 1.
[37] Joseph P. Farrell, *The Nazi International*, pp. 63-83.

the American side, was aided by ITT CEO Sosthenes Behn, with help from none other than Allen Dulles.[38]

We need to pause and consider the full implications of this little-known or appreciated fact. On the German side, the motivation of the anti-Hitler plotters was first of all, their inside knowledge of impending German success with the atom bomb,[39] their reluctance to allow Hitler the possibility of using it, a possibility that would have brought severe Allied reprisals and the complete destruction of Germany. Secondly, this group wished to conclude a separate peace with the Western Allies to allow them to transfer military resources to the Eastern front, and stem the Soviet advance into Eastern Europe. With an atom bomb in their hands, the plotters assumed this would have given them negotiating leverage with the Allies.

This latter motivation squared well with the views of the American corporate elite, and hence, explains their willingness to aid in the plot. It does not, however, explain how the American faction planned to deal with the Roosevelt Administration, which had made the unconditional surrender of Germany its war objective. The answer to this reveals the only possibility that the American faction could have entertained: they hoped, with Hitler's removal, that Roosevelt's re-election chances later that year would be curtailed, and failing that, they may have had plans to otherwise remove him from office. In this respect, it should be recalled that the same corporate interests had, before America's entry into the war, had actually plotted a military coup to remove Roosevelt, a plot that was exposed by Marine Corps general Smedley Butler.

To put it succinctly, the American faction's cooperation with the Anti-Hitler faction of the Nazi government reveals the American component of the breakaway civilization. Dean Acheson, for example, stated that the BIS would be needed to help rebuild Germany after the war, and he could not have been oblivious to the heavy Nazi presence and influence in the bank.[40]

Indeed, as early as the summer of 1942, the BIS was functioning as the choke point for Nazi currency manipulations in anticipation of

---

[38] Higham, op. cit., pp. 112-113.

[39] See my *Reich of the Black Sun: Nazi Secret Weapons and the Cold War Allied Legend* (Adventures Unlimited Press, 2004), p. 157.

[40] Higham, *Trading With the Enemy*, p. 13.

the Reich's defeat, in an effort to ensure the survival of the Party organization and its goals:

> In the summer of 1942, Pierre Pucheu, French Cabinet member and director of the privately owned Worms Bank in Nazi-occupied Paris, had a meeting at the BIS with Yves Bréart de Boisanger, Pucheu told Boisanger that plans were afoot for General Dwight D. Eisenhower to invade North Africa. He had obtained this information through a friend of Robert Murphy, U.S. State Department representative in Vichy. Boisanger contacted Kurt von Schröder. Immediately, Schröder and other German bankers, along with their French correspondents, transferred 9 billion gold francs via the BIS to Algiers. Anticipating German defeat, they were seeking a killing in dollar exchange. The collaborationists boosted their holdings from $350 to $525 million almost overnight. The deal was made with the collusion of Thomas H. McKittrick, Hermann Schmitz, Emil Puhl, and the Japanese directors of the BIS.[41]

In other words, the chairman of I.G. Farben, and senior members of the Reichsbank and Gestapo, were already laying the foundations for vast currency transfers, and a vast postwar financial empire, for the postwar Nazi International. Nazi deposits of gold—much of it looted and plundered from Europe and Holocaust victims—in the BIS allowed the Nazis to begin converting this gold to liquid foreign currency assets for operations after the war.[42]

We must now examine one particular group within the American faction must more closely...

3. The Rockefeller Link and Its Implications
a. Martin Bormann's Check-Cashing Episode Revisited

In my book, *The Nazi International*, I recounted a curious incident of an unusual check that was cashed in the early 1960s, revealed by the former CBS journalist, Paul Manning, an associate of CBS newsman Edward Murrow. Manning recorded the curious incident as follows, referring to FBI files on Martin Bormann's whereabouts in Latin America:

---

[41] Higham, *Trading with the Enemy*, pp. 10-11.
[42] Ibid., p. 17.

...John Edgar Hoover assigned the investigation to his most experienced and skillful agent in South America, who proved that he was just that by eventually obtaining copies of the Martin Bormann files that were being held under strict secrecy by Argentina's Minister of the Interior in the Central de Intelligencia. When the file (now in my possession) was received at FBI headquarters, it revealed that the Reichsleiter had indeed been tracked for years. One report covered his whereabouts from 1948 to 1961, in Argentina, Paraguay, Brazil and Chile. *The file revealed that he had been banking under his own name from his office in Germany in Deutsche Bank of Buenos Aires since 1941; that he held one joint account with the Argentinian dictator Juan Perón, and on August 4, 5, and 14, 1967, had written checks on demand accounts in First National City Bank (Overseas Division) of New York, The Chase Manhattan Bank, and Manufacturers Hanover Trust Co., all cleared through Deutsche Bank of Buenos Aires.*[43]

The implications of this event are staggering, and reveal the full extent of the breakaway civilization, for on the one hand, it is apparent that official agencies of the U.S. government are committing resources to discover the whereabouts of the infamous Nazi Party *Reichsleiter*, yet, clearly his existence is known to private American banking interests connected with the Rockefeller interests!. In other words, those interests are acting counter to the goals and objectives of the American government, and to that extent, symbolizes the American component of the breakaway civilization. It therefore requires a closer look.

b. The Pre-War Rockefeller Group-Nazi Links

The Nazi-Rockefeller links suggested by "the Bormann check-cashing affair" in fact pre-dated the war, and were maintained during the war, by both parties. The Chase bank, at the time of the American entry into World War Two, was the United States' largest and by any accounts its most powerful bank. It was the lynchpin in the enormous Rockefeller corporate empire, as it handled the accounts for the Rockereller empire's other large corporate concern, Standard Oil. Additionally, it was the bank that also handled ITT's accounts, the accounts for the American branches of I.G. Farben and its

---

[43] Paul Manning, *Martin Bormann: Nazi in Exile*, pp. 204-205, emphasis added, cited in my *Nazi International*, p. 304.

subsidiaries, and thus, had close contacts with the BIS, and the corporate and Gestapo elite of Nazi Germany.[44]

Here, as Charles Higham's meticulous research points out, the relationship becomes very deeply intertwined with the Gestapo, and the BIS, and reveals even more sinister postwar implications:

> As war approached, the links between the Rockefellers and the Nazi government became more and more firm. In 1936, the J. Henry Schröder Bank of New York had entered into a partnership with the Rockefellers. Schröder, Rockefeller and Company, Investment Bankers, was formed as part of an overall company that *Time* magazine disclosed as being "the economic booster of the Rome-Berlin Axis." The partners in Schröder, Rockefeller and Company included Avery Rockefeller, nephew of John D., Baron Bruno von Schröder in London, and Kurt von Schröder of the BIS and Gestapo in Cologne. Avery Rockefeller owned 42 percent of Schröder, Rockefeller, and Baron Bruno and his Nazi cousin 47 percent. Their lawyers were John Foster Dulles and Allen Dulles of Sullivan and Cromwell. Allen Dulles (later of the Office of Strategic Services) was on the board of Schröder. Further connections linked the Paris branch of Chase to Schröder as well as the pro-Nazi Worms Bank and Standard Oil of New Jersey in France. Standard Oil's Paris representatives were directors of the Banque de Paris et des Pays-Bas, which had intricate connections to the Nazis and to Chase.[45]

The implications of the Rockefeller-Allen Dulles-BIS-Gestapo links revealed here are nothing less than staggering, for it was Dulles who, of course, negotiated the bargain with Nazi General Reinhard Gehlen, head of Germany's military intelligence group for all of Eastern Europe and the Soviet Union—the *Fremde Heere Ost*, or Foreign Armies East—the bargain that later left the immense Nazi military intelligence organization intact after the war, and still under Gehlen's operational command, while incorporating it as the "Soviet Desk" of the future CIA until such time as West Germany would assume jurisdiction over the organization.[46]

---

[44] Higham, *Trading With the Enemy*, p. 20.
[45] Higham, *Trading With the Enemy*, p. 22.
[46] For more on this aspect of the story, see my *SS Brotherhood of the Bell*(Adventures Unlimited Press, 2006), pp. 75-79.

With the addition of the Rockefeller interests into this equation, and with the postwar creation of the various American intelligence agencies enacted by the 1947 National Security Act—the CIA and the NSA—means that both the Nazi International and the corporate and banking interests of the USA were not only influential within those organizations, but that those organizations constituted one nexus of interaction between them, in addition to the banking connections already surveyed. *The breakaway civilization had, in other words, created its own intelligence group, grafted an already existing Nazi one into it, and created a steady source of funding for it: the American taxpayer.*

In addition to this, the Rockefeller group maintained a network of interlocking directorships and relationships with I.G. Farben. The chairman of Standard Oil of New Jersey, Walter C. Teagle, for example, along with its president William S. Farish, maintained close ties with I.G. Farben's Hermann Schmitz, and actually became the director of American I.G. Chemical Corp, Farben's American subsidiary, and sat on its board along with Edsel Ford.[47]

This arrangement allowed I.G. Farben to protect its patents from seizure by the American government, by simply transferring them to Standard Oil joint ownership, with an actual agreement being signed in The Hague that after the war, regardless of its outcome, the patents would be returned to Farben.[48] In addition to this, the Rockefeller interests also began the first murky beginnings of yet another source of independent funding that will play such a prominent role later in this chapter as a source of covert funding, for it sponsored both legal and illegal drug smuggling through an allied corporate interest, the pharmaceutical company, Sterling Products.[49] This was done through airline connections between Europe and Latin America, chiefly through the L.A.T.I. airline, via Brazil and Argentina, and by Standard Oil ships which had, under Farish's direction, changed registry from the U.S.A., to Panama. Under this flag, they were granted immunity from seizure by the then U.S. Under-Secretary of the Navy, James V. Forrestal, who additionally

---

[47] Higham, *Trading With the Enemy*, p. 33.
[48] Ibid., p. 37.
[49] Ibid., p. 38.

was a member of the Nazi-Rockefeller nexus, as a vice-president of the American Farben subsidiary, General Aniline and Film![50]

In other words, the postwar Nazi concentrations in Latin America had, by dint of the pre-war nexus between the American and German cartelists and corporate elite, ample protection for its activities. But there is yet another telling link between the American and Nazi factions in this history of this breakaway civilization and its activities:

c. The American and Nazi Elites: A Common Ideological Culture

It is a commonplace among researchers of the Rockefeller-Nazi connection that the two interests are divided by a common ideology, for on the American side of that equation, that corporate elite viewed itself *as* an elite both of *class* and of *race*, fit to rule over the vast masses of "human resources" in its corporate empires, while the same attitude prevailed in Nazism as well. Charles Higham aptly summarizes this ideological commonality: "They understood each other's language and their aims were common."[51]

But it goes beyond a common ideology, and again, into a common *goal and activity*. Researchers Glen Yeadon and John Hawkins, in their seminally important work *The Nazi Hydra in America*, point out yet another connection not only in ideology but in actual scientific and sociological technology and practice by observing that the Rockefeller interest was an early sponsor of eugenics research and sterilization programs, which formed the model for the later Nazi race laws. Additionally, both factions sponsored actual "genetics" research.[52]

d. Oil: Beginnings of the Texas and Radical Islam Connections

There is yet another prewar nexus between the American corporate elite in general, the Rockefeller interests in particular, and

---

[50] Ibid., pp. 38-39.
[51] Higham, *Trading With the Enemy*, p. 46.
[52] Glen Yeadon and John Hawkins, *The*

the Nazis that is continued after the war, and this is the link between Standard Oil and the then emerging Texas oil industry.[53]

A similar nexus emerges during the prewar period between American petroleum interests, the Nazis, and radical Islam, an interest again fraught with long-term implications for the activities of the breakaway civilization and its factions:

> From these sources, from German Foreign Office document 71/51181 (July 22, 1942) and from recently declassified secret reports prepared by British Intelligence on Walter Schellenberg of the Gestapo, it is possible to determine the extent of Nazi influence on (the house of) Ibn Saud in the middle of the war. The Grand Mufti of Jerusalem was, until the time of Italy's collapse as an Axis partner, living in Rome, working with the agents of Kurt von Schröder's friend and associate Ambassador Franz con Papen in Ankara, Turkey, to send out agents through the Arab states. In Saudi Arabia fanatical Arabs were trained as Nazis at German universities and schools. From a headquarters in a carpet shop in Baghdad, Dr. Fritz Grobba, German minister to Iraq, ran espionage rings, subsidized Arabic newspapers and clubs in the Saudi Arabian capital of Jidda. The German TransOcean New Agency functioned as an espionage and propaganda agency in Jidda. The Nazi spy Waldemar Baron von Oppenheim, until recently in the United States and Syria, was headquartered in Saudi Arabia. Many Nazis flocked in disguised as tourists or technicians. They constructed roads and built factories. They formed German-Arab societies and learned (the) Arab (sic) language so as to address crowds and whip them up into a fanatical support of Hitler. Ibn Saud, as always, played both ends against the middle, protesting admiration for Roosevelt and Churchill while authorizing his personal representative Rashid Ali El-Kilani to continue to represent him in Berlin and address the Moslem society there. [54]

Again, the implications here are profound, for such Nazi-radical Islamic contact could not have occurred without the knowledge and tacit approval of the large American and British petroleum interests on the Arabian peninsula, and this affords a clue into the postwar relationships we have seen emerging in the previous pages, for each

---

[53] Higham, op. cit., p. 76. For the importance and long-term significance of this Texas oil-Nazi nexus, see my *LBJ and the Conspiracy to Kill Kennedy* (Adventures Unlimited Press, 2011), pp. 151-172; 290-294.

[54] Higham, *Trading With the Enemy*, p. 84.

faction—the Nazi and the American corporate faction—would view each other in different ways. The American faction would come to view its postwar Nazis as its compliant tools, as the soldiers on the ground to execute the tactical planning and operations it deemed necessary. Similarly, the Nazi faction would view its American corporate contacts as compliant instruments to represent, and launder, its vast financial empire. It was a marriage strictly of convenience, as we shall now see in reviewing the postwar continuation and adjustment of these arrangements.

B. The Post-War Tapestry

The foregoing survey has been necessary to reveal just how, during the postwar period, the basic form and structure of the breakaway civilization's major factional relationships remained more or less intact.

1. Money Laundering and Blackmail

At one point, it was estimated that approximately 15,000 Nazis lived in the U.S.A. alone.[55] Additionally, the pre-war nexus between the Rockefeller interests and the corporate power structures behind Nazism were continued. Researcher and former Justice Department member John Loftus, for example, states that Chase Bank owned nearly a third of Thyssen-Krupp in 1973.[56] Thyssen, as is now well-known, had pre-war relationships with Prescott Bush and the Bush family, and of course, Krupp was Germany's notorious armaments maker.[57]

But the relationships go much deeper, and are inclusive of the activities of the breakaway civilization to cloak its postwar financial

---

[55] John Loftus, *America's Nazi Secret* (Trine Day, 2011), p. iii.

[56] Ibid., p. 4, n. 5.

[57] The complexities of this Bush-Thyssen relationship are too numerous to go into here, and have been covered by many other researchers. It is, however, worth noting that Loftus makes yet another connection: "Brown Brothers Harriman had so many corrupt ties to the Nazi regime that it became the only bank in New York State history ever to obtain permission to shred its war time and prewar files. It certainly had the influence to pull this off—two of its Nazi investment clients, Nelson Rockefeller and Averell Harriman, had become Governors of New York." (Loftus, op. cit., p. 17).

activities with the Nazis. In *The Nazi International* I briefly outlined the meeting held in August 1944, at the behest of Nazi Party *Reichsleiter* Martin Bormann, at the *Rotes Haus* Hotel in Strasburg. There, the Nazi and corporate leadership of Germany schemed the final stages of the strategic evacuation plan of the Nazi party, and its postwar survival as a kind of underground, extraterritorial state.[58] I also noted that when CBS journalist Paul Manning queried Allen Dulles on Bormann's whereabouts in Latin America, that Dulles indicated he was "on the right track." As I indicated in that book, the postwar investigations of the Nazi *Rotes Haus* meeting were anything but complete.

One reason for this "incompleteness" stems from the role of Sullivan and Cromwell, the prestigious Wall Street law firm, in representing U.S. businesses with Nazis ties, and in particular, to the role of one its most famous members, Allen Dulles, in that venture. The arrangement was convenient, for as Loftus notes, while some of the firm was representing corporations "whose assets had been seized under the Trading with the Enemy Act because they operated as Nazi fronts," other members of Sullivan and Cromwell "volunteered as the Justice Department's prosecutors, officially titled the Alien Property Custodians."[59] Dulles, as OSS station chief in Zurich, also used his position "to protect himself and his clients from investigation for laundering Nazi funds back to America."[60] No wonder Bormann could count on the success of his flight capital plan, for before the war was even over, the financial links that had existed during the prewar period were being re-forged, as we have seen, exactly according to the Nazis' own postwar plans.[61]

---

[58] Farrell, *The Nazi International*, pp. 63-83.

[59] Loftus, *America's Nazi Secret*, p. 2.

[60] Ibid., p. 5.

[61] Loftus goes further, and notes that the "British SIS reported that Dulles's American clients, including the Rockefellers, were helping the Nazis by laundering oil supplies through neutral countries. When FDR demanded that (the Department of) Justice indict the corporations, DOJ settled for a minor financial penalty. In defense of DOJ, it must be noted that Dulles's corporate cartel did threaten to withhold oil supplies for D-Day unless all charges were dropped."(op. cit., p. 7, n. 11) This included an investigation led by William J. Rockler, who was investigating Hitler's paymaster, Dr. Hermann Josef Abs, later CEO of Deutsche Bank and a principal attendee at

But this is just the tip of the iceberg of postwar Nazi-American corporate relationships. Originally, President Roosevelt entrusted the postwar investigation of American-Nazi financial relationships— Operation Safehaven— to his Secretary of the Treasury, Henry Morgenthau. Morgenthau was, of course, the originator of the Morgenthau Plan, a notorious "revenge" document calling for the complete de-industrialization of Germany and its division into smaller merely agricultural states. He was replaced as the head of Operation Safehaven after the war by none other than Allen Dulles, who used his position to recruit Nazis. From there, it gets even murkier:

> Although Dulles destroyed the Safehaven index, a few of Morgenthau's original files escaped Dulles's shredder, and can be found in the wartime State Department POst Files. For example, in the Switzerland Post files I discovered the Operation Safehaven investigation of Dulles himself, where he was accused of laundering money for the Nazis.... The Safehaven files were stolen by Eleanor Dulles and given to the Zionist intelligence service. They then blackmailed Nelson Rockefeller into pressuring the Latin American nations to supply the extra votes in the UN to create the State of Israel.[62]

---

early Bilderberger meetings. (See Loftus, op. cit., p. 8, and my *Babylon's Banksters*, pp. 64-70).

[62] Loftus, *America's Nazi Secret*, p. 12, n. 20. Loftus also notes that the real reason Roosevelt wanted the Nazi bankers put on trial at Nuremberg was in order for them to point the finger at their American counterparts, so that charges could then be brought against them for treason. (Loftus, op. cit., p. 13). As it was, this was wishful thinking on Roosevelt's part, for this would have exposed a crucial component of the postwar structures that the Nazis needed to ensure their survival and recrudescence.

It is also worth observing that the postwar Deutsche Bank mandarin, Dr. Hermann Josef Abs, was not only an early Bilderberger attendee, but during the early 1980s was appointed to a special Vatican council investigating the Banco Ambrosiano and Roberto Calvi banking scandals that so rocked the Vatican, having implications, according to some, for the mysterious and untimely death of Albino Luciani (Pope John Paul the First). (See Charles Higham, *American Swastika: The Shocking Story of Nazi Collaborators in our Midst from 1933 to the Present Day* [Doubleday and Company, 1985, p, xiv.) Higham expresses his disbelief and puzzlement over Abs' appointment by the Holy See to this commission, but it should not be at all surprising, since with the election of Pope John Paul II, his close

This is not yet the place to go into the Rockefeller-Latin America-Nazi nexus, but suffice it to say this episode is revealing of another interesting feature of the postwar structure of the breakaway civilization, for it is an indicator that within the corporate power structures revolving around New York and the City of London, there is a rupture, or fissure, between the Rockefeller interests and the Rothschild interests, a rupture revealed by the close relationships between the former and the Nazis, and it does not take a Nazi rocket scientist to figure out why that fissure exists.

2, Nazi Penetration of the West and the Potential of Captured Programs

The collusion elaborated above reveals yet another significant and crucial fact for the idea of a breakaway civilization, in that it discloses the extent to which official U.S. government agencies and official policy could be, and were, captured by external interests and agendas inimical to those of the government itself. We are, in short, looking at captured programs, and the beginnings of the existence of a parallel structure existing inside those programs and agencies, using them as a host, and for its own purposes. We have noted, for example, Dulles' recruitment of Nazis. These were recruited for the State Department's Office of Policy Coordination, headed by Frank Wisner,[63] in effect meaning that after Truman's 1948 upset victory over Republican Thomas Dewey, that there were two CIAs, the official one which hunted Nazis, and the other unofficial one, linked to Wisner and Dulles, that recruited them.[64] As Loftus notes, the very compartmentalized structure of American government agencies and intelligence functioned as a way of screening these Nazi programs and cloaking their activities.[65] And of course, once one enters into such arrangements with the Nazi devil, the possibility always exists that the Nazi component will turn on its American handlers and

---

advisor, Josef Cardinal Ratzinger (now Pope Benedict XVI), became one of the most influential advisors to the new pontiff.

[63] It is worth noting here that the OPC was implicated by Colonel Fletcher Prouty in the assassination of President Kennedy, adding yet another hidden rogue intelligence-Nazi connection to the murder.

[64] Loftus, *America's Nazi Secret*, p. 21.

[65] Ibid., p. 34.

blackmail their compliance at the threat of the exposure of the whole program, as indeed did happen.[66]

One is consequently looking at the potential of captured programs in two senses, the first being the penetration of official agencies by a breakaway civilization comprised both of an American and of a Nazi component, and the second being the blackmail of the American component by the Nazi one, or vice versa, according to the dictates of circumstances of the moment.

3. The Breakaway Civilization, Radical Islam, and Psychological Warfare: Terrorism

One of the most controversial aspects of the postwar history of the breakaway civilization and its activities is John Loftus' research into the links between the American corporate elite, the Nazis, and the Muslim Brotherhood, links that continued up to the tragic events of 9/11, so here we must review his case in more detail. Terrorism—i.e., the calculated application of violence—has long been a tool of psychological warfare operations, of *Weltanschauungskrieg.* Loftus begins by noting that

> The truth... is that the Muslim Brotherhood was the original Arab Nazi movement, working for British intelligence to crush the infant state of Israel. In the 1980s it was hired by American intelligence to recruit the *Muhajedeen* in Afghanistan, and it is now the parent organization of every Sunni terrorist group in the Middle East.[67]

The relationship between American corporate interests and radical Islamic elements, according to Loftus, goes back to the 1920s:

> During the 1920s three countries were targeted for takeover by the Robber Barons: Germany, Russia and what is now known as Saudi Arabia. The tactics were the same: American cartels bribed their way into friendly governments and then protected their investments by hiring local mercenaries—paid terrorist groups who watched over their interests.
>
> In Saudi Arabia, the terrorists for hire were known as the Ikhwan al Muslimeen, the Muslim Brothers, or more colloquially,

---

[66] Ibid., p. 49.
[67] Loftus, *America's Nazi Secret*, p. viii.

the Muslim Brotherhood. The Robber Barons armed this group of fanatical Wahhabists, who drove the peaceful Hashemite rulers out of Mecca and Medina and installed the House of Saud. The Saudis named the country after themselves, created an oil company with their American investors (Aramco), and then promptly threw the Ikhwan terrorists out of Saudi Arabia. The Saudis were not stupid after all.

The Ikhwan settled primarily in Egypt, where they joined the Egyptian Muslim Brotherhood created by Hassan Al Banna in 1928. He was a devout admirer and correspondent with young Adolf Hitler. "In heaven Allah, on earth Hitler" was their battle cry. Hassan's Muslim Brotherhood became a fully-integrated arm of the German intelligence and propaganda networks during WWII. They specialized in acts of terrorism and assassinations of Allied troops, promising German General Rommel that he would not find a single Allied soldier left alive when he arrived in Cairo. [68]

After the war, of course, Nazism survived, and became the on-the ground troops for the CIA-sponsored overthrow of Egypt's King Farouk, under the leadership of SS colonel Otto Skorzeny, installing Gamel Abdul Nassar, who turned on his Nazi supporters, threw them out, and invited the Soviets into Egypt.[69] At this juncture, the American corporate-intelligence component convinced the Saudis to take back the Brotherhood. This they did, employing them, as Loftus notes, throughout the Saudi kingdom as schoolteachers in "a perfect storm of Nazi racism and Wahhabbi bigotry."[70] The 1950s also saw the election of Dwight Eisenhower, and the installation of John Foster Dulles as Secretary of State, and his Nazi-recruiting brother, Allen, as director of the CIA.

All of this Nazi recruitment was handled through the State Department's Office of Policy Coordination, a haven for postwar Nazi intelligence recruits, and a department of the American government with direct links to Nazi General Reinhard Gehlen's military intelligence organization based in Pullach, outside of Munich. When U.S. Army counter-intelligence began to suspect the OPC's reliance on "former" Nazis, the day-to-day control of its operations was shifted back to Gehlen directly.[71] Thus, effectively, this means that

---

[68] Loftus, *America's Nazi Secret*, pp. 13-14.
[69] Farrell, *The Nazi International*, pp. 191-200.
[70] Loftus, *America's Nazi Secret*, p. 15.
[71] Ibid., pp. 30-31, 33, 45.

when the Muslim Brotherhood was recruited by the Reagan administration during the 1980s, the "Arab Nazis" were reactivated as proxies in the war against the Soviets in Afghanistan.[72]

All this throws conventional analysis of the events of 9/11 into a potential cocked hat, for at one level, the surface level of Arab terrorists hi-jacking airplanes and flying them into buildings, one is dealing with a network that had been in existence from prior to the war, and a network with deep connections both to the American corporate and intelligence worlds, and to the Nazis themselves.

At a second deeper level, one may be dealing, as the 9/11 truth movement so often argues, with inside knowledge and the tacit permission of a rogue element within the American intelligence and corporate parapolitical structure. But I believe that the physics signatures of the collapse of the Twin Towers and other evidence in New York City on that day do *not* point to the use of controlled demolitions to bring down the towers, but to the existence of a very sophisticated and exotic directed energy weaponry, a thesis which I share with the 9/11 researcher Dr. Judy Wood.[73]

(And that fact points to a third, deeper layer of involvement on that day, one I believe to be the signature of the activity of this breakaway civilization, and perhaps suggesting that the postwar marriage of convenience between the American corporate elite and the postwar Nazi International had finally broken down. Obviously, such a case would have to be argued in much greater detail, the task, perhaps, for a future work devoted to that subject. For now, however, it is worth noting that the Twin Towers constitute symbols of that Anglo-American corporate power and their long association with the fraternity that so embodies that elite, Freemasonry, and with the "twin pillars" Jachin and Boaz that adorn any Masonic lodge. The strike, in other words, was a strike against the symbols of that corporate power, sending very strong and deliberate messages to it: "we have perfected the technology we have been investigating since the war." It was, in my opinion, the announcement of divorce.)

---

[72] Ibid., p. 24.

[73] See her superb gathering of 9/11 evidence and arguments for the directed energy weapon hypothesis: Judy Wood, B.S., M.S., Ph.D., *Where Did the Towers Go?: Evidence of Directed Free-Energy Technology on 9/11.*

4. The Skorzeny Connection

The use of terror on this scale, and to this implied degree of technological sophistication, returns us once again to the crucial figure of SS colonel Otto Skorzeny, who first proposed use of advanced technology in connection with a *Weltanschauungskrieg*, and to his postwar activities.

It was Skorzeny who played a central role in Bormann's plan to evacuate liquid and hard assets in the form of cash and various bullions out of Europe to safe havens in South America.[74] As such, Skorzeny was an early target of America's war-end intelligence efforts, not so much to bring him to trial for war crimes, but to employ him in its own postwar anti-Communist efforts.[75] As such, Skorzeny is the link between Bormann's Nazi International in South America, Gehlen's postwar group of Nazi spies in Eastern Europe based out of Pullach, and American intelligence, and had in fact even met with America's OSS chief, General William Donovan after the war in Nuremberg.[76] Yet, as all of these links were forged, Skorzeny maintained contact with the SS elements behind the Iron Curtain that had ostensibly gone over to serve the Communist cause![77] Skorzeny was also related to Hjalmar Schacht, having married his niece and was in frequent contact with Schacht himself both from his headquarters in Spain, and later during the aftermath of the overthrow of King Farouk.[78] It was during that aftermath, when the Nazis had not yet been thrown out of Egypt by Nasser, that Skorzeny and his Nazis, with Nasser's approval, conducted pogroms and murders against Egyptian Jews, confiscating over $100 million of Jewish property in the "New Egypt."[79]

The nexus of postwar terrorist operations, then, can be traced to Skorzeny's branch of the Nazi International, and its deep connections both to radical Islamicism, and to the elite of the American corporate world and rogue groups within American intelligence.

---

[74] Charles Higham, *American Swastika: The Shocking Story of Nazi Collaborators in Our Midst from 1933 to the Present Day* (Doubleday and Company, Inc., 1985), pp. 247-248.
[75] Ibid.,p. 243.
[76] Ibid., p. 249.
[77] Ibid.
[78] Ibid., pp. 250-251.
[79] Ibid., p. 253.

5. The Final Source of Deepest Black Funding:
Drugs and the Nazi International

Thus far, our survey of the history and activities of the financial matrix of the breakaway civilization has highlighted two sources of funding, or "instruments of surplus creation" to use Quigley's nomenclature, namely, Nazi plunder from a looted Europe, moved into and laundered through Western Banks, largely in New York, and the implicit funding of its activities through the American taxpayer. These activities were, however, supplemented by a third component of funding, one guaranteeing a steady source for financing its goals and activities, and one, moreover, that was independent of any government's oversight or scrutiny. That source was through the criminal underground, and the growing worldwide trade in illegal drugs.

This story begins in the 1970s, when a major effort was mounted by rogue elements within American intelligence, and by the postwar Nazi International, to restructure the entire global heroin trade, closing off the old "French Connection" through Marseilles, and re-orienting it through the Southeast Asian, Mexican, and Latin American drug cartels.[80] Placing the lucrative Latin American and Mexican cartels' trade in league with the postwar Latin American Nazis and Fascists gave this component of the breakaway civilization a virtually inexhaustible source of money to fund its activities, from terrorism to research.

This group had pulled off a number of spectacular robberies in Europe, including the theft of gold bullion from the Société Générale de Nice, had been implicated in various assassination attempts on French President Charles DeGaulle, and had connections to terrorist and Fascist groups in Italy, Lebanon, and Britain. So pervasive and deep were these connections that "a number of newspapers, even including the *New York Times*, mentioned speculations" that it might be the activity of a "Fascist International."[81]

---

[80] Peter Dale Scott, "Foreword," to Henrik Krüger, *The Great Heroin Coup: Drugs, Intelligence, and International Fascism* (Boston, South End Press: 1980), p. 3.

[81] Ibid., p. 9.

By the time of the ITT-Nazi-CIA sponsored coup against Chilean President Salvadore Allende in 1973, this group had made deep penetration into the Cuban exile community (a fact already in evidence as early as the Bay of Pigs fiasco), and had scattered connections throughout Argentina, Chile, and Brazil. [82]

The Nazi component of the breakaway civilization moved quickly to solidify its ties and influence over the international drug trade. As this drug trade was being restructured in the early 1970s, Miami became a haven for the activity of European Fascists, and this led researcher Henrik Krüger to begin asking some interesting questions. Those questions, and his answers, are worth citing in some detail:

> What are European Fascists doing in Miami before and after major operations? Why are Miami-based Cuban exiles executing contracts on young Spaniards? Why was the main station of the CIA-supported Fascist front World Service in Miami? Why did bank robber Spaggiari contact the CIA in the United States?
>
> Miami is the center of a huge conspiratorial milieu whose personnel wind through the Bay of Pigs, attempts on Castro's life, the JFK murder and the great heroin coup, and which is now reaching out with a vengeance to Latin America and Europe.
>
> To trace the roots of this milieu we must refer to the immediate aftermath of World War II, when the CIA began its close cooperation with Adolf Hitler's espionage chief, Reinhard Gehlen, and the Soviet general, Andrei Vlassov, of Russia's secret anti-Communist spy network. Vlassov's organization was absorbed into Gehlen's, which evolved into a European subsidiary of the CIA. U.S. and German agents mingled in Berlin and West Germany, paving the way for inroads into U.S. intelligence by former Nazis, SS agents, and Russian czarists.
>
> Headquarters of the CIA/Gehlen/Vlassov combine, staffed in the mid-fifties by 4000 full-time agents, were in Pullach, near Munich. There Gehlen sang to the tune of more than one piper, having remained in touch with the old Nazi hierarchy relocated in Latin America, whose coordinator, Otto Skorzeny, was in Spain. Skorzeny had infiltrated the Spanish intelligence agency DGS, and effectively controlled it single-handedly.
>
> With the onset of the Cold War, Gehlen's agents were recruited by the CIA for assignments in the United States, Latin America and

---

[82] See p. 10 of Scott's Foreword.

Africa. One agent, reportedly, was Frank Bender, allegedly alias Frank Swend, a key figure in the Bay of Pigs invasion.[83]

But this isn't the half of it.

From his headquarters in Albufera, Spain,[84] Skorzeny's goal in penetrating and allying with the powerful Latin American drug cartels was not only to provide a limitless source of funding, but to create nothing less than an alliance of right wing terrorists with connections to the old anti-Gaullist OAS in France, and Spanish, Argentine, Italian, Brazilian and Central American Fascists.[85] These groups "and other Nazi and Fascist powers throughout Europe and Latin America, envisioned a new world order built on a Fascist Iron Circle linking Beunos Aires, Santiago, Lima, la Paz, Brasilia and Montevideo."[86]

With this alliance, the Nazi International embarked on a campaign of terror and assassination in South America known as Operation Condor, with oblique CIA approval, a grim reminder of Skorzeny-led commando oeprations behind American lines during World War Two, also known as Operation Condor, all the while cloaking its activities as those of the radical left![87] The end result of this campaign was, of course, the consolidation of the South American drug cartels, and a new source of funding for the breakaway civilization. [88]

And speaking of Latin America, there is one final connection we must now explore...

---

[83] Henrik Krüger, *The Great Heroin Coup: Drugs, Intelligence, and International Fascism,* pp. 204-205.

[84] Ibid., p. 209.

[85] Krüger, *The Great Heroin Coup,* p. 209.

[86] Ibid.,p. 210.

[87] Ibid.,pp. 212-213. On p. 214, Krüger notes that some members of this vast organization were even successfully elected to the first European Parliament in 1979.

[88] There are, of course, any number of books on the American component's involvement in this drug trade, detailing connections with Iran-Contra, the Mena, Arkansas affair, INSLAW, and so on. My point here has been to emphasize the role of the Nazi International in these events, to supplement the already existing literature detailing other aspects of this story.

6. The Argentina-Rockefeller-Nazi Connection

Argentina, as I have reported in *The Nazi International*, was home to a major postwar Nazi research effort in advanced technology ostensibly investigating controlled fusion, but in reality, connected to its wartime Bell project and investigations of anti-gravity and zero-point energy.[89] But it is in Argentina that one discovers yet another nexus between the American corporate elite and the postwar Nazi International:

> Nelson Rockefeller's role in Latin America during the War was to coordinate US intelligence and covert operations in the days before the creation of the CIA. He was the direct liaison between President Franklin Roosevelt and British Prime Minister Winston Churchill's personal intelligence head for the Americas, Sir William Stephenson, who directed a front company called British Security Coordination or BSC. Notably, Stephenson's clandestine headquarters for his covert activity was in room 3603 in Rockefeller Center, in New York City, not far from Nelson's office.[90]

We have already noted the statements of John Loftus that the files of Rockefeller associate Allen Dulles were used by various Zionist organizations to blackmail the Rockefeller interest into using its influence in Latin America to secure enough UN votes to recognize the State of Israel.

As researcher F. William Engdahl notes, "This included the pro-Axis regime of Juan Peron in Argentina. Rockefeller and Washington pressured Peron to officially declare war on Germany and Italy, even though it was two weeks before the war's end. That allowed Argentina to vote with the winning side."[91] But this was, with due respect to Mr. Engdahl, not the real reason for the behind-the-scenes maneuvering of the Rockefeller interests in Argentina's declaration of war.

We have already noted, throughout this chapter, that the American and Nazi components of the breakaway civilization were beginning to reconstitute their prewar links even before the war

---

[89] Farrell, *The Nazi International*, pp. 249-350.

[90] F. William Engdahl, *Seeds of Destruction: The Hidden Agenda of Genetic Manipulation* (Global research 2007), p. 109.

[91] Ibid., p. 111.

ended, and these links especially included the Rockefeller interest. We have seen also the role of Allen Dulles in laundering Nazi money, and in recruiting Nazis into the American bureaucratic infrastructure of postwar American intelligence.

Given the fact that the Nazis were conducting postwar research into advanced technologies in Argentina, and given the Rockefeller influence both in laundering Nazi plunder and in coercing the Argentine declaration of war, we are therefore justified in concluding that the real purpose of this, as far as the Rockefeller group was concerned, was to provide an Argentine homeland for Nazis that it did not wish to see come to America, and to maintain a degree of influence over their advanced technologies. In short, it wished to keep the most advanced technologies out of the hands of the American government, a goal which the Nazis themselves also shared. It was, once again, a marriage of convenience.

C. Conclusions

We are now, finally, in a position to summarize the financial matrix in which the crystal of the breakaway civilization grew. Summarizing the features of the financial relationships surveyed in this chapter, we take note of the following points:

1) Nazism, in its beliefs and ideology, and its genocidal pratice, constituted itself as a breakaway civilization, and for a brief moment, took Germany and the rest of Europe down that path;

2) The nexus of financial relationships between the American and German corporate elites prior to World War Two constituted, and viewed themselves as, a Fraternity or Empire of Money, willing and fit to rule over the rest of humanity within their sphere of influence. As such, this breakaway society was both a parasitic and a producing society, controlling the necessary instruments of surplus and invention, as revealed by the numerous links between that elite and the scientific and academic world. These connections, as noted, included a deep study of the techniques of psychological operations and social engineering, and the use of those operations *in conjunction with the development of advanced technology*, in order to

175

engineer the interpretation and perceptions of that technology in broader society. In the case of Adamski, the fascist connections of his associations and the fascist nature of his "teaching" strongly suggest that much of the early contactee literature was an operation of this sort;

3) Additionally, we have seen the emergence of a postwar permanent intelligence-gathering structure with deep connections both to the Nazi and to the American components of this breakaway civilization. In effect, this gave that civilization the ability to gather intelligence and to conduct ongoing black operations, including psychological operations inclusive of terrorist actions;

4) This breakaway civilization, through its American and British components, also maintained close ties with major media organs and outlets, allowing softer forms of psychological warfare and social engineering to be practiced on a wide population;

5) Via its easy access to large banking institutions and a deliberately feudalist structure of central banks clustered around the Bank for International Settlements, this Empire of Money also had access to the instruments of surplus, as well as instruments by which to launder money from almost any source. This deliberately feudal structure is also a clue, again, to the breakaway mentality of the Fraternity, since it views itself in mediaeval fashion as the lords over the serfs;

6) The above facts also highlight the nature of the mechanisms of funding for its activities and research, since, as we have indicated, there are three different sources for this financing:

a) Overt funding through taxation of the general populace in the various countries hosting the Fraternity and its institutions, which funding is used to contract its activities and research;

b) Covert, or "black budget" funding, in budgets that remain parallel to the official budgets of states, a phenomenon revealed in Nazi Germany by the parallel SS industrial structure, and in the USA by the black budget funding of secret research such as the Manhattan project. Such sources of funding do, however, depend upon the collusion of officials and agencies of that part of the state representing its budgetary oversight, and is thus never entirely "black";

c) Underground, or criminal sources of funding, which, as we have seen in this brief survey, include the worldwide traffic in illegal drugs, a trade which was massively restructured in the 1970s with the assistance of the postwar international Fascist organization. This implies that its most direct and basic source of funding is from these enterprises;

7) Finally, we have seen yet another link between the American and Nazi components of this fraternity, and pre- and post-war radical Islamic elements, a link persisting up to 9/11, and bearing profound implications for the proper interpretation of that event.

It is worth observing that this basic constellation of relationships is exactly the same structure as I outlined and argued existed behind the assassination of President John F. Kennedy.

With all this said, however, we must now address an entirely different question in relationship to the breakaway civilization, and its possible structure: what are its core and peripheral areas? To answer that will require yet another chapter, and yet another look at the profound historical analysis techniques of Dr. Carroll Quigley.

Hjalmar Schacht with Adolf Hitler

I.G. Farben's Wartime Chairman, Hermann Schmitz

9

AS ABOVE, SO BELOW:
THE GEOGRAPHIC AND TOPOGRAPHIC MATRIX OF THE
UNDERGROUND BLACK WORLD

*"In the imperialist wars of Stage 4 of a civilization the more peripheral states
are consistently victorious over less peripheral states. In Mesopotamian
civilization the core states like Uruk, Kish, Ur, Nippur, and Lagash were
conquered by more peripheral states like Agade and Babylon. These in turn
were conquered by peripheral Assyria, and the whole of western Asia was
ultimately conquered by fully peripheral Persia."*
Dr. Carroll Quigley[1]

As is evident from the previous epigraph, Dr. Quigley's historical analysis of the rise and fall of civilizations included the idea that there were "core" areas within each civilization, and "peripheral" ones. Briefly stated, the "core" area of a civilization was the region, society, or more recently, the nation, that stamped its culture, ideology, and social structures most indelibly on the rest of the societies that shared it. The core regions were, in this sense, the most influential. The peripheral areas were denoted by a *partial* adaptation of the cultural values of the core.

This conception bore certain consequences and implications for Quigley's analysis of modern history, in that, so far as western civilization was concerned, the "core" area during the period leading up to and away from the two world wars encompassed the nations of the United Kingdom, France, and the United States, with central and eastern Europe—Germany and the successor states to the Austro-Hungarian empire—forming important peripheral states, partially influenced by the culture of the west but, in their political and social organization, departing from the core by not being true representative democracies.

The key conception behind both "core" and "peripheral" societies within a civilization was *location*: both occupied clearly definable regions. But in the case of the breakaway civilization we have been examining, we are not in such an easy position, for as is by now evident, the structure of this civilization is parasitic: it exists

---

[1] Caroll Quigley, *The Evolution of Civilizations*, p. 154.

alongside of, and *within*, host societies or nations, and indeed has an international extent, crossing the borders and boundaries of normal national organization. How, then, one would define the "core" and "periphery" of such a civilization? Where would one *locate* it?

A. The Historical Matrix of World War Two

The clue, again, begins during World War Two, and again, specifically in Nazi Germany, for here the circumstances of history combined to create the unusual conditions necessary for the emergence of a breakaway civilization, firstly, in the acceptance of an ideology vastly at variance with the surrounding values of "Western Civilization," and secondly, in the creation of a "state within a state" that the SS represented, and by *its* creation, in turn, of the actual *physical locations* to carry on its secret "breakaway" activities, from genocide to black projects research, with the two activities often tied to the very same facilities. It was within these facilities of a "State within the State" that we discover both (1) the instruments of the generation of surplus, (2) the instruments for invention in the black research projects undertaken by the *Kammlerstab* of SS General Hans Kammler, and other bureaucracies of the SS, and (3) the combined "producing" and "parasitic" qualities of the civilization that we have remarked upon previously.

1. The Importance and Significance of the Kammlerstab to the Evolution of the Breakaway Civilization

Before we look more closely at the actual physical *plants* of this breakaway civilization, it is worth pausing to consider the significance of the *Kammlerstab* once again, for it affords yet another important clue into the nature of the breakaway civilization, both in its "Nazi," and in its "American", postwar components. As I first observed in *Reich of the Black Sun*, the *Kammlerstab* was essentially a "think tank," a super-secret research group tasked very deliberately to think *outside the box* of conventional scientific models, for the Nazis, this effectively meant that scientists were expected to develop paradigms of physics different from the relativistic physics model of "Jewish physics" that were the regnant standard model. They were expected to develop the basic outlines of technology trees to lead to second, third, and even fourth generation weapons of all sorts, and to lay the groundwork of what was needed to achieve them.

2. The Ideological and Scientific Culture of the Kammlerstab and a Modern Parallel

An *ideological culture of scientific research and development* was thus established that was vastly different from the surrounding civilization, a culture in which science itself was drafted to serve a political agenda of empire-building and hegemony via technological means. This mentality is reflected in the *locations and physical plants*, and in the *sociology* that they engender. Indeed, as we shall discover in the next chapter, this "sociology of weaponry" was itself a crucial area of investigation for Dr. Quigley. We find the modern parallel of the *Kammlerstab* in modern America, for example, in such agencies as The Defense Advanced Projects Research Agency, or DARPA, whose mission brief—thinking outside the box and charting the necessary steps in the technology trees—seems to be directly modeled on the example of the *Kammlerstab.*

3. The Direct Interface Between the Kammlerstab and The Cartelized Corporate World

There is also another feature of the *Kammlerstab* that is also quite crucial to point out in connection with the Nazi-corporate interfaces we have examined in previous chapters, and that is its *direct* relationship with the main corporate representative connected with its secret research and its ability to tap into the vast labor pools represented by the concentration camps. In *Reich of the Black Sun* I observed that Kammler himself was the actual designer of the Auschwitz camp,[2] was directly in command of the SS Buildings and Works department,[3] and that I.G. Farben had constructed a large synthetic rubber or Buna plant at Auschwitz, which was most likely a plant for the enrichment of uranium and other radioactive elements on a vast scale,[4] utilizing the latest technologies, perhaps even

---

[2] Farrell, *Reich of the Black Sun*, pp. 102ff.
[3] Ibid.
[4] Ibid, pp. 25-52.

including laser isotope enrichment, to do so.[5] In other words, within the structure of wartime Nazi secret research, we discover the *direct* relationship of the "state within a state," the SS, with the international corporate world represented by I.G. Farben, a relationship bypassing the ordinary bureaucratic structures of the German government itself. This, again, will bear enormous consequences for the postwar structure of the breakaway civilization.

B. The Breakaway Civilization and the Underworld

As is now well-known, prior to and during World War Two, the German government, and later the SS, constructed a number of enormous underground complexes, from communications centers, to entire factories and research facilities. In so far as these facilities are connected to the SS, they represent the actual *physical locations* for the emergence of a peripheral civilization in the very midst of the core or host civilization surrounding it, and that for a very important and obvious though often overlooked reason. Like all obvious things, it is easy to overlook precisely because it is so very obvious. But before looking at that obvious reason, we will first look at a sampling of Nazi and American underground installations, and the technologies for constructing them, in order to highlight the significance of that obvious thing, and its implication for the possibility of a breakaway civilization.

1. The Nazi Pentagon: The Underground Bunker Complex of Zossen

Hans George Kampe is a researcher who wrote possibly the only short verbal and graphic history of what must surely be one of the first examples of the breakaway civilization's obsession with security, and secure communications: the "Nazi pentagon," the huge underground complex of bunkers located in the German town of Zossen, south of Berlin. Neither the enormity of these structures nor the scope of Kampe's research can hardly be given due justice in this short review, but a look at some of the features of this vast underground bunker complex is in order, for its features also disclose prominent aspects of the sociology of the breakaway

---

[5] Farrell, *The Philosophers' Stone*, pp. 205-234.

civilization, evident in the structures it has built, and in the technology required to build them.

Consider, for example, this charming, typically German, rural farmhouse:

Rural Farmhouse over the North Terminus Entrance, Zossen Bunker Complex[6]

Beneath the peaceful, charming exterior, however, lay a hardened concrete framework, and a bombproof entrance to a staircase and elevator descending some 10 meters into a huge underground world of bunkers piled three stories deep, teletype, telegraph and telephone exchanges, storage rooms, corridors hundreds of meters long, battery rooms, generator power plants, sewage facilities, radio communications facilities... in short, a self-contained underground world, accessed through various "farmhouses" on the surface dotted around the village of Zossen:

---

[6] Hans George Kampe, *The Underground Military Command Bunkers of Zossen, Germany: History of Their Construction and Use by the Wehrmacht and Soviet Army 1937-1994*, trans. from the German by Don Cox (Atglen, Pennsylvania, Schiffer Military/Aviation History, 1996), frontispiece.

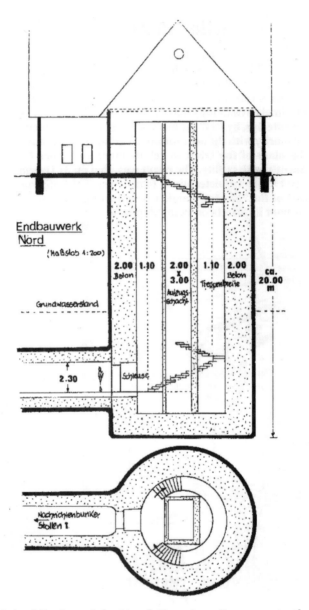

Endbauwerk
Nord
(Maßstab 1:200)

The Original Design of the North Terminus Entrance to the Zossen Zeppelin Bunker Complex[7]

---

[7] Kampe, *The Underground Military Command Bunkers of Zossen, Germany*, p. 12.

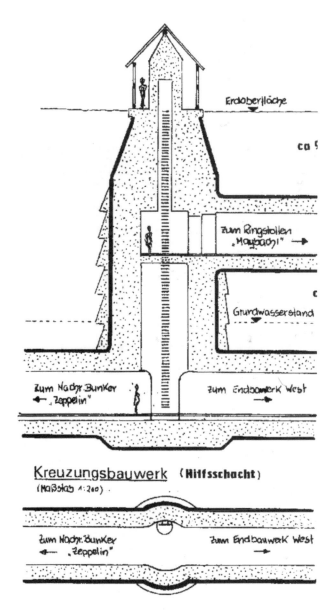

The Original Design for the Junction Complex At Zossen[8]

---

[8] Kampe, *The Underground Military Command Bunkers of Zossen, Germany*, p. 13.

This vast underground world was home to state of the art communications equipment, to secure the Wehrmacht's communications in all circumstances. The scale of the complex, and of the technologies housed in its bunkers can only be appreciated by Kampe's pictures:

One of the over Four Hundred Line Amplifying Relay Stations in the Underground Bunkers of Zossen[9]

---

[9] Kampe, *The Underground Military Command Bunkers of Zossen, Germany*, p. 22.

The Army Headquarters Self-Dialing Exchange in the Zeppelin Communications Bunkers at Zossen[10]

The Voice Frequency Telegraph Center in the Zeppelin Bunker Complex at Zossen[11]

---

[10] Kampe, *The Underground Military Command Bunkers of Zossen, Germany*, p. 21.

[11] Ibid., p. 23.

The enormous scale of just the Zeppelin communications complex is revealed by the floor plan of the complex accessed through the "farmhouse":

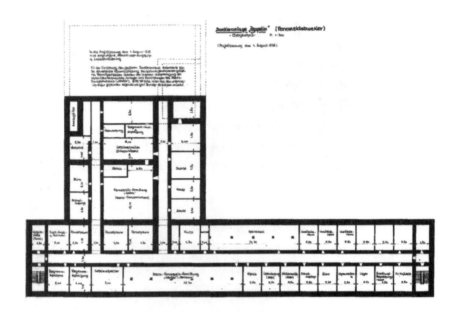

The Upper Floor of Junction Section of the Zeppelin Complex, in its original design[12]

The lower story of this junction complex contained connecting tunnels to other bunker complexes at Zossen, each a self-contained functional entity, each connected to the others, and each accessed by the sort of deceptive camouflaged entrance such as the "farmhouse" leading into this particular complex.

2. The Underground Factories and the Manufacturing, Assembly, and Launch Facility at Ebensee

In addition to these types of complexes, as is now well-known, Nazi Germany constructed a number of large underground

---

[12] Kampe, *The Underground Military Command Bunkers of Zossen, Germany*, p. 13.

manufacturing and research facilities for its various secret weapons projects. What is seldom appreciated, however, is the enormity of some of these facilities, which is yet another of those obvious facts with enormous and overlooked implications for the conception of a breakaway civilization. As the Allied armies swept into the Reich, its counterintelligence teams were sent to vacuum the Reich of every conceivable technological innovation.

However, in the case of the technology and engineering of the underground complexes themselves, this, obviously, could not be down. But detailed plans and schematics of these sites, and in some cases, artists' renditions, were made when the original German plans could not be recovered. One of these was the enormous rocket manufacture, assembly, and launch complex for the A-10 *Amerikaraket*, or "America rocket," at Ebensee, a complex whose sheer enormity indicates that, as far as the Nazis were concerned, the rocket bombardment of the continental United States was an immanent possibility. The scale of the launch facility itself is indicated from this 1945 artist's drawing of the complex entrance:

Artist's Rendition of the Ebensee Complex Entrance and Launch Facility[13]

---

[13] Friedrich Georg, *Hitlers Siegeswaffen: Band 2: Star Wars 1947: Teilband B: Von der Amerikarakete zur Orbitalstation—Deutschlands Streben*

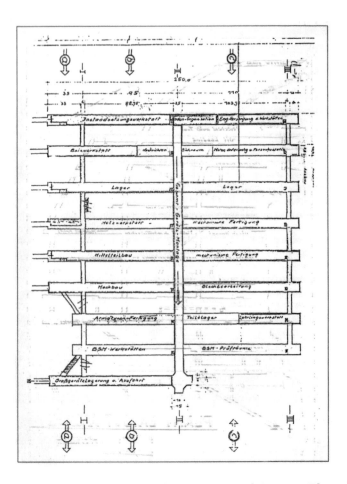

The British and American BIOS/CIOS Captured German Plan of the Ebensee Distillation Facility B for Rocket Propellant Production[14]

nach Interkontinentalwaffen und das erste Weltraumprogramm (Schleusingen, Germany: Amun Verlag, 2004), p. 130.
    [14] Ibid., p. 35.

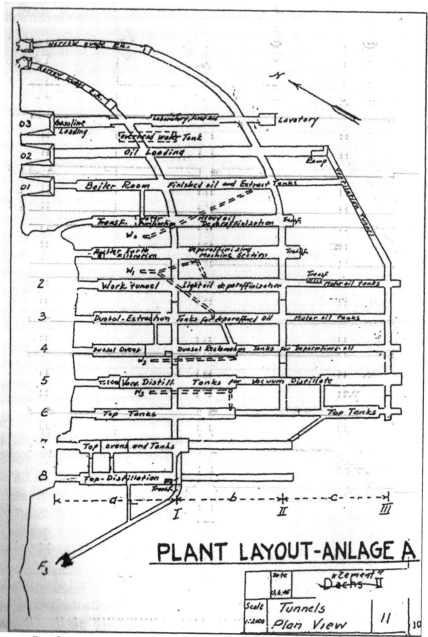

Production Facility A of the Ebensee A-10 Rocket Complex[15]

---

[15] George, *Hitlers Siegeswaffen, : Band 2: Star Wars 1947: Teilband B:*

What is to be noticed about this SS facility is not only its enormity but its self-containment, for here in one enormous complex was all that was necessary both for the production *and launch* of an enormous intercontinental rocket. In short, we are looking at the "state within the state" that was the SS, and its immanent ability to literally wage an altogether *different type* of warfare—utilizing then still unconventional technologies—from that of its host civilization, Nazi Germany itself.

3. A Few Modern American Counterparts
a. The Skunk Works, Pure Research Facilities, and Other Installations

The American side of this story is equally, if not more, fascinating and revealing of the possibilities of a breakaway civilization. We may gain our entry into this discussion by looking at some of the more well-known underground installations that are connected both to the private corporate sector and to deeply black covert projects research.

Richard Sauder, Ph.D., has published his extensive research into underground basses in an important study, *Underground Bases and Tunnels*, and a careful review of his research is essential here in order for its vast implications for the hypothesis of a breakaway civilization to be fully appreciated, implications Sauder himself is alive to:

> History teaches us that when a country has an exceptionally powerful military, and when that military carries out secret policies and agendas like the U.S. military does (think of the illegal Iran-Contra affair, of super-secret nuclear bomb testing in Nevada, of the astronomical amounts of money given to the Pentagon every year for so-called "black projects"), then there is an ever present danger of that military taking control of the government. That control could be taken quickly—or gradually. Noisily or quietly. [16]

Von der Amerikarakete zur Orbitalstation—Deutschlands Streben nach Interkontinentalwaffen und das erste Weltraumprogramm, p. 34.

[16] Richard Sauder, Ph.D., *Underground Bases and Tunnels: What is the Government Trying to Hide?* (Adventures Unlimited Press, 1997), p. 7.

The extent of black budget funding for the construction of the sites that Sauder refers to is substantiated by official U.S. government statements and publications:

> In 1987, Lloyd A. Duscha, the Deputy Director of Engineering and Construction for the U.S. Army Corps of Engineers, gave a speech entitled "Underground Facilities for Defense—Experience and Lessons.".... Mr. Duscha subsequently launched into a discussion of the Corps' involvement, back in the 1960s, in the construction of the large NORAD underground base beneath Cheyenne Mountain, Colorado... And then he said: *"As stated earlier, there are other projects of similar scope, which I cannot identify, but which included multiple chambers up to 50 feet wide and 100 feet high using the same excavation procedures mentioned for the NORAD facility."*[17]

Such techniques, Sauder notes, were developed by private engineering and construction corporations, particularly for "hydroelectric powerhouses" which are often located deep underground.[18]

Sauder notes that the U.S. Army Corps of Engineers distinguishes between two basic types of underground constructions: (1) those constructed in deep shaft-type fashion, and (2) those which are tunneled into mountains.[19] As Sauder also notes, in 1985 the Corps of Engineers admitted in an official publication that there were essentially no technological limitations to the construction of such underground facilities, "under virtually any ground conditions, the main constraint" being primarily financial limitations.[20]

Cost appears to have been of little concern to the vast corporate underground research centers in California, well-known to most researchers as the "skunk works" of major American defense and aero-space firms:

---

[17] Sauder, *Underground Bases and Tunnels*, p. 10, citing Lloyd A. Duscha, "Underground Facilities for Defense—Experience and Lessons," in *Tunneling and Underground Transport: Future Developments in Technology, Economics, and Policy*, ed. F.P. Davidson (New York: Elsevier Science Publishing Company, Inc. 1987), pp. 109-113, emphasis Sauder's.

[18] Sauder, op. cit., pp. 11-12.

[19] Ibid., p. 13.

[20] Ibid.

Lockheed's Helendale, California "Skunk Works" Facility. The Runway-like Feature is not a runway.

Close-up of the Entrance "Bunker" to Lockheed's Helendale, California Facility

While we do not know the extent of these facilities, nor how deeply underground they go, there are certain features they all have in common, and there are certain rumors accompanying them:

The Northrop facility is located near the Tehachapi Mountains, 25 miles to the northwest of Lancaster (California). THere are rumors that the installation there goes down as many as 42 levels, and that there are tunnels linking it with other underground facilities in the area. I do not know whether these rumors are true or not. There are also reports of many strange flying objects in the vicinity, of many shapes and sizes. Some are reportedly spherical, others are alleged to be triangular, elongated, boomerang or disk shaped. And they are said to range in size up to hundreds of feet in diameter. The facility itself is engaged in electronic or electromagnetic research of some sort. There are large radar or microwave dishes and strange-looking pylons to which various objects can be affixed, ostensibly for the purpose of beaming electromagnetic radiation at them These pylons rise up from underground, out of diamond-shaped openings in the middle of long paved surfaces that resemble aircraft runways, but which, in fact, are not used by aircraft.

...The McDonnell Douglas facility is located at the now closed Gray Butte airport, northeast of Llano, California. It too has "runways" that are not runways, with diamond-shaped openings through which huge pylons with strangely shaped objects mounted on them are raised to the surface. These objects sometimes resemble elongated disks or flying saucers and have been seen to glow and change colors. Glowing spheres have also been seen by people in the area at night. However the nature and function of the spheres is not known.

...The Lockheed installation is adjacent to what used to be the Hellendale (sic et passim), auxiliary airport, six miles to the north of Hellendale, California. Just like the McDonnell Douglas and Northrop facilities it also has the runway-like features, which large diamond-shaped doors through which huge pylons rise from underground with strange objects attached. This facility has an obvious underground entrance.[21]

---

[21] Sauder, *Underground Bases and Tunnels*, pp. 67=68.

195

It is now known that most of these facilities were crucial in the development of stealth technologies, with the pylons and radar dishes being used to test radar cross-sections. [22]

In short, these facilities were being used for research purposes, and we may reasonably assume that stealth research was not the only research being conducted at them, given the expense of constructing what must be large underground complexes with the machinery to hoist the pylons. Similar pure research facilities are alleged to have been constructed at the Manzano Mountain near Albuquerque, New Mexico, and at Los Alamos National Laboratories, the latter for "pure physics" research.[23] In Los Alamos' case, proposals were advanced for mile-or-deeper facilities for doing experiments in particle physics and gravity research,[24] the latter fact, as we shall see in the next chapter, connecting to the work of American physicist Thomas Townsend Brown.

Sauder notes that a number of these facilities, especially those dedicated to continuity of government operations and functions, come totally equipped underground lakes, cafeteria, hospitals, streets and sidewalks, dormitories, radio and TV studies, independent power generation, and tunnels for vehicles, in short, with all the amenities of the "surface civilization,"[25] a fact that testifies once again to the fact that the breakaway civilization—if indeed there be one—is literally an "underworld", a peripheral civilization existing literally beneath the surface of the core civilizations.

It is important to mention that in its planning of these facilities, both government and private corporations have developed three technologies for independent sources of power, completely separate from the public power grid system, in diesel generating plants, nuclear plants, and fuel cell technologies,[26] a fact that again implies that, should those with control over these installations choose to break away from the surface host civilization, they could do so. Additionally, private corporations such as the Federal Reserve

---

[22] It was Northrop Grumman that recently built a mock-up of the Nazi Horten Brothers' Go229 flying wing and tested it at its radar cross section facility. See http://www.thehowlandcompany.com/Bluefire_Tejon.htm.

[23] Sauder, *Underground Bases and Tunnels*, p. 29.

[24] Ibid., p. 66.

[25] Ibid., pp. 49-51, see also pp. 31-33.

[26] Ibid., pp. 19, 73.

maintain their own facilities for the emergency maintenance of their corporate accounts and records.[27]

There is a final possibility for such underground installations and a breakaway civilization, one with profoundly disturbing parallels to Nazi Germany, and here it is necessary to allow Sauder to speak to this possibility in his own words:

> I will simply observe that many people absolutely disappear in this country every year, never to be heard from again. No bodies are found, no trace of them ever surfaces. I don't know where these people go; I don't know what happens to them. I can offer no proof that any of them are held in secret underground prisons. I cannot even offer proof that there *are* secret underground prisons. However, it occurs to me that at the end of WW II many German citizens were surprised to find out that there were concentration camps, run by the Nazis, in which millions of their neighbors (Jews, Gentiles, Gypsies, mentally-impaired, homosexuals, political prisoners) had been incarcerated, tortured, forced into slave labor—and killed.[28]

The possibility is more than disturbing, since former Reich Armaments Minister Albert Speer himself records a deliberate kidnapping project of the SS—over and above the Nazi genocide—to round up suitable slave-laborers and test subjects for its deeply black projects.[29]

What we have seen thus far—government and private corporate research facilities, whole vast underworld installations with all the amenities of civilization—strongly indicates that the *infrastructure* for a breakaway civilization exists.

b. The Rumored Tunnel System and Its Implications

But part of the infrastructure of normal "surface" civilization consists in the fact that its centers are connected by a variety of communications links, including transportation links. Indeed, as Sauder notes, there has been for years a persistent rumor that the

---

[27] Sauder, *Underground Bases and Tunnels*, pp. 52-53.

[28] Ibid., p. 70.

[29] Albert Speer, *Infiltration: How Heinrich Himmler Schemed to Build an SS Industrial Empire*, p. 316.

various underground installations of this "underworld" are indeed linked by an equally hidden and underground system of tunnels, allowing vehicular traffic to flow smoothly, and unnoticed, between its centers.[30]

But does such a system exist?

While there is no proof, there are a number of strong indicators that suggest it does. During the late 1970s and early 1980s, the "United States military had extensive plans to construct a very deep, hundreds-of-miles-long, underground tunnel system somewhere in the western United States,"[31] in connection with its MX-mobile ICBM system.[32] Moreover, several Federal contracts were actually awarded for preliminary studies or actual site selection and excavation testing for the system,[33] an indicator that tunneling work went ahead for some other purpose, even though ostensibly the MX missile program was cancelled:

> ...the documents, articles and contracts...suggest it is entirely possible that the military, working through the Ballistic Missile Office at Norton Air Force Base, with the probable assistance of the Army Corps of Engineers and private companies such as Robbins, Earth technology, and others, has secretly built an extensive, very deeply buried tunnel system and nuclear missile complex, somewhere in the United States, perhaps somewhere in the West.
>
> If it has been made, this system may be, in its totality, hundreds of miles long and thousands of feet underground. If it exists it is certainly very well hidden. And if it exists it may very well explain either partly or wholly the recurrent rumors in UFOlogy about a secret tunnel system in the southwestern United States.[34]

In my opinion, given the indicators thus far, and the detailed planning for continuity of government operations, it would seem very *unlikely* for such a tunnel system connecting key installations, even if separated by hundreds of miles, *not* to be built.

---

[30] Sauder, *Underground Bases and Tunnels*, p. 6.

[31] Ibid., p. 72.

[32] Ibid., pp. 74, 76-77. Sauder notes on p. 73 that a committee, the U.S. National Committee on Tunneling Technology was established, one of whose functions was "to coordinate U.S. tunneling technology activity with those of other nations."(p. 73).

[33] Ibid., pp. 78-80.

[34] Ibid., p. 80.

In Sauder's opinion, this possibility raises, once again, the specter of psychological operations surrounding such facilities and systems, operations designed, once again, to cloak their true function, and perhaps the technologies associated with them:

> From the standpoint of disinformation there is another possibility: that the military has really built a tunnel system of the sort described here, but has tried to hide its existence under a tabloid-style cover story of alien tunneling activities. According to this hypothetical scenario the military would count on the "alien" connection to be sufficiently ridiculous in the public eye that if word of the tunnels ever surfaced in the media they could be discounted as the fevered imagining of daffy UFOlogists and other flaky characters, and nothing more. In that way, the Pentagon could carry out its underground agenda and prying eyes would be deflected by the threat of public humiliation and ridicule.[35]

Sauder is correct, simply because, as we have already indicated with Adamski and the much more serious schemes of Skorzeny, plans were laid as early as World War Two to couple advanced technologies to a *Sonderkampf*, a special psychological operation to socially engineer people's perceptions. Only in one respect does Sauder perhaps miss the wider scope of the implications of the breakaway civilization that his research implies, namely, that such operations may have *two* simultaneous goals: (1) to cloak its activities and implied technologies, and (2) to plant a meme within the culture that such technologies are "godlike" and "alien" to mankind, *making its wielders commensurately "godlike."*

c. Camouflage and Security

This cloaking activity is a telltale sign of the possibility that one is dealing with a breakaway civilization, and hence, we must now examine its other camouflaging efforts, which include the actual camouflage of covert construction methods, through private or corporate proxies buying the land for such installations,[36] to the types of camouflage activity we saw associated with the Nazi Zossen

---

[35] Sauder, *Underground Bases and Tunnels*, pp. 80-81.
[36] Ibid., pp. 15-16.

communications bunkers.[37] Such camouflage "could literally be just about anywhere: under a military base; under a major hotal; under a prominent government build; under old, abandoned mine workings; under virtually any mountain or hill; under a national park, or perhaps in a national forest; in a small town; or in the middle of a large city—maybe even deep under an Alaskan glacier."[38]

Allied to this camouflage effort is security, and a variety of means are now common to gain access to these facilities, or, conversely, to prevent unwarranted or unauthorized access, from quadruple belts of chain link fences with concertina wire and lethally electrically charged fences at the Manzano Mountain underground nuclear research and storage facility in Albuquerque,[39] to retinal and palm print scanners,[40] to a host of other security measures such as motion detectors, armed security guards, and even mine fields.

Monzano Mountain, Albuquerque, New Mexico, Known to be Home to Miles of Underground Tunnels and Galleries for Nuclear Weapon Storage and Research

---

[37] Sauder, *Underground Bases and Tunnels*, pp. 15, 69.
[38] Ibid.,p. 69.
[39] Ibid., p. 25.
[40] Ibid., p. 26.

The implication of such security procedures, however, for the hypothesis of a breakaway civilization are often overlooked, for like all obvious things, it is easy to do so. It is one of the functions of a government to secure the borders of its society from other societies, and thus, such security procedures in effect amount to a *border*, a boundary between two societies, and it will be evident that the distinction between a border between a government's secret installations and its public society, and a border between two entirely separate *societies*, is very thin.

d. The Nexus of Interests

In the previous chapter, we observed the nexus between governmental structures, a political ideology (Fascism), and the private corporate world that constituted the unusual circumstances in which the breakaway civilization emerged. In this respect, Sauder makes the highly trenchant observation that this nexus is *best* exhibited in the actual construction of the underworld infrastructure itself:

> That nexus of interests was comprised of (a) big business; (b) military agencies; and (c) private individuals who were in on the deal (and who very likely benefitted from insider speculation in the local real estate market). Underground base researchers would do well to look for this nexus of interests and pattern of activity elsewhere, as similar groups are likely to have played key roles in planning and constructing underground facilities...[41]

In other words, the postwar pattern we saw emerging toward the very end of World War Two is alive and well.

---

[41] Sauder, *Underground Bases and Tunnels*, p. 17, see also p, 23 for some specific information on agencies, academic institutions, and corporations involved.

*e. The Implications of Doomsday and Continuity of Government
Planning:
The Apocalyptic Ideology*

There are a number of other parallels between the wartime Nazi model and the postwar American one, notwithstanding their many connections to each other, not the least of which is that many American think tanks, such as DARPA and the Rand Corporation, appear to be modeled on SS General Hans Kammler's "think tank," the *Kammlerstab*. Additionally, as Sauder astutely observes, most of the installations with which we have been concerned, have been either for the purpose of secret research and technological development, or with gaming out, and preparing for, various apocalyptic scenarios, including nuclear war.[42] This is an important point, for it means that in addition to having a "survivability infrastructure" it also has an apocalyptic view of the future, which is coupled to the very technologies it possesses. This matrix of infrastructure, technology, and ideology is a powerful combination that could lead to a *Weltanschauungskrieg* in the fullest sense of the word, i.e., in the careful preparation of world-apocalyptic events through techniques of social engineering, and then to the "fulfillment" of those created expectations via its access to the technologies themselves via gamed-out and computer-tested scenarios. If this sounds farfetched or fanciful, recall the peculiar pronouncements of the Nazis in the postwar period, of Adamski, and of his own suggestive fascist connections and doctrines.

f. Technologies of Tunnel Boring

No survey of Sauder's excellent research would be complete without a mention of the excavating and boring technologies he recounts in his book. And here, we are dealing, as we shall see, *directly* with the hypothesis of the possibility of a breakaway civilization. In a conventional tunnel excavating or boring machine, a cylindrical machine has a cutting rotating head, in which are located several superhard alloy drilling and grinding bits which dig into the rock. This excavated rock, called "muck" in the trade, is moved by

---

[42] Sauder, *Underground Bases and Tunnels.*, pp. 22, 43, 60-61.

conveyor belts to the end of the machine where it is hauled away.[43] The process, particularly through hard rock, is costly, and time consuming.

It should come as no surprise, however, that underworld installations for the secret and covert research of advanced technologies should also investigate advanced technologies for creating more such installations! Sauder cites a 1964 Bechtel Corporation study in which new tunnel boring technologies are mentioned, including electrical disintegration, microwaves, electron beam guns, various flame jet technologies, lasers, water jets, and, significantly, nuclear plasmas,[44] about which more in a moment.

(1) The Water Jet Boring Technology

Before turning to the plasma boring technology, it is worth considering two others mentioned by Sauder. The pulsed water jet cannon "essentially grinds away the rock face by directing a high-pressure, pulsed, water jet against it."[45] In other words, the water-jet boring technology is nothing but "high speed" or "time lapsed" erosion.

(2) The Flame Jet Boring Technology

According to Sauder, in 1968 United Aircraft Research Laboratories compiled a feasibility study of the possibilities represented by flame-jet excavation. As envisioned by the laboratory, the machine would advance on conventional caterpillar treads while directing very high temperature jets against the face. The jets would loosen and partially vitrify the rock while a conventional boring head would drill and grind it away. The flame-jet method would leave a smooth wall,[46] and it was estimated that it would save "from 44% to 28% of the cost of the drill and blast

---

[43] Sauder, *Underground Bases and Tunnels*, p. 85. For a list of prominent manufactures of such machines, see p. 86.

[44] Ibid., p. 90. On p. 91 Sauder also cites a study of United Aircraft Research Labs to use a hybrid technology consisting of a conventional boring machine with cutting and grinding head, which uses pulsed lasers to soften or weaken the rock surface prior to boring.

[45] Ibid., p. 92.

[46] Ibid.

method."[47] But this was by no means the most exotic technology envisioned, and perhaps manufactured, for the construction of the underworld's installations.

(3) Nuclear Subterrenes and a NASA Study

By far the most exotic tunnel boring and excavating technology was the "nuclear subterrene" proposed and actually designed by the Los Alamos National Laboratory, whose scientists even filed a number of patents on the device, and then, as Sauder quips, "the whole thing just sort of faded away. Or did it?"[48] These "subterrenes" work by applying the extremely hot plasma from a portable nuclear reactor to the dirt or rock face, actually completely vitrifying the rock or dirt as it proceeds, "and leaving a neat, solidly glass-lined tunnel behind them,"[49] actually making it possible for these machines to bore tunnels into soil not normally considered safe for such tunnels, since the hardened glass-like or ceramic-like walls left behind provide an natural reinforcement to the structure in almost any conditions. Additionally, this process leaves no "muck" behind that must be carted away. The nuclear subterrene literally "slices through rock like a nuclear powered, 2,000 degree Fahrenheit earthworm, boring its way deep underground."[50]

According to Sauder both the United States Atomic Energy Commission and the United States Energy Research and Development Administration took out patents on such machines in beginning in 1972 and a later one in 1975.[51]

---

[47] Sauder, *Underground Bases and Tunnels*, p. 93.
[48] Ibid., p. 94.
[49] Ibid.,
[50] Ibid., p. 95.
[51] Ibid., pp. 95-96.

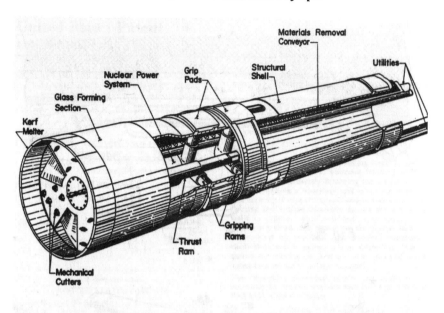

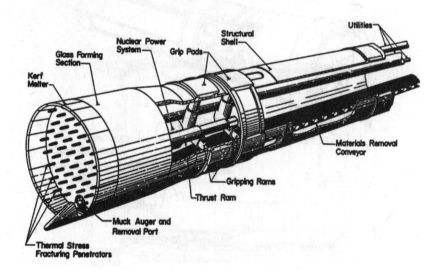

Two Types of Nuclear Subterrene Boring and Excavating Machines[52]

---

[52] Sauder, *Underground Bases and Tunnels*, photo insert section.

United States Patent [19]

Altseimer et al.

[11] **3,881,777**

[45] **May 6, 1975**

[54] **APPARATUS AND METHOD FOR LARGE TUNNEL EXCAVATION IN SOFT AND INCOMPETENT ROCK OR GROUND**

[75] Inventors: **John H. Altseimer; Robert J. Hanold,** both of Los Alamos, N. Mex.

[73] Assignee: **The United States of America as represented by the United States Energy Research and Development Administration,** Washington, D.C.

[22] Filed: **Jan. 25, 1974**

[21] Appl. No.: **436,402**

[52] **U.S. Cl.** 299/33; 175/11; 176/DIG. 3; 299/14
[51] **Int. Cl.** E21c 9/04
[58] **Field of Search** .... 299/33, 14; 175/11, 16; 61/45 R

[56] **References Cited**

UNITED STATES PATENTS

| 3,334,945 | 8/1967 | Bartlett | .... 299/33 |
| 3,396,806 | 8/1968 | Benson | .... 175/11 |

| 3,667,808 | 6/1972 | Tabor | .... 299/33 |
| 3,693,731 | 9/1972 | Armstrong et al. | .... 175/11 |

Primary Examiner—Frank C. Abbott
Assistant Examiner—William F. Pate, III
Attorney, Agent, or Firm—John A. Horan; Henry Heyman

[57] **ABSTRACT**

A tunneling machine for producing large tunnels in soft rock or wet, clayey, unconsolidated or bouldery earth by simultaneously detaching the tunnel core by thermal melting a boundary kerf into the tunnel face and forming a supporting excavation wall liner by deflecting the molten materials against the excavation walls to provide, when solidified, a continuous wall supporting liner, and detaching the tunnel face circumscribed by the kerf with powered mechanical earth detachment means and in which the heat required for melting the kerf and liner material is provided by a compact nuclear reactor.

The invention described herein was made in the course of, or under a contract with the U. S. ATOMIC ENERGY COMMISSION.

3 Claims, 5 Drawing Figures

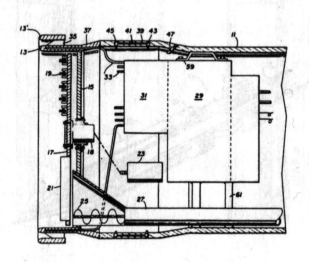

1975 U.S. Patent for a Nuclear Subterrene Excavating and Boring Machine[53]

---

[53] Reproduced by Sauder, *Underground Bases and Tunnels*, photo insert.

Some federal agencies, however, speculated on an exotic use for this exotic technology, and here, it is best site Sauder for the implications of this use to sink in fully:

> 1980s documents from Los Alamos National Laboratory and from Texas A&M University (under contract to NASA) indicate that there are plans to use "nuclear subterrene tunneling machines" to melt tunnels under the Moon's surface, to make living, working, mining and transportation facilities for a lunar colony.
>
> A 1986 Los Alamos report calls for using a fission powered, nuclear subselene to provide the heat to "melt rock and form a self-supporting, glass-lined tunnel suitable for Maglev or other high-speed transport modes," The report recommends burrowing beneath the surface because of the harsh lunar environment. It further mentions that the tunnels would "need to be hundreds, or thousands of kilometers long..." The actual subselenes would be automatic devices, remotely operated. In 1986, Los Alamos estimated each subselene could be built for about $50 million and transported to the Moon for anywhere from $155 million to $2.323 million... It should be noted that the report did not specify how the nuclear subselenes and their crews would be transported to the Moon.[54]

Indeed, that is the mystery, for by the time of these plans, NASA had long abandoned the massive Saturn V boosters of the Apollo program, and had no similar deep space capability, having opted for the space shuttle system for low earth orbit heavy lift capabilities.

This implies three possibilities:

1) NASA was conducting hypothetical studies for a future project when a deep space launch capability was again operational;
2) NASA had a hidden technology of deep space launch capability and was conducting practical studies(or at least was aware of such capabilities in the hands of some other agency or group); or,
3) NASA was publicly stating "future possibilities" that had already begun.

With respect to the latter two possibilities, Sauder observers that the Texas A&M study proposed a combination tunneling technology,

---

[54] Sauder, *Underground Bases and Tunnels*, pp. 100-101.

using a conventional drill-and-grinding rotating head, but a nuclear plasma to melt the surrounding tunnel walls and then passing the remaining muck out the back,[55] and then makes one more highly provocative remark: "The rest of the melted much(called regolith) is passed out of the back of the tunneler and then carried to the surface for disposal by the dump trucks that follow the tunneler through the tunnel."[56] For those who are unfamiliar with the name, an early space anomalies researcher, George Leonard, wrote a book in the 1970s—*Somebody Else is on the Moon*—in which, on the basis of official NASA photographs, he maintained that one could detect precisely the type of "mining excavations" mentioned in the Texas A&M study.

While I have always been extremely skeptical of Leonard's book, analytical techniques, and conclusions, the combination of his claims plus the subsequent NASA sponsored study of the possibility of subselene lunar nuclear excavation does raise the possibility that these technologies were being developed not only for the creation of an "underworld" infrastructure, but of an "overworld" one as well.

C. Conclusions and Reflections:
The Obvious Things: Camouflage, Deception, and Security

We are now in a position to summarize what this review of underground installations implies for the hypothesis of a breakaway civilization.

Firstly, the facilities surveyed, both Nazi and American, indicate the creation of a physical plant and infrastructure capable of three of the crucial activities of a civilization in Quigley's inventory: manufacture, invention(research), and the creation of surplus.

Secondly, the sheer enormity of these facilities, plus the possibility of their interconnection by equally hidden and underground means, implies that the nerve centers of this underworld are connected, just as in any ordinary society cities and centers of commerce are connected.

Thirdly, the measures taken to camouflage these facilities, by outright camouflage and by psychological operations techniques designed to cloak their activities and sew contexts within the core

---

[55] Suader, *Underground Bases and Tunnels*, p. 101.
[56] Ibid., p. 102.

civilization for their misinterpretation, strongly suggest that we are, in fact, dealing with a breakaway civilization. Additionally, the security surrounding such installations is commensurate if not identical to borders between societies or nation-states in the core civilization, indicating, again, that the strong possibility exists that we are dealing with a breakaway civilization.

Finally, the fact that psychological operations appear to be indicated in connection with these installations and the advanced technologies they both represent and research, plus the fact that they are connected with an inherently apocalyptic view of the future, a view which brought them into existence, strongly suggests that the ideological culture of this society or breakaway civilization is different from that of the core civilization.

But the careful reader would, here, strongly object, to certain assumptions made in this chapter, namely, the equivalence of a breakaway *society* with a breakaway *civilization.* Indeed, he would be correct to do so. As we noted in the first chapter, the essence of Richard M. Dolan's idea of the breakaway civilization is its possible possession of a technology greatly in advance of that of the core civilization surrounding it, and by implication, its suppression of the knowledge and existence of that technology. It is this final issue we must now, briefly, consider.

A Large, Conventional German Tunnel Boring Machine[57]

---

[57] Sauder, *Underground Bases and Tunnels,* photo insert.

10

TESLA TO TOWNSEND:
THE 1950s PATTERN OF COORDINATED
SUPPRESSION:
CONCLUSIONS TO THIS STUDY

*"Nevertheless, unknown to the many newcomers being indoctrinated
into the field of electrogravitics, this multicompany R&D effort was
merely supplementing a highly classified effort that had already been
in progress since the end of World War II. This preexisting project,
known as Project Skyvault, was actually ahead in achieving the goal of
a manned antigravity craft."*
Dr. Paul A. LaViolette[1]

Paul A. LaViolette is a scientist who has researched and
published on an extraordinary range of topics, everything
from physics metaphors contained in ancient and esoteric
systems, to the non-random distribution of pulsars throughout the
Milky Way galaxy when viewed from the Earth. He has also
published a superb, and supremely valuable, study of suppressed
physics and technologies related to antigravity, *Secrets of Antigravity
Propulsion: Tesla, UFOs, and Classified Aerospace Technology*, an
indispensable guide for those concerned with off-the-books physics
and technologies.

It is also, however, an indispensable book for a consideration of
Dolan's hypothesis of a breakaway civilization and its technologies,
for when its insights are combined with the wartime and postwar
researches of the Nazi International, and further, combined with our
findings presented previously in this book—namely, that the prewar
corporate nexus between large German and American corporations
was reconstituted during and after the war, this time with the Nazis
thrown into the mix—then the picture that emerges is one of
coordinated action to suppress public awareness of the physics
being developed, and the technologies being engineered on the basis
of that physics.

---

[1] Paul A. LaViolette, Ph.D., *Secrets of Antigravity Propulsion: Tesla, UFO's
and Classified Aerospace Technology* (Bear and Company, 2008), pp. 81-82.

We therefore assume, in this concluding chapter, the following things:

1) that a relationship existed during the immediate postwar period, and continuing at least through the 1950s, between the Nazi International and American corporate and banking components of the "military-industrial complex;"

2) that each component constituted a crucial element within the matrix of the breakaway civilization, that each component would wish to suppress any competition—in line with its prewar cartel and monopoly ideology—and that this means, effectively, that each component would take responsibility within its own sphere of influence to suppress the public development and knowledge of scientific theories and associated technologies that it itself was covertly researching and developing;[2]

3) that each component would also engage in psychological operations designed both to conceal its activities and technologies, and to plant memes within the broader culture leading to a context that would promote the deliberate misinterpretation and obfuscation of its technologies; and thus,

4) the "coincidental" emergence during the 1950s of contactee stories, the postwar statements of Nazis, along with the "near simultaneous" and "coincidental" disappearance of certain technologies and subjects from the open literature, is not coincidental at all, but the coordinated action of this postwar breakaway civilization and each of its components, pursuing psychological operations, and suppression of pubic scientific inquiries and areas of technological development it wishes to monopolize for itself.

As we noted at the outset, the core issue in Richard Dolan's hypothesis of a breakaway civilization is advanced technology, and the implicit idea that such technology has been secretly advanced far

---

[2] This pattern of each component policing its own sphere of activity and "jurisdiction" as it were is the same pattern that I observed at work with the various components involved in the JFK assassination in *LBJ and thr Conspiracy to Kill Kennedy: a Coalescence of Interests.*

beyond the technological level of open society, to such an extent that the covert bureaucratic infrastructure conducting this research has, in effect, become a wholly different type of civilization, with a *wholly different scientific paradigm.*

But is there, in fact, such a paradigm? And if so, what are its implications?

A. Suppressed Physics
1. LaViolette's Anecdotal Story

There is indeed such a hidden paradigm, if one is to believe the statements of those involved with the black projects world, or those connected with it secondhand. And there are deep sociological implications and consequences. But before we can understand those implications and consequences, we need to understand exactly what has been said about that hidden underworld, an underworld that includes not merely subterranean installations, but also underground concepts and paradigms.

Dr. LaViolette recounts a story that, for him, opened a door onto the possibility of a vastly different, covert, and off-the-books physics, one far different from the "public consumption" physics learned in universities:

In 1992, I had an interesting telephone conversation with a man who is one of the group of informants... whose stunning revelations about the B-2 bomber were published in *Aviation Week & Space Technology.* Although he gave me his full name, I will identify him as Ray for reasons of confidentiality. Ray claimed to have worked on a number of black R&D projects and to have been in contact with certain other black-world researchers. *He told me that the physics theories that academics and most laboratory physicists currently understand, teach, and write about are grossly in error. A very advanced and much more accurate theoretical framework has been developed by scientists of the black-programs community, but its fundamentals presently remain classified. From the standpoint of the new physics, modern physics concepts used in the conventional world, such as relativity theory, quantum electrodynamics, and quantum mechanics are referred to as "classical concepts," that is, they are treated as terribly outdated.*[3]

---

[3] LaViolette, *Secrets of Antigravity Propulsion*, p. 115, emphasis added.

If true, LaViolette's story is a strong indicator that an entirely *different* scientific and engineering culture exists within the black projects underworld, than exists *publicly*, and this is a powerful argument that one is dealing, in classic Dolan-esque fashion, with a breakaway civilization, in that it has an entirely different scientific ideology, and even, as we shall see subsequently, a unique sociology that results from its technological achievements.

Indeed, LaViolette continues, giving a glimpse into what the nature of that paradigm might be:

> According to Ray, unlike today's "Classical" physics, the new physics **does not begin with physical observables** in developing its treatment of physical phenomena. Rather, it postulates the existence of an underlying reality **consisting of an inherently unobservable subtle substance** called an *ether*, or alternatively *aether*, which fills all space. It then defines all of its fundamental quantities at that subphysical level. Physical observables then emerge as mathematical solutions to equations defined in terms of these more basic ether processes. This new physics regards time and space as absolutes and views Einstein's notion of relative time and space as fundamentally incorrect.[4]

Whatever the merits of this story—and one must always entertain the possibility that "Ray" was continuing in some sort of psychological disinformation operation, giving just enough true elements along with a deliberate lie—a brief closer look at the suggested physics is necessary.

The first thing to be noted about Ray's allegations is that the "off-the-books" physics *deliberately dispenses with Einstein's relativity theories, exactly as the Nazi scientists working in the Reich's black projects prior to and during World War Two had done. In other words, the scientific, physics culture of the two worlds is, in this respect, exactly the same.* This in turn argues plausibly that some sort of Nazi influence continued to be felt within the American component of the breakaway civilization long after the war, a point to which we shall return in a moment.

The point to be noted about Ray's allegations is the return to the nineteenth and early twentieth century idea of an *aether*, a physical

---

[4] LaViolette, *Secrets of Antigravity Propulsion*, p. 116, boldface emphasis added, italicized emphasis in the original.

non-observable with certain specific *properties of information processing*. And this leads us to a fresh consideration of what I have referred to in previous books as a "topological metaphor" of the physical medium found in some ancient metaphysical texts.[5] This should not surprise us, since the mathematical description of such a medium would have to rely upon higher order topological languages to describe its processes.

We may envision this physical non-observable, in mathematical terms, as the empty hyper-set, or $\emptyset$. At the outset, we note that it *is a nothing*, a physical non-observable, and thus, in the conceptions of the ancient metaphysical systems with which the Nazis were so familiar, it is not only a nothing, but also an infinity, neither definable, but paradoxically, a "countable entity", a "One." At this juncture, in quasi-physical terms, it is quanticizable, and yet, since there is nothing else, it is also a continuum.

We then imagine that we bracket a certain region of this nothingness. Immediately when we do so, we have introduced a *change into the system*, and therefore, introduced the notion of time. Simultaneously with this, we introduce three distinct "nothings" (notice how number itself arises from this process), the first region of nothing, $\emptyset_1$, a new region of nothing, $\emptyset_2$, and a common "surface", itself a nothing, between the two: $\partial\emptyset_{1,2}$. (The partial derivative symbol ∂ is used in topology to denote the surface of something). Thus, the topological metaphor that I have outlined in previous books appears to be at least *similar* to the notions that Ray described to Dr. LaViolette.[6]

---

[5] See my *Giza Death Star Destroyed* (Adventures Unlimited Press, 2005), pp. 106-113, 206-243; *The Philosophers' Stone* (Feral House, 2009), pp. 43-50, 259-266; and Scott D. de Hart's and my *The Grid of the Gods* (Adventures Unlimited Press, 2011), pp. 70-79, 181-184, 276-287.

[6] For physicists, the change between the two states may itself be denoted as a delta t(time), Δt, change between sets of information, with the initial state or $\emptyset$ followed by the three resulting nothings, i.e., $\Delta t\ \emptyset = \{\emptyset_1, \emptyset_2, \partial\emptyset_{1,2}\}$. By giving Δt the definition of the resultant set with the three members, we are in effect also stating that time, in this mathematical method of analysis, is not a scalar, as it is in most systems of mathematical physics. Such a method would also tend to suggest that the complex verbal systems of natural languages, which approach time in a complex series of systems interrelationships, is capable of mathematical formalism. We might equally describe such an approach as a kind of "hyper-relativistic"

But there are other anecdotal evidences of the development of such an off-the-books physics and technology from other sources, including, incredibly enough, the statements of the former head of Lockheed-Martin's Skunk Works, Ben Rich.

2. The Curious Statements of Ben Rich:
The Implications of Hidden Technologies and Hidden Physics[7]

Ben Rich, the well-known chief of Lockheed's "skunk works," the secret development facility responsible for, among other things, the development of stealth technology and America's F-117 stealth fighter, was born in Manilla, the Philippines on June 18, 1925. Fascinated with aircraft and aircraft models from his youth, his family moved to the United States in May, 1941, in response to the gathering war clouds with the Japanese Empire that would burst with such sudden ferocity with the Japanese attack on Pearl Harbor later that year on December 7.

Obtaining a Bachelor of Science degree in mechanical engineering from UCLA in 1950, Rich went to work for Lockheed's Burbank facility as a specialist in thermodynamics, aerodynamics, propulsion, and design. By 1955, he had so distinguished himself he was moved to Lockheed's Advanced Development Projects, the "skunk works," then under the capable and brilliant direction of Clarence "Kelly" Johnson, the man he would eventually replace. There, Rich worked

---

approach, since one of the emergent properties of this information-processing and algorithmic approach is that $\varnothing$, both in its initial state and first differentiation, is non-local, as is the treatment of time itself. It is here that I have some difficulty with some of the statements "Ray" made to LaViolette, for in my own private experiments with this type of approach, the possibility does emerge of locally relative time dependent on the frame of reference of the physical observer and the local "rotation moment" of space time. To put it succinctly, one is dealing with a "both-and" situation, not an "either-or" one.

[7] This section originally appeared as a members' only "white paper" on my website, www.gizadeathstar.com. I would, again, here like to thank my friend and colleague Michael Schratt for graciously allowing me to quote from an article of his, "Ben Rich and the Secret of the Skunk Works" that appeared in *Open Minds* magazine this year. All quotations of Mr. Rich that appear here appear in Mr. Schratt's article, and have also been cited in numerous articles by other researchers.

on the development of Top Secret advanced aircraft, the high altitude U-2 and even more exotic SR-71 Blackbird among them. When Johnson retired in 1975, Ben Rich succeeded him as the director of Lockheed's "skunk works," a position he held until his retirement on Dec. 31, 1990. Ben Rich died on Jan. 5, 1995, but between the time of his retirement and his death, he made a number of astonishing public and private statements, the subject of our study here.

a. A Catalog of Ben Rich's Astonishing Statements

For simplicity's sake, we will catalog Rich's statements, italicizing the statement itself, and then providing the context in which each was made.

1. *"The Air Force has just given us a contract to take ET back home."* This statement was made by Rich during a slide presentation he was giving on September 22, 1992, at the United States Air Force Museum in Dayton, Ohio. It is worth mentioning—though most readers will probably already be aware of it, that Dayton, Ohio is home to Wright-Patterson Air Force base, reputedly the place where recovered and alleged extra-terrestrial craft, including the Roswell craft, and the Kecksburg craft, were initially taken for examination. Wright-Patterson based the Air Technical Intelligence Command, Project Bluebook, and a large contingent of Paperclip Nazis after World War Two.

2. *"We now have the technology to take ET back home."* This nearly verbatim statement was made by Rich about half a year later, on March 23,1993, at a lecture using virtually the same presentation as he made to the US Air Force Museum the previous year. The presentation was made to the UCLA School of Engineering Alumni Association.

3. *"We did the F-104, C-130, U-2, SR-71, F-117 and many other programs that I can't talk about. We are still working very hard, I just can't tell you what we are doing."* This statement was likewise made during Rich's 1992 presentation to the US Air Force Museum.

4. *"We already have the means to travel among the stars. But these technologies are so locked up in black programs, that it*

> *would take an act of God to ever get them out to benefit humanity."* This statement was made during Rich's presentation in 1993 to the UCLA School of Engineering Alumni Association.

5. *"If you can imagine it, Lockheed Skunk Works has done it."* This statement was made by Rich to a small informal gathering at UCLA after his formal presentation.

6. *"We have some new things. We are not stagnating. What we are doing is updating ourselves without advertising. There are some new programs, and there are certain things, some of them twenty or thirty years old that are still breakthroughs and appropriate to keep quiet about. Other people don't have them yet."* This statement was made by Ben Rich to *Popular Science* magazine reporter Stuart F. Brown in the October 1994 issue.

7. *"I wish I could tell you about the projects we are currently working on. They are both fascinating and fantastic. They call for technologies once only dreamed of by Science fiction writers."* Rich made this statement in presentation to the AIAA (American Institute of Aeronautics and Astronautics) on September 7, 1988 in Atlanta, Georgia.

8. *"We now know how to travel to the stars."* This statement, again, was made during his 1993 UCLA presentation.

And last, but not least, there was one final comment, and for our purposes as we shall see, it is the most significant one:

9. *"There is an error in the equations, and we have figured it out, and now know how to travel to the stars, and it won't take a lifetime to do it."* This statement immediately followed number 8 above, and was made at the 1993 UCLA presentation.

In addition to these comments by Ben Rich, it is also worth noting that others in the black projects industry made similar statements. Michael Schratt states in his article that an unnamed Lockheed retired engineer was quoted in the February 1988 issue of *Gung-Ho* magazine, in an article titled "Stealth and Beyond," as saying "Let's just put it this way… we have things flying in the Nevada desert that would make George Lucas drool."

Schratt goes on to state:

> The same *Gung-Ho* article continues with an earth-shaking comment made by an Air Force officer who was involved in the development of the SR-71 (blackbird): "*We are testing vehicles that defy description. To compare them conceptually to the SR-71 would be like comparing Leonardo da Vinci's parachute design to the space shuttle.*" One retired Colonel chimed in with the following statement which also appeared in the same article: "*We have things that are so far beyond the comprehension of the average aviation authority as to be really alien to our way of thinking.*"

All of these quotations lead Schratt to ask a very logical question: are they "veiled confirmation of the so-called 'secret space program'"?

b. Interpretive Possibilities

Before we proceed to answer that most important question—indeed, the central question posed by Rich's remarks—we must examine the interpretive possibilities suggested by this catalog of remarks. Looking carefully at Rich's statements, there are three broad classes into which they fall:

1. Statements implying the general nature of a fantastic though hidden and secret technology, with no indications of the capabilities or nature of that technology (statements 3,5-7);
2. Statements implying the general nature of a fantastic though hidden and secret technology, with the clear statement that this technology is capable of an interstellar capability (statements 1-2, 4, 8); and,
3. A single statement implying that the Lockheed scientists found *an* error "in the equations" that underwrites the fantastic technologies alluded to in all the other statements. Note that Rich is specific, and speaks of *an* error in the singular, though he does not:
   a. Specify the *nature* of that error, if it lies in the general philosophical and physical assumptions or if it is of a more specific and formal mathematical nature;
   b. Specify which *kind* of equations he is referring to: the field equations of electromagnetism, the tensor equations of relativity? We have no idea. Rich *does*

219

provide a clue, however, in that he refers to a *single* error in *equations*, implying a *set* of equations describing a particular phenomenon. This argues that the "singular error" may been of a generalized philosophical nature that crept into the formalization of an entire set of equations.

c. We are now in a position to examine the interpretive possibilities that Rich's statements give rise to.

d. We may begin our examination by a bit of a thought experiment. Imagine we are foreign agents infiltrated into each of Rich's presentations to monitor them, analyze and assess them, and report back to our home country. The first and most obvious possibility that we must entertain is that Rich may be lying, that he is stating things as a part of a psychological operation to make America' potential enemies think that the USA has technologies far in advance of anything in any terrestrial arsenal. But as with every disinformation operation, there must be a kernel of truth operating in order for the false perception to take hold and influence decision-making.

e. In this case, that kernel of truth is provided by Rich's and Lockheed's track record of accomplishing feats of aerodynamic engineering well in advance of the public technologies of any given period. Consider only the U-2, the SR-71 Blackbird, or the F-117 stealth fighter. The mere fact, in other words, that someone of Rich's stature would make such statements means that they have to be taken seriously, and all possible interpretive paradigms and possibilities evaluated carefully. One must not, therefore, leap to the conclusion that he was telling the complete unvarnished truth, nor may one entirely dismiss them as being a complete pack of lies and total falsehoods.

c. The Error in the Equations: A Hidden Physics and Secrets

f. It is in this context that our would-be agent and analyst will turn his attention to the one piece of internal evidence that Rich gave as support for all the other fantastic statements that he made, namely, that "There is *an* error (singular) in the *equations* (plural), and we have figured it out, and now know *how to travel to the stars,* and it won't take a lifetime to do it." The context of Rich' statement indicates that, whatever this error was, and if genuine, it prevented mankind from traveling to the stars, and that fixing it theoretically enabled that possibility. We may therefore rule out the possibility that the equations in question are those dealing with standard aerodynamic of lift, drag, and so on. *Some other types of equations altogether are implied.*

g. Thus the question becomes: are there areas in which there are indications of an error in the equations that would theoretically enable inter-stellar travel? *In other words, can one argue a prima facie case that Rich was telling the truth here?* And if he *was* telling the truth here, then are there indications that an actual technology is being developed from that basis?

As noted, Rich made his statement in the specific context of knowing "how to travel to the stars" and this means that the "error in the equations" cannot be in the form of an error in any of the conventional equations of aerodynamics, fluid flow and so on.

In short, Rich's statements imply that one has to reverse-engineer an entire hidden history of physics and electrodynamics, for they clearly imply that there *is* such a history.

This raises the whole point of *secrecy* and just how long advanced secrets may be closely held and hidden from public view. Within UFOlogy the argument is often made that secret human technology could not be that advanced from that in the public view, nor would it have remained classified for so long. But the clear implication of Rich's statements is quite the opposite, for he not only clearly implies the existence of such technology but that it is so deeply secret that it has remained so for decades; he is also implying a hidden *physics.* The question is, when was "the error in the equations" known and why were the scientists looking for it?

d. Maxwell's Equations

221

As I have pointed out in many of my published books, the original form of James Clerk Maxwell's equations unifying electricity and magnetism were originally written in a geometric language known as quaternions. But additionally, when one turns to the literature of those physicists who are increasingly dissatisfied with the standard models, one finds other criticisms, even of their standard formulation in the partial derivative form learned by most students of physics, and as they were revised by Oliver Heaviside.

One of the most trenchant observations of such problems was noted by the physicist Thomas E. Phipps, Jr., in an excellent book entitled *Old Physics for New*, a highly mathematical work. There he notes two crucial things, namely, that Maxwell's own formulation of his theory does not adequately take into consideration sink motions, but only source motions, but more importantly, notes that induction is mathematically misrepresented by one form of equation (partial derivative form) when another form alone adequately accounts for the *changing shape of circuit parameters* that is being penetrated by a magnetic flux.[8] While all this may seem abstruse and incomprehensible, it basically boils down to the fact that in the quest for mathematical formalisms that are "beautiful," physicists essentially abandoned observation for the pursuit of theoretical beauty.

In the context of Rich's statements then, and their implication that there was an error in the equations, it is likely that the Lockheed engineers discovered this very simple mathematical change, one that, in effect, did *away* with the all important *observer* of the effect, in this case, the effect being the electromagnetic field itself.[9] In this case, the circuit parameters, *only fully describable by the change in notation from partial to full derivative form, function as the physical observer of the field effect; change the parameters of the circuit, and one changes what is observed.* And that, of course, means that circuit parameters *directly* affect the local engineering or observation of space-time, exactly was was stated by the electrical engineer Gabriel Kron.[10] *Physics, in other words, went very early astray by means of this*

---

[8]Thomas E. Phipps, Jr. *Old Physics for New* (C. Roy Keys, Inc., 2006), p. 16.
[9]Phipps, op cit., p. 3.
[10]For a fuller discussion of this point relating to the change from partial to full derivatives, see Phipps, pp. 10-11.

change.

So from the standpoint of Rich's statements, *two* conceptual and philosophical errors were introduced because of this change of mathematical languages: (1) the change from quaternion geometry to linear algebra lost the idea of a non-translational stress in the physical medium, a stress that might conceivably be manipulated for an "antigravity" effect, and (2) the change from partial to full derivative form lost the observer – the *circuit parameters* – and the direct effect these had on the field to be observed.

In other words, even on this short and necessarily cursory examination, *one need go no further* than the parameterizations of Maxwell's theory of electromagnetism to discover two major changes in the mathematical formalisms of the theory that strongly support Rich's contention that "there was an error in the equations," an error making possible a technology to take us to the stars.

Those changes in the formalisms of the theory would, of course, lead to further theoretical developments, including, of course, Einstein's Special and General Relativity theories, and the subsequent attempts in the 1920s to formulate unified field theories between electromagnetism and gravity. But if the first foundations of electromagnetic theory were themselves vitiated by two seemingly minor changes in the mathematical formalism, then this would mean that many of the assumptions and parameters of the theoretical edifice built upon them also would have to be revisited and rethought from the ground up. For the moment, it need only be noted that, given this analysis, *it must be concluded that Rich was not simply stating something untrue, nor stating a piece of disinformation to mislead the public, other scientists, or engineers. His statements must be given great weight because the actual history itself suggests that such errors were made.* The history is known and commented on by physicists willing to break with accepted dogmas and examine the history of the theoretical edifice (often at great cost to their own careers).

This fact, plus the fact of the other statements Rich made, leads me to conclude that Lockheed's engineers not only discovered these and similar errors, but that they went on to work out a new, hidden, off-the-books theoretical structure of physics, and to begin the engineering of actual technologies based upon it. We are, in other words, looking at the possibility of an actual, practical, field propulsion technology, utilizing electromagnetism in a practical way to achieve antigravity effects.

3. Quigley Again:
The Sociology of Weaponry and the Implications

But what does all this imply for the hypothesis of a breakaway civilization? The first, and most obvious, thing is that we are in fact dealing not merely with a breakaway *society*, i.e., with a rogue group at more or less the same pitch of development as the civilization it is breaking away from, but with a *civilization* with a *distinctively different science and technological matrix*, and that in turn imposes its own *sociological organization.*

Here we must once again return, for a brief moment, to Dr. Carroll Quigley. In a bibliographical appendix accompanying Quigley's *Evolution of Civilizations*, William Marina notes that

> At the time of his death, Quigley was at work on a study which had occupied him for years and which might be called the sociology of weaponry; that is, the way in which the structure and development of civilizations are to a considerable extent a reflection of the weapons systems and military organization prevalent within a society.[11]

Marina notes that drafts of this study, almost two thousand pages long, were among Quigley's papers remaining at Georgetown University.[12]

A few weeks before his untimely death, Quigley spoke to this subject in a lecture to the School of Foreign Service at Georgetown:

> Also related to the problem of internalized controls is the shift of weapons in our society. This is a profound problem. I have spent ten years working on it throughout all of history, and I hope eventually to produce a book if I can find a publisher. There will be endless analyses of Chinese history and Byzantine history and Russian history and everything else, and the book is about nine-tenths written, I'd say, in the last ten years. The shift of weapons in any civilization and, above all, in our civilization, from shock

---

[11] William Marina, "Selective Bibliography," in Quigley, *The Evolution of Civilizations*, p. 423.
[12] Ibid., pp. 423-424.

weapons to missile weapons, has a dominant influence on the ability to control individuals...

In our society, individual behavior can no longer be controlled by any system of weaponry we have. in fact, we do not have enough people, even if we equip them with shock weapons, to control the behavior of that part of the population which does not have internalized controls. One reason for that, of course, is that the twenty percent who do not have internalized controls are concentrated in certain areas. I won't go into the subject of controls. It opens up the whole field of guerilla resistance, terrorism, and everything else; these cannot be controlled by any system or organized structure of force that exists, at least on the basis of missile weaponry. And, as I said, it would take too many people on the basis of shock weaponry. We have now done what the Romans did when they started to commit suicide: we have shifted from an army of citizen soldiers to an army of mercenaries, and those mercenaries are being recruited in our society, as they were in Roman society, from the twenty percent of the population which does not have the internalized controls of the civilization.[13]

This requires careful parsing.

First, it is to be noted that Quigley is *not* speaking of the breakaway civilization, but of the core western civilization—the one most of us are living in—and of the sweeping sociological changes that shock weapons, i.e., automated weaponry from machine guns to precision munitions, have introduced. His point is that such weapons have so drastically expanded firepower that it would require a huge force to be armed if the twenty percent of the population that "lacked internalized controls" were to revolt.

Secondly, this fact, plus the fact that strategic weaponry—in Quigley's time, thermonuclear weaponry—is useless against such a contingency, has led to the employment of that very population "lacking internalized controls" as the core of its military, in order to head off a social crisis, and to use the military as a means of social engineering.

Weapons technology, in other words, creates certain conditions of governmental and social organization. In the case of a society possessing the advanced physics and technologies of antigravity, it is inevitable that it would produce certain sociological and cultural attitudes, since, as Adamski's "ETs" warned, weaponized gravity

---

[13] Quigley, *The Evolutions of Civilizations*, p. 424.

would potentially greatly and exceed the destructive power of the largest thermonuclear weapons, and require new sociological structures, among them, *the need to restrict access to such technologies to prevent them from falling into the hands of those lacking "internalized controls."* Quite literally, it would, from the ideological standpoint of that American-Fascist matrix, *require* the development of a breakaway civilization, the semi-permanent bifurcation of human society defined along the lines of the types of technologies to which each component has access.

And what are these "internalized controls"? For Quigley, they represent the constraints of conscience and moral development, oftentimes formed by religion. In a post-modern world, however, such constraints are increasingly under assault, and have to be replaced by something else. In this respect, it is intriguing to note that, both in Adamski's case, in the case of the implied psychological operations associated with advance technologies, and in the case of Skorzeny's *Weltanschauungskrieg*, it appears that the strategy adopted was to couple the appearance of advanced technologies with a modern, materialistic counterpart to the threat of metaphysical and spiritual evil standard in many religions, in short, with aliens or extraterrestrials whose intentions for humanity are ambiguous at best.

But this is not the only activity that a breakaway civilization would evidence, the other, as alluded to previously, would be to monopolize its control over such technologies, and thus, to suppress information about them, and the scientific principles upon which they are founded, from the general public. While volumes could be written about this entire subject, we shall concentrate here upon three unique cases, and the less-than-coincidental pattern of the occurrence of their suppression in the 1950s. In doing so, we are strongly suggesting that the occurrence of contactee allegations, the statements of Paperclip Nazis concerning the "extraterrestrial presence," and the suppression of certain types of physics experimentation, were the coordinated activity of this breakaway civilization to protect its research and development monopoly over these advances.

B. The Less-Than-Coincidental Pattern of the 1950s:
Anti-Gravity, Richter, and Townsend Brown

Saucers, Swastikas, and Psyops

1. The Tesla Precedent

Most people are aware that the banker J.P. Morgan suppressed Nikola Tesla's Wardenclyffe Project for the wireless transmission of electrical power.[14] What needs to be underscored here is that this is the first documentable case of the interference with the invention of new energy technologies by the American corporate and banking interest we have surveyed previously. This pattern will be repeated, with a vengeance, during the immediate postwar period and extending into the 1950s, as we shall now see.

2. Project Skyvault
a. Nick Cook on the 1950s "Coincidence"

The curious disappearance of the subject of antigravity discussion during the 1950s was first brought to light by *Jane's Defence Weekly* consultant and aerospace journalist Nick Cook in his highly-acclaimed *Hunt For Zero Point*, and it is worth recalling what he stated about the matter:

> In 1957, George S. Trimble, one of the leading aerospace engineers in the US at that time, a man, it could safely be said, with a background in highly advanced concepts and classified activity, had put together what looked like a special projects team; one with a curious remit.
>
> This, just a year after he started talking about the Golden Age of Anti-Gravity that would sweep through the industry starting in the 1960s.
>
> So what went wrong?
>
> In its current literature, the stuff pumped out in press releases all the time, the US Air Force constantly talked up the 'vision': where it was going to be in 25 years, how it was going to wage and win future wars and how technology was the key.
>
> In 1956, it would have been as curious as I was about the notion of a fuelless propulsion source, one that could deliver phenomenal performance gains over a jet; perhaps including the ability to accelerate rapidly, to pull hairpin turns without crushing the pilot and to achieve speeds that defied the imagination. In short, it would have given them something that resembled a UFO.

---

[14] See my *Babylon's Banksters*, pp. 136-155.

> I rubbed my eyes..... The evidence was suggesting that in the mid-1950s there had been some kind of breakthrough in the anti-gravity field and for a small window in time people had talked about it freely and openly, believing they were witnessing the dawn of a new era, one that would benefit the whole of mankind.
>
> Then, in 1957, everyone had stopped talking about it. Had the military woken up to what was happening, bringing the clamps down?[15]

Indeed, articles on antigravity research were fare for the mainstream media throughout the 1950s, even making the front page of the *New York Herald Tribune* for Sunday, November 20, 1955, and notably, the article refers to George S. Trimble, Jr., at that time "the vice-president in charge of advanced planning of Martin Aircraft Corp."[16]

b. The 1955 New York Herald Tribune Article

In confirmation of Cook's hypothesis that the discussion of the subject in open literature was suddenly and deliberately terminated, the *New York Herald Tribune* article begins with an astonishing revelation:

> *The initial steps of an almost incredible program to solve the secret of gravity and universal gravitation are being taken today in many of America's top scientific laboratories and research centers.*
>
> *A number of major, long-established companies in the United States aircrafts and electronics industries also are involved in gravity research.* Scientists, in general, bracket gravity with life itself as the greatest unsolved mystery in the Universe. But there are increasing numbers who feel that there must be a physical mechanism for its propagation which can be discovered and controlled.
>
> Should this mystery be solved it would bring about a greater revolution in power, transportation and many other fields than even the discovery of atomic power. The influence of such a discovery would be of tremendous import in the field of aircraft

---

[15] Nick Cook, *The Hunt for Zero Point: One Man's Journey to Discover the Biggest Secret Since the Invention of the Atom Bomb* (Century, 2001), p. 11.

[16] Thomas Valone, PhD, *Electr-gravitics II: Validating Reports on a New Propulsion Methodology* (Intergrity Research Institute, No Date), p. 85. The entire *New York Herald Tribune* article is reproduced on pp. 85-89 of Valone's book.

design—where the problem of fighting gravity's effects has always been basic.[17]

The article mentions specifically Dr. Charles T. Dozier, a scientist with General Dynamics, and of course, George S. Trimble of Martin, as well as Dr. Vaclav Hlavaty of the University of Indiana, as being involved in some of this research.[18]

But then the article gives an astonishing revelation, and a clue to the mystery earlier alluded by Ben Rich, namely, that there was an error in the equations, and also alluded to by Dr. LaViolette's source, "Ray," who maintained that the off-the-books physics began not with observations, but with a series of equations of the non-observable medium. Here are the article's bombshells:

> Martin Aircraft has just put under contract two of Europe's leading theoretical authorities on gravity and electromagnetic fields—Dr. Burkhard Heim of Goettingen University, where some of the outstanding discoveres of the century in aerodynamics and physics have been made and Dr. Pascual Jordan of Hamburg University, Max Planck medal winner whose recent work was called: 'Gravity and the Universe' has excited scientific circles throughout the world.
>
> Dr. Heim, now professor of theoretical physics, at Goettingen and who was a member of Germany's Bureau of Standards, during World War II, is certain that gravity can be overcome. Dr. Heim lost his eyesight and hearing, and had both his arms blown off at the elbows, in a World War II rocket explosion. He dictates his theories and mathematical calculations to his wife.[19]

Now we must pause to consider these bombshells in detail.

c. The Implications of Burkhard Heim and Pascual Jordan's Presence in These Projects

---

[17] Ansel F. Talbert, Military and Adviation Editor, "Conquest of Gravity: Aim of Top Scientists in U.S.", *New York Herald Tribune*, Sunday, November 20, 1955, 1, 36, p. 1, emphasis added. Cited in Valone, *Electro-Gravitics II*, pp. 85, 88.

[18] Ibid.

[19] Ibid., cited in Valone, op. cit., p. 87.

229

The first point to be noted is that the presence of Dr. Vlaclav Hlavaty and Dr. Burkhart Heim indicates that the American corporate components of this breakaway civilization were investigating theories of the unification of gravity and electromagnetism that were hyper-dimensional theories, in that both men were then proposing such theories.

The second point to be considered carefully is the presence of Burkhardt Heim and Pascual Jordan in these efforts of American aerospace corporations to decipher the code of gravity.

As I detailed in *The Philosophers' Stone: Alchemy and the Secret Research for Exotic Matter*, Burkhart Heim's theory is an unusual departure from the then-regnant standard model of physics in several respects, and here it is necessary to cite my remarks and quotations there at length:

> ...Heim did not reject one fundamental insight of Einstein, both in his General Theory of Relativity and more importantly, in his subsequent versions of the Unified Field Theory, namely, that physical forces could be described geometrically. Thus, forces not only were functions of the geometry, the geometry *was* the forces. But there is one crucial insight to Heim's version of the theory, borrowed from the standard model of quantum mechanics, and that is "the two important ingredients that Einstein did *not* use," namely "a discrete spacetime and a higher dimensional space, provided with special, additional features."[20] Thus, Heim's theory is a logical extension of the insight of quantum mechanics *and* the various Unified Field Theories of the 1920s and 1930s in that all physical interactions are described as geometries, and in the crucial insight that space-time *itself* is quantized, that is, that it is built not of ever smaller infinitely divisible units, but of discrete "smallest possible" units of space and time.[21]

---

[20] Ibid.

[21] Dröscher and Häuser point out in a previous paper, also presented to the AIAA, that "Spacetime itself is quantized. The current area of a **Metron**," which is Heim's term for the smallest possible unit of quantized space-time , "τ is $3Gh/8c^2$ where G is the gravitational constant, h denotes the Planck constant, and c is the speed of light in vacuum. The **Metron** size is *a derived quantity and is not postulated.*" (Walter Dröscher and Jochem Häuser, "Physical Principles of Advanced Space Propulsion Based on Heim's Field Theory," *38th AIAA/ASME/SAE/ASEE Joint Propulsion Conference and Exhibit,*

Thus, Heim's theory is not only a "completely geometrized unified field theory" but it is one with profound implications, for it gives rise "to a novel concept for an advanced space transportation technology, permitting, in principle, *superluminal* travel."[22] This unification is accomplished, in its extended version, by an 8-dimensional quantized "and *spin-oriented space.*"[23] As a result, its predictive power is enormous, for it not only predicts fundamental particle properties such as masses and lifetimes,[24] but also that "a transformation of electromagnetic wave energy at specific frequencies into gravitational like energy is possible."[25]

In coming to this view, Heim followed the principle of General Relativity and universalized it. In General Relativity, matter bends space-time itself, or, to put it differently, matter *is* a "bend" in the fabric of space-time; "matter and space-time curvature are equal."[26] Since the geometry and matter itself are equivalent, and to that extent, since matter is caused by the geometry of space-time distortion, then the essence of Heim's Theory is that every physical interaction or fields including gravity, electromagnetism, and the strong and weak forces of quantum mechanics are distortions in what otherwise would be a non-distorted undifferentiable space-time. Heim first presented this view "in 1952 at the International Congress on Aeronautics in Stuttgart, Germany,"[27] a date rather close to the end of World War Two, and not without its own suggestive implications, as will be seen. Heim further formally developed these ideas in the first versions of his theory during the late 1950s and early 1960s, the precise period in which Leonard Cramp's book appeared, outlining his views for the first time to an English-speaking general public.

...

This insight leads in turn to the next fundamental component of the extended 8 and 12 dimensional versions of his theory. Dröscher and Häuser present this aspect of his theory in the following manner:

AIAA 2002-4094, 7-10 July, 2002, pp. 6-7., boldface emphasis in the original italicized emphasis added).

[22] Ibid., p. 3, emphasis in the original.

[23] Ibid., emphasis added.

[24] Ibid., p. 4. These predictions have, in part at least, been recently verified.

[25] Ibid., p. 3.

[26] Ibid., p. 5.

[27] Ibid.

> According to Heim, the whole universe comprises a grid of
> *Metrons* or metronic lattice. Space that does not contain
> any information consists of a discrete Euclidean grid...
> However, empty space must be **isotropic** with regard to
> spin orientation. If all metronic spins of a 6D volume
> pointed outward or inward, such a world would not have a
> spin potentiality. Therefore, cells with all spins outward
> have to have neighboring cells with all spins inward and
> vice versa. This alternative spin structure satisfies the
> isotropy requirement, but provides empty space with spin
> potentiality.... Thus empty space is void of physical events,
> but has inherent potentiality for physical events to
> happen.[28]

In other words, the normal void of space itself, absent any
information distortions such as mass or matter, is a pure potential
for "things to happen," it *is* the transmutative medium of the
ancients. As a void it is a non-differentiated nothing, since there is a
balance of spin orientations in all its cells.

It is thus when that balance or equilibrium is unbalanced and
enters into non-equilibrium, where a preponderance of spin
orientation of one or the other type prevails, that all physical
interactions, and all matter, arises. Non-equilibrium and spin are
the very *mechanisms* not only for the differentiations of creation,
but therefore are also the very mechanisms of the unification of
physics, or, to put it in alchemical terms, for the "em-bodiment" of
the medium itself within normal matter. Thus, Heim's theory
incorporates and corroborates the fundamental insights of Jordan
and Kozyrev, for particles themselves for they are "geometrical
entities that possess an internal structure which is changing
cyclically in time...Elementary particles are not point entities, but
do consist of **Metrons.**"[29] Thus, in a sense peculiarly paralleling
some ancient views, "space and time are not the container for
things, but are, due to their dynamic (cyclic) nature, the things
themselves."[30] In Heim's hands, this dynamic view leads to a truly
extraordinary cosmology, because the higher dimensional space is
composed of such a lattice of "metrons" there are no "singularities"

---

[28] Dröscher and Häuser, "Physical Principles of Advanced Space
Propulsion Based on Heim's Field Theory,", p. 6.

[29] Dröscher and Häuser, "Physical Principles of Advanced Space
Propulsion Based on Heim's Field Theory,", p. 7.

[30] Ibid.. for the actual mathematical description of particles in Heim
theory, see p. 12.

or infinities that plague the standard models, and that have to be gotten rid of by the fancy mathematical accounting trick of renormalization.[31] The universe thus began as a single metron covering its entire surface (the undifferentiated medium), and as the number of metrons increased, their size decreased.[32]

In short, the spin-orientation and active force characteristics of time itself is the fundamental pillar of Heim's theory.

If all this is beginning to sound familiar, hold on, there's more.

In the 12-dimensional extension of Heim's original theory, there are

five semantic units, namely, the subspaces R^3 (space), T^1(time), S^2 (organization), I^2 (information) and G^4(steering of I^2) where superscripts denote dimension. Except for the 3 spatial dimensions, all other coordinates are imaginary. Several metric tensors can be constructed from these subspaces... Analyzing the metric tensors acting in R^4, the theory predicts *six fundamental interactions,* instead of the four experimentally known ones.[33]

These two additional interactions are the basis behind the claim that the theory holds out the promise of a breakthrough in physics and in propulsion and energy technologies.

The first of these reactions, a weak gravitationally *repulsive* action, which is analogous to the standard model's "dark energy," Heim calls by the peculiar term "quintessence," a term with its own alchemical associations, as has been seen, and thus perhaps suggestive of influences at work on Heim's thinking other than the purely physics-related, namely, the alchemical. But there is also a "gravitophoton" reaction that "enables the conversion of electromagnetic radiation into a gravitational like field."[34]

It will have been noted by the careful reader that Heim's hyper-dimensional space it actually comprised of five sub-spaces, one of which is our normal three dimensional space. Put differently, our three dimensional space is influenced by distortions in the higher nine dimensional space composed of its sub-spaces, recalling esotericist Manly P. Hall's observation that the successful

---

[31] Ibid., p. 16.

[32] Ibid.

[33] Ibid., p. 1, emphasis in the original.

[34] Dröscher and Häuser, "Guidelines for a Space Propulsion Device Based on Heim's Quantum Theory", p. 5.

confection of the Philosophers' Stone must be realized by one operation occurring simultaneously in four separate worlds.

It is precisely Heim theory's prediction of a direct gravitational-electromagnetic coupling that Dröscher and Häuser propose as the basis "for the novel space propulsion concept" that will be presented momentarily.[35]

...

Taking as their point of departure a series of experiments sponsored jointly by the European Space Agency and the U.S. Air Force, Dröscher and Häuser summarize the experiments and its implications as follows:

> In a recent experiment (march 2006), funded by the European Space Agency and the Air Force Office of Scientific Research, Taimer et al. report on the generation of a toroidal (tangential, azimuthal) gravitational field in a rotating accelerated (time dependent angular velocity) superconducting Niobium ring. IN July 2006, in a presentation at Berkeley university (sic), Taimar showed improved experimental results that confirmed previous experimental findings. Very recently, October 2006 and February 2007 the same authors reported repeating their experiments employing both accelerometers as well as laser ring-gyros that very accurately measured the gravito-magnetic field. The acceleration field was clearly observed, and its rotational nature was determined by a set of four accelerometers *in the plane of the ring.*
>
> *Since the experiment generates an artificial gravitational field, which is in the plane of the rotating ring...it cannot be used as a propulsion principle.* It is, however, of great importance, since it shows for the **first time that a gravitational field can be generated other than by the accumulation of mass.**[36]

Again, the mention of superconductors recalls Hudson's observations of mass loss anomalies in his strange material, and of physicist Hal Puthoff's explanations for them.

But note what Dröscher and Häuser conclude about the configuration of the experiment: since the artificial gravitational

---

[35] Ibid., p. 7.

[36] Dröscher and Häuser, "Current Research in Gravito-Electromagnetic Space Propulsion," *Institut für Grenzgebiete der Wissenschft* (Innsbruck, Austria), p. 10, italicized emphasis added, boldface emphasis in the original.

field was generated in the plane of the rotation of the superconductor, and not in the plane parallel to the axis of rotation, no practical propulsive benefit could accrue from the experiment. And this, precisely, is where Heim's unique theory steps in:

...(Theoretical) considerations obtained from (Extended Heim Theory) lead to the conclusion that an experiment should be possible to generate a ***gravitational field acting parallel to the axis of rotation of (a) rotating ring***... and thus, if confirmed, could serve as a demonstrator for a **field propulsion principle.**[37]

The authors then propose an apparatus for testing this hypothesis consisting of two counter-rotating systems *arranged, as per the predictions of Heim's theory, **one on top of the other**, exactly as I have conjectured was the actual internal configuration of the Nazi Bell's counter-rotating drums!* [38]

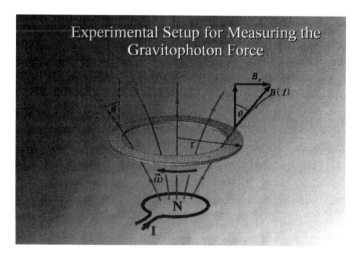

Dröscher and Häuser's Proposed Apparatus for the Testing of a Field Propulsion Principle in a Plane Parallel to the Axis of Two Stacked Counter-rotating Systems

That this theory would predict so specifically such effects, within such a short time after the end of World War Two, with its suspicious resemblance to the actual proposed configuration of the

---

[37] Ibid., boldface emphasis in the original, italicized boldface emphasis added to the authors' original emphasis.
[38] See my *Secrets of the Unified Field,* pp. 268-282.

Bell's internal counter-rotating drums, is suggestive that there is perhaps more in play in the formation of Heim's theory than meets the eye. And this is only confirmed by the mystery of what sort of research Heim was actually engaged in during the war.[39]

Now let us summarize what we have with respect to Heim's theory:

1) The theory begins with higher-dimensional definitions of a *quantized* but fully geometrized space-time;
2) The theory is able to make predictions from first principles concerning the mass and spin properties of fundamental particles;
3) The theory significantly departs from Einstein's relativistic hypothesis of a space-time *continuum*, and in this sense, Einstein's theory may be viewed, ala "Ray's" revelations to Dr. LaViolette, as a "classical" theory;
4) The theory is *testable*, and indeed, since it views space-time as a series of *cells with rotation moment or spin characteristics*, and as such it bears unique and direct conceptual relationships to the Nazi Bell project.

In short, we are looking at the distinct, direct, and strong possibility that Heim theory itself became the basis for the elaboration of the type of off-the-books-physics mentioned by "Ray" to Dr. LaViolette, and of an "error in the equations" mentioned by Ben Rich, for it adequately fulfills the parameters outlined by each man!

So much for Heim, but what about Pascual Jordan?

Here once again the story is very interesting, for Jordan was one of the seminal contributors to the development of quantum mechanics, and additionally, an ardent Nazi. But for our purposes, his significance lies also in an interesting contribution he made to the development of the idea of a coupling between gravity and electromagnetism:

It seems likely that yet another scientist played some role in this project, although his name did not appear in the original interrogation protocols; his unique works could constitute part of the theoretical basis of the experiments. It's about professor

---

[39] Farrell, *The Philosophers' Stone: Alchemy and the Secret Research for Exotic Matter* (Feral House, 2009), pp. 321-326.

236

Pascual Jordan, one of the most outstanding physicists of the Third Reich (whose career was as enigmatic as Gerlach's!). During the war he worked on a theory which described the phenomenon of "separation of magnetic fields," linking the isolation of magnetic fields with gravitational effects. Shortly after the war it was "perfected" and combined with the works of another scientist – presently it is known as the Jordan-Thiry theory. It is considered as one of the most fundamental achievements of the XXth century physics and Jordan was an almost certain candidate to receive the Nobel prize in 1954. Eventually, however, he was disqualified after his role during the war was revealed... the Jordan-Thiry theory forms the basis to analyze relativistic plasma vortices...[40]

Remember that point about plasmas, for we shall return to it shortly. For the present moment, again, it is critical to realize the value of someone like Jordan—in spite of his Nazi past—to the American program via his discovery of coupling effects between magnetism and gravity.

It is to be noted, additionally, that the presence of these two German scientists—one of them, Jordan, an ardent Nazi—in these postwar American antigravity projects occurs a mere two years before the whole subject appears to have gone deeply black.

d. Skyvault

We now return to the crucial research of Dr. Paul Laviolette. LaViolette also mentions another source, and project in antigravity research, also dating from the crucial period of the late 1950s, Project Skyvault:

> One evening in 1986, a friend and I went out for a beer. Like myself, he had a keen interest in alternative, cutting edge science. The topic of our conversation eventually turned to electrogravitics, and at this point my friend shared an interesting story. He told me that during the late 1950s, his father had worked as a physicist at the Rocketdyne Aerospace Corporation in Southern California and had

---

[40] Igor Witkowski, "Supplement 3, to be inserted on page 260 of the English edition," of *The Truth About the Wunderwaffe* for pending German edition, personal communication to the author. Witkowski cites Jordan specifically in reference to "magnetic fields separation" that played such a prominent conceptual role in the Bell project

been involved in some sort of super-secret antigravity research. At that time, my friend had been just a young boy. He said his father normally told him nothing about what he did at work because of an oath of secrecy he had taken, but one evening, after returning home from work he had been unable to contain himself. Very exuberantly, he had exclaimed, "We got it to work, we got it to work!" When my friend inquired what it was that was made to work, his father drew him a picture showing a lens shaped craft suspended in midair. He said, "We got it to lift off!" He would not say anything more about it, but that moment stuck in my friend's mind and now he shared it with me. I knew my friend well enough to know that what he told me was entirely genuine.[41]

We will present more evidence in a moment why this story should be taken seriously, but for the present, it suffices to note that once again the crucial period of the late 1950s is singled out, this time by a completely different author, as a period of deeply black covert research activity into antigravity by a major American defense contractor.

LaViolette was later contacted by entirely different source, whom he identifies only by the name "Tom," who corroborated details of this story:

The story he later told me about the Skyvault project was quite astounding. He said that he first heard about it in the fall of 1974, when working for an engineering firm in Texas. His supervisor, with whom he had come to be very good friends, one day told him about a top-secret government project that *he had worked on between 1952 and 1957 while at North American Aviation,* a company that was later renamed North American Rockwell. The project had been initiated by the Defense Department through North American's Rocketdyne division. Although Tom's boss had already passed away, Tom did not wish to reveal his name, so to facilitate the discussion, we will call him Murray. Well, Tom had heard from Murray that the purpose of this project was to develop an antigravity vehicle that used microwave beams as its means for propulsion. It is uncertain whether Skyvault was the official name

---

[41] Paul A. LaViolette, Ph.D., *Secrets of Antigravity Propulsion: Tesla, UFOs, and Classified Aerospace Technology* (Rochester, Vermont: Bear and Company, 2008), p. 190. LaViolette presents a summary of Rocketdyne's corporate history on pp. 190-191.

of the project, but at least this is what the scientists at Rocketdyne used to call it.

Although Project Skyvault was initiated by the government in the early 1950s, investigations into this exotic microwave propulsion technique actually dated back to the late 1940s. Murray, who held a Ph.D., said that in those earlier days he had worked on projects that were associated with an initial phase of this research and that later he had continued this work at Rocketdyne, where he worked up until the 1960s. This microwave antigravity propulsion research project was still in progress in 1974...[42]

Again, the project fits into the same time-frame, the 1950s, but appears to have begun during World War Two.

But can microwaves theoretically be used for propulsion?

According to LaViolette, it can, utilizing a principle known as the microwave soliton effect resulting from phase conjugation. While it is not necessary to go into the principles of phase conjugation here,[43] we may effectively view this principle to involve powerful microwave standing waves between a resonator cavity on a presumed craft, and the ground, producing a propulsive lift.[44]

But there are two other indicators of research into antigravity and the structure of space-time that went deeply black during the crucial 1950s.

3. Thomas Townsend Brown and His Statements in " Project Winterhaven"

The name of Thomas Townsend Brown is well known to those researching the rise—and sudden disappearance—of antigravity as a subject of discussion in open literature. What most do *not* know are the curious statements he made on the subject, statements that, when viewed within a very wide context, suggest that his work was suppressed not only by agencies of the government and therefore, possibly by the breakaway civilization, but also by the American corporate component of that entity.

---

[42] LaViolette, *Secrets of Antigravity Propulsion*, p. 192, emphasis added.
[43] For LaViolette's summary of this principle, see pp. 227-229.
[44] Ibid., pp. 234-235.

American Experimental Physicist Thomas Townsend Brown

These statements occur in a formal research proposal drafted by Brown and submitted to the U.S. Government for consideration, a proposal composed in 1952, and officially entitled "Project Winterhaven: A Proposal for Joint Services Research and Development Contract."[45]

Before looking closer at this project, we must understand what led to it. Brown, as most know, began experimenting with electrogravitics as a young man, when he noticed an effect that subsequently was named after him and his mentor Paul Biefeld: the Biefeld-Brown effect. When Brown would turn on the electric current to a cathode ray tube, the tube would momentarily jerk in the direction of the positive pole.

Brown subsequently conducted a lifetime of work of this phenomenon, eventually constructing disks of dielectric material and charging the leading edges of these disks positively, with the

---

[45] For our purposes here, I will refer to the page numbers of the original report. The entire proposal is available in Thomas Valone, PhD, *Electrogravitics II: Validating Reports on a New Propulsion Methodology* (Integrity Research Institute, No Date), pp. 102-115.

result that the disks would move more or less silently, with a faint hissing sound, in the direction of the positive polarity. This idea he patented in a 1960 patent for an "Electrokinetic Apparatus".

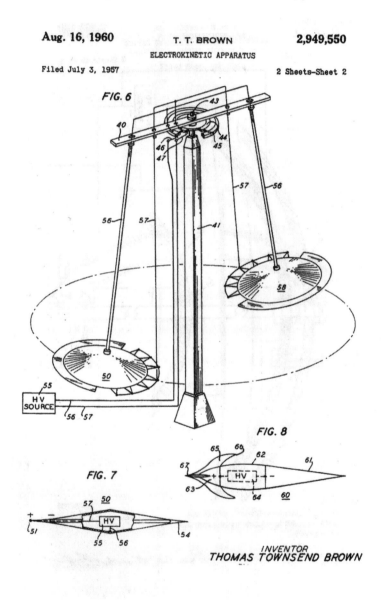

Brown's 1960 Electrokinetic Apparatus Patent

Thomas Townsend Brown with one of his Electro-Kinetic Disks

Brown was well suited to this type of research, serving in the US Navy during World War Two, experimenting with degaussing technologies and radar, as well as being connected in the popular imagination with the alleged Philadelphia Experiment, an early attempt to render an entire ship invisible to radar via electromagnetic means.[46] By Nick Cook's reckoning Brown's "curriculum vitae" from this period indicates that "there was no question that Brown was ... well plugged into the military's research and development community, and that his opinions were given great credit."[47] During the years of his research into this effect, Brown performed tests in France of his disks in high vacuum, eliminating the possibility that the propulsive effect was due to the creation of an ion wind in the atmosphere.

But to resume his story, after World War Two, Brown moved to Pearl Harbor and again resumed his research into the effect that he was now convinced was electrogravitic in nature. At this juncture, Brown's research during the period from 1945-1952 is shrouded in obscurity, but at some point he moved from Hawaii to Los Angeles,

---

[46] Cook, *The Hunt for Zero Point*, pp. 24-25.
[47] Ibid., p. 24.

and according to Nick Cook, established the Townsend Brown Foundation.[48]

What *is* known is that once back in California, Brown's foundation was paid "an unannounced visit by Major General Victor E. Bertrandis of the US Air Force."[49] There, Brown performed demonstrations of his disks for the General, who was impressed with the results.[50]

It was during this period that Brown made a formal pitch to the military to fund what he called "Project Winterhaven: A Proposal for (a) Joint Services Research and Development Contract" of the phenomenon. The proposal was straightforward:

> For the last several years, accumulating evidence along both theoretical and experimental lines has tended to confirm the suspicion that a fundamental interlocking relationship exists between the electrodynamic field and the gravitational field.
>
> It is the purpose of Project WINTERHAVEN to compile and study this evidence and to perform certain critical or definitive experiments which will serve to confirm or deny the relationship. If the results confirm the evidence, it is the further purpose of Project WINTERHAVEN to examine the physical nature of the basic "electro-gravitic couple" and to foresee and develop possible long-range practical applications.
>
> The proposed experiments are to be limited at first to force measurements and wave propagation. They are to be expanded, depending upon results, to include applications in propulsion or motive power, communications and remote control, with emphasis on military applications of recognized priority.[51]

Note that Brown foresees the results being applicable to communications, a point to which we shall return shortly, but Brown specifically states in his research proposal that the experiments and research organization established to experiment in electrogravity

---

[48] Nick Cook, *The Hunt for Zero Point*, p. 29. Some researchers have maintained this foundation was established in 1938 in Ohio.

[49] Ibid., p. 29.

[50] Ibid., pp. 30-31.

[51] Thomas Townsend Brown, "Project Winterhaven: A Proposal for (a) Joint Services Research and Development Contract," Townsend Brown Foundation, No Date, p. 1.

should be divided into two basic tracks, one investigating the use of the effect for motive purposes, and the other for communications.[52]

Brown also makes the observation that such a coupling effect between electromagnetism and gravity was first suggested in *unpublished* notes of Sir Oliver Heaviside in the late nineteenth century.[53] In other words, Brown was obliquely suggesting the same thing we have encountered elsewhere, that there was a little-known history of such concepts in physics, concepts that may have been deliberately kept out of view. This, in fact, is stated clearly in the Winterhaven proposal, which notes that "In recent years, as additional data of a confirming nature became available, the research has been associated with government research projects of a highly classified status, and publication has been precluded,"[54] a statement that strongly suggests Brown himself was involved in some of this research, and that also suggests that the chase for antigravity was well underway in the early 1950s, even before the subsequent mid-1950s disappearance of discussion of the subject in the open literature.

In its review of his electrified disks, the Winterhaven Proposal document notes that the disks contained "no moving parts" and that in atmospheric tests "they emit a bluish-red electrical coronal glow and a faint hissing sound."[55]

Then comes a bombshell, which readers familiar with my previous books, *The Philosophers' Stone, Babylon's Banksters,* and *The Grid of the Gods* will recognize instantly:

> However, there are certain variable factors which are not completely understood. For example, there are tidal effects apparently caused by the Sun and Moon which influence to a small extent the power developed. There are anomalous sidereal effects which seem to be related to the passage of the Earth through

---

[52] Thomas Townsend Brown, "Project Winterhaven," p. 1.1. Elsewhere Brown states more explicitly the nature of the coupling his research had uncovered by stating that experiments would be conducted in order to prove or disprove the hypothesis that "a gravitational field can be effectively controlled by manipulating the space-energy relationships of the ambient electrostatic field."(p. 5.)

[53] Ibid., p. 2.

[54] Ibid., p. 3.

[55] Ibid., p. 7.

diffuse clouds of cosmic dust or electrified particles ejected from the Sun.[56]

In other words, Brown, during his research, had apparently observed variable effects on his devices that were dependent upon the relative positions of the Sun and Moon and the output of the solar wind, results that sound very similar to what was noticed by Russian astrophysicist Nikolai Kozyrev,[57] and variable effects on solar coronal activity that were correlated to planetary positions, noticed by RCA engineer J.H. Nelson.[58]

However, just a little later in the Winterhaven proposal, Brown states that his early experiments' results "were surprising for the reason that they failed to reveal a directional effect with respect to the gravitational field of the Earth, but showed only a dependence upon the mass (m) of the electrified bodies," an effect that "provided a theory for a gravitational drive virtually independent of the gravitational field of the Earth."[59]

How would one reconcile these two statements, for obviously, Brown is guarding his language? The answer seems to lie in the possibility that relative planetary positions, moon position, and solar wind activity, are correlated in the ever-changing electrodynamic nature of the solar system itself, and in the possibility that these in turn also produce dynamic torsion effects. This, in effect, is what Brown himself later states: "The tentative theory implies that the basic relationship between the electrodynamic field and the gravitational field is revealed 'during the process of charging or discharging electric capacitors.'"[60] This coupling effect Brown also subsequently notes could eventually "be utilized in a completely new method of wireless communication."[61]

This coupling effect, and the communications opportunities it presented, lead Brown to drop yet another bombshell, and again, it is one that readers of my previous books will recognize:

---

[56] Thomas Townsend Brown, "Project Winterhaven," p. 7.

[57] See my *The Philosophers' Stone*, pp. 153-155ff., and *The Grid of the Gods*, pp. 23-27.

[58] See my *Babylon's Banksters*, pp. 114-119.

[59] Thomas Townsend Brown, op. cit., p. 8.

[60] Ibid., p. 12.

[61] Ibid., p. 14.

> At the outset, development of the electrogravitational communication system obviously could provide a secret, almost wholly untouchable, channel for classified military communications. Message transmissions could be put through without breaking military radio silence, at a time when all electromagnetic transmissions are prohibited. Due to the high penetrability of the gravitational wave, communications could conceivably be maintained between submerged submarines, between submarines and shore installations or between bomb-proof shelters and similar underground installations without the use of external wires.
>
> ...
>
> Due to the tremendous momentary displacement of air and the gravitational disturbance resulting there from, there is reason to believe that the electrogravitational receiver may be one of the few devices capable of instant long-distance detection and ranging of atomic bomb explosions.[62]

Brown is suggesting, in guarded language yet again, that nuclear explosions send out a *longitudinal pulse in the medium* ("instant long-distance detection and ranging of atomic bomb explosions") that is of a superluminal nature, and that this is a result of the momentary geometry created at the center of the explosion, a geometry that *couples* electromagnetic and gravitational fields.

It is worth pausing to note what Dr. LaViolette says about this phenomenon, for it once again takes us back to Tesla's wireless transmission of power via a kind of "electro-acoustic" or electrical longitudinal wave via his "impulse magnifying transformers":

> Superluminal propagation speeds have also been observed in atomic bomb tests. Scientists working for the military have known since the early bomb tests in the late 1940s that the electromagnetic pulse shock wave from a nuclear explosion propagates outward at superluminal velocities when measured near the explosion epicenter. The enormous energy released in the explosion accelerates the fireball's free electrons radially outward at a relativistic velocity, generating a radially propagating shock

---

[62] Thomas Townsend Brown, "Project Winterhaven," p. 25. It is worth noting that many UFOlogists have pointed out that UFOs seemed to have arrived in large numbers *after* atomic bomb tests over various defense installations, as if somehow the tests had been *detected* by "someone."

pulse that, like a shock discharge from...(a) magnifying transmitter, moves outward at superluminal speeds.[63]

Brown's Winterhaven proposal was ultimately rejected, and Brown made his way to the Bahnsen Laboratories, where he continued his private investigations of the phenomena, including research into Adamski-style disks.

But as Nick Cook points out, Brown's subsequent association in the popular literature with the Philadelphia experiment, plus the military's rejection of his Winterhaven proposal, may not be as clear-cut as they seem, for his association with the Philadelpia Experiment

> helped to perform a very important function.
> By 1980, it had managed to tip Brown over the edge; make him a wholly discredited figure in the eyes of science.
> That left me with the uncomfortable feeling that the story had been carefully stage-managed. If so, why? And why so long after the supposed events had taken place?[64]

Cook is not just proposing a possibility, for Brown's association with the Philadelphia Experiment was first popularized in the book on the subject by Charles Berlitz and William Moore, both of whom had intelligence contacts, Moore, of course, eventually confessing that he had allowed himself to be used as a disinformation agent within the UFOlogy community by intelligence agencies, thus strongly raising the possibility that he was acting as such when their book coupling Brown to the Philadelphia Experiment was written.

This, for Cook, raises the possibility that when Brown proposed Project Winterhaven, that he, like the aerospace companies later openly discussing antigravity research in the popular media, were discussing things already under investigation by the military "until someone, somewhere, ordered them into silence."[65] Additionally, while Brown's project may have been rejected, some of the results of his years of research nevertheless ended up being, as Brown himself stated in the proposal, "highly classified."[66]

---

[63] Paul A. LaViolette, *Secrets of Antigravity Propulsion,* p, 184.
[64] Cook, *The Hunt for Zero Point,* p. 29.
[65] Ibid., p. 35.
[66] Ibid., pp. 6-7.

So what do we now have? Clearly, in Brown's Winterhaven proposal, we have the strong suggestions that there are electro-gravitic coupling effects, effects that in turn are variable according to the locally changing geometries of the solar system, and that these small effects are also directly tied to the geometries of nuclear explosions, suggesting in turn that their yields are variable with the same local system geometries.

All of this leads to yet *another* suppressed project, this time, of a Nazi scientist working in Argentina....

4. Dr. Ronald Richter's Argentine "Fusion" Project

While I have written extensively elsewhere of the "controlled fusion" project of Nazi scientist Dr. Ronald Richter in Argentina,[67] a brief review is in order here. After Juan Perón disclosed the existence of Richter's project to control thermonuclear fusion in 1951, boasting that Argentina had learned the secret of the hydrogen bomb, Perón, and Richter, were both roundly denounced in the world's press, and nowhere more so than in the American media, as frauds. As is now known, Perón established a commission to investigate Richter and his claims, and placed the scientist under permanent house arrest in Buenos Aires, and the project was dismantled.

However, as I outlined in *Nazi International*, while this was taking place, the US Air Force subsequently conducted secret interviews of Richter in the mid-1950s, and learned that Richter was actually attempting to manipulate the zero point energy—Richter's term!—through rotating and electromagnetically stressed plasmas involving lithium-7 reactions.

The US Air Force's review of Richter was ambivalent, with some scientists still insisting that his claims were fraudulent, but with others stating that Richter was some sort of "mad genius" working two decades in advance of everyone else. The problem, as co-author Scott D. de Hart and I pointed out in *The Grid of the Gods*, is that Richter knew of lithium-7 thermonuclear reactions, which threw official US explanations for runaway yields in its Castle Bravo nuclear test into a cocked hat. The Castle Bravo test was, of course, the infamous hydrogen bomb test of the early 1950s whose actual

---

[67] See my *Nazi International*, pp. 249-350.

yield far exceeded the pre-test calculated yield. Scientists later offered the lame explanation that they had not considered that all the lithium-7 in the device would contribute to the reaction. Both Richter, and his Argentine scientist opponents, knew years in advance of these reactions, which were fairly standard and well-known thermonuclear chemistry.[68]

Richter, in his interviews with the US Air Force, not only made it clear that lithium-7 was a primary component in his experiments, but also indicated that it was his opinion that plasmas accessed a cellular type structure in space—shades of Burkhart Heim!—and thus could momentarily act as transducers of the zero point energy under the proper geometrical conditions.

And Thomas Townsend Brown was saying essentially the same thing, and that the whole coupling effect could also be used for propulsion and communication.

And all of it, as George Adamski was talking to "extraterrestrials" about the planetary federation and the dangers of weaponized gravity, and as Nazi scientists involved with the Bell project were opining disingenuously about off world aliens, went deeply black, all of it, consistent with the activity of a breakaway civilization trying to protect its secrets.

C. Conclusions

We are now in a position so summarize the results of this essay, and to project some speculations that seem warranted from those conclusions.

1) Throughout this study, we have noted various efforts aimed at the camouflage of its activity and research, from the construction of secret facilities with disguised entrances, to the more subtle forms of camouflage indicated by possible psychological operations designed to deflect attention away from human development of the advanced technologies represented by antigravity research;

2) Additionally, we have noted that this civilization, like all governments, is protecting its "borders" and security by monitoring access to its facilities, which represent a

---

[68] See our *The Grid of the Gods*, pp. 1-36.

"geographic" location that is scattered over the earth, but that is largely underground;

3) Additionally, we have noted that this civilization has all the "instruments of surplus" noted by Quigley as being necessary for the sustaining of a civilization, methods of surplus whose financing mechanisms are largely covert, in the form of black budgets, and even more hidden, through the connection with criminal activity connected with the drug trade, a trade in turn heavily penetrated by some sort of postwar international Fascist organization. It is thus entirely feasible that this latter source of "surplus" represents a component of the breakaway civilization's *independence* from the host society;

4) Moreover, we have seen that there is a tripartite *structure* of various components to this civilization, composed of

a) private corporate and banking interests closely allied with the Morgan-Rockefeller interest and the American aerospace development firms,;

b) the American military, and finally;

c) the prewar German cartels, most notably I.G. Farben, and subsequently the Nazi party and the SS;

5) Within this wider context, the significance of the Morgan suppression of Nikola Tesla's invention of wireless power transmission appears not as the isolated case of suppression, but as the first significant *private corporate and banking example* of the wider pattern of such suppression by all factions and components of the structure;

6) We note in particular that Thomas Townsend Brown's elaboration of the key concepts of "electrogravitics" closely parallels similar physics conceptions elaborated by Russian astrophysicist Nikolai Kozyrev, and that both men's ideas were suppressed and deeply classified, giving rise to the possibility of an off-the-books physics and technology arising from it, ideas corroborated by statements of Ben Rich and others closely involved in advanced aerospace research. We also note the similarity of these ideas to the types of open systems physics discussed in connection with banking interests in *Babylon's Banksters.*, and to what I have called the ancient "topological metaphor of the medium". This confluence of ideas, again, strongly suggests the possibility

that we are indeed dealing with a breakaway civilization, and one that may in fact be *very* ancient in its ultimate origins.

7) We note that, insofar as the Nazi and American components of this research are concerned, the former began to investigate the antigravity possibilities in the 1940s, whereas the American component appears to have begun in earnest in the 1950s, possibly as a response to "catch up" with the former;

8) The strong possibility thus arises that we are looking at the matrix for a two-track space program, since the breakaway civilization appears to have access to, and to have developed, advanced and very different physics conceptions and technologies than the public sector;[69]

9) Beginning with Adamski, the "meme" was very early planted that mankind would have to surrender its independence and sovereignty as a safeguard against weaponized gravity, and this raises the next possibility;

10) Beginning at the end of World War Two, and specifically among the *Nazi* component of the emerging matrix of the breakaway civilization, SS Colonel Otto Skorzeny proposed a *Weltanschauungskrieg* or psychological operation conceived in conjunction with the careful display of advanced technology. Given the statements of Adamski, the Paperclip Nazis, and the emerging ET mythos, and following the insights of Dr. Jacques Vallee, it would appear that this operation was conceived not merely as a cloak for the development of the technology, but also that the technology itself was perceived in an alchemical, psychotronic fashion, as a means of altering human perceptions and the ability to interpret aspects of the UFO phenomenon correctly, deflecting such developments from a terrestrial to an extraterrestrial origin. This raises the possibility that the technology was perhaps perceived to give the potential for

---

[69] Dr. LaViolette observes that a source told him that the USA had, beginning in the early 1960s, a system of early warning satellites in orbit not just around the Earth, but around Mercury, Venus, Mars, and "other planets" in the solar system, designed to give early warning against an alien threat, thus indicating that the secret space capabilities of the USA were far in advance of what was being publicly disclosed. See *Secrets of Antigravity Propulsion*, pp. 396-397.

massive deception operations, such as staged ET contact or invasion events;

11) We have also noted that there are significant indications of yet another component of a breakaway civilization, namely, a different ideological and scientific culture prevailing secretly within it, utilizing paradigms of science very different from the public consumption physics promoted in the open host civilization, with the statements of Ben Rich being the most prominent public admission of this possibility, a possibility further corroborated by the presence of Nazi scientists Burkhart Heim and Pascual Jordan in 1950s antigravity research undertaken by the American military. It must be pointed out, once again, that the *earliest* public record of the possibility of the emergence of a very different paradigm of physics is in fact with the Nazi proscription of "Jewish physics," i.e., the relativistic paradigm of Einstein, a clear statement of a breakaway scientific ideological culture. In the postwar period, with the manifest crimes of the Third Reich and its many patent failures in various areas of science, this in itself could afford the basis for an effective psychological operation of suppression of those areas of successful development of alternative paradigms falling outside the relativistic paradigm.

12) The fact that such technologies give off strong radiations— some of them which we have examined, in the microwave range—also had inevitable neurophysiological effects, effects most likely observed by those researching and developing these technologies. These effects would have included disorientation and possibly even hallucination, and thus the idea may have been born to use the technologies in psychological warfare operations.

In short, I believe it is now clear that the possibility raised by Richard Dolan of a breakaway civilization is not only possible, but that the conditions exist for it to do so.

Moreover, it would seem clear that various activities undertaken with respect to UFOs would seem to indicate that at least *some* of these are psychological operations, one clear activity of *civilizations in conflict with other civilizations.* This last statement indicates one final possibility, that one single most prominent activity of civilizations, hinted at by Quigley's "sociology of weaponry," namely, war.

We have not, in this book, discussed the war-making powers and possible actual *wars* of this breakaway civilization for the very simple reason that this, in itself, would require a book of its own. But the fact remains that war is one of the principal organizing principles of any civilization, and this raises yet another prospect and possibility. The waging of an actual war would be the clearest sign that this civilization exists. But what would one look for?

I believe the answer was hinted at in the second chapter, and by Adamski's "ET" himself: one would look for the signatures of a weaponized electrogravitics. In the scheme of things, one would be looking for a technology able to manipulate phenomena on a planetary, or possibly even stellar, scale.

The Russian astronomer Kardashev proposed a classification scheme for civilizations based on their abilities to manipulate energies. A Type 1 civilization would be capable of manipulating and engineering the energies of an entire planet. A Type 2 civilization would be capable of doing the same with stars, and a Type 3 civilization, the most advanced, would be capable of manipulating those of an entire galaxy.

Given what we have encountered in this chapter, it is clear that the physics being proposed by Brown and others is capable of at least type 1 or 2 manipulations, and this would mean the breakaway civilization is truly a breakaway civilization in yet another sense as well, for as the larger world wallows in fossil fuels and all the economic- and geo-politics thereof, it would have literally pulled away from that civilization in its technological capabilities. The possibility of such engineering and manipulation raises the prospect that such technologies could reasonably be disguised as natural activities; after all, Mother Nature provides the perfect "plausible deniability."

All this to say that such capabilities would be most manifest in the types of military operations it was able to mount. One would have to look for certain things, reading the tea leaves of recent events, and ascertaining if the signatures of those events evidenced the types of physics being outlined here.

Is such a war being waged, covertly, right under our noses?

Unfortunately, that possibility must await its own exposition. Here it suffices only to recall that Colonel Skorzeny proposed it ...near the end of World War Two.

Where that war has come since the 1950s would require another volume, for if indeed that breakaway civilization is waging a war against the rest of humanity, or if there is covert warfare between its various factions, then it would require a close examination of the technologies, their signatures, and the situations in which they may have been used.

That is the task for another work. For the moment, it is clear that the possibility of a breakaway civilization exists, and moreover, given the activities and relationships we have surveyed, it is in my opinion a likelihood.

BIBLIOGRAPHY
WORKS CITED OR CONSULTED

Adamski, George. *Flying Saucers Have Landed.* George Adamski Foundation. 1955. No ISBN

Adamski, George. *Inside the Spaceships.* George Adamski Foundation. 1955. No ISBN.

Baumann, H.D., *Hitler's Fate: The Final Story..* London. Athena Press. 2008. ISBN 978-1-84748-135-1.

Brown, Thomas Townsend. "Project Winterhaven: A Proposal for Joint Services Research and Development Contract." The Townsend Brown Foundation. No Date. No ISBN. (Typewritten manuscript).

Cook, Nick. *The Hunt for Zero Point: One Man's Journey to Discover the Biggest Secret Since the Invention of the Atom Bomb.* London: Century. 2001. ISBN 0-7126-6953-1.

Dolan, Richard M. *UFOs and the National Security State: Chronology of a Cover-up 1941-1973.* Hampton Roads Publishing Company, Inc. 2002. ISBN 978-1-571-74-317-6.

Dolan, Richard M. *UFOs and the National Security State: The Cover-up Exposed: 1973-1991.* Keyhole Publishing Company. 2009. ISBN 978-0-9677995-1-3.

Engdahl, F. William. *Seeds of Destruction: The Hidden Agenda of Genetic Manipulation.* Global Research. 2007. ISBN 978-0-9737147-2-2.

Farrell, Joseph P. *Babylon's Banksters: The Alchemy of Deep Physics, High Finance and Ancient Religion.* Feral House. 2010. ISBN 978-1-932595-79-6.

Bibliography

Farrell, Joseph P. *The Giza Death Star Destroyed: The Ancient War for Future Science.* Adventures Unlimited Press. 2005. ISBN 978-1-931882-47-9.

Farrell, Joseph P., and de Hart, Scott D. *The Grid of the Gods: The Aftermath of the Cosmic War and the Physics of the Pyramid Peoples.* Adventures Unlimited Press. 2011. ISBN 978-1-935487-39-5.

Farrell, Joseph P. *LBJ and the Conspiracy to Kill Kennedy: A Coalescence of Interests.* Adventures Unlimited Press. 2011. ISBN 978-1-935487-18-0.

Farrell, Joseph P. *Nazi International: The Nazis' Postwar Plan to Control Finance, Conflict, Physics and Space.* Adventures Unlimited Press. 2008. ISBN 978-1-931882-93-4.

Farrell, Joseph P. *Roswell and the Reich: The Nazi Connection.* Adventures Unlimited Press. 2010. ISBN 978-1-935487-05-0.

Farrell, Joseph P. *The Philosophers' Stone: Alchemy and the Secret Research for Exotic Matter.* Feral House. 2009. ISBN 978-1-932595-40-6.

Farrell, Joseph P. *Secrets of the Unified Field: The Philadelphia Experiment, the Nazi Bell, and the Discarded Theory.* Adventures Unlimited Press. 2008. ISBN. 978-1-931882-84-2.

Farrell, Joseph P. *The SS Brotherhood of the Bell: The Nazi's Incredible Secret Technology: NASA's Nazis, JFK, and Majic-12.* Adventures Unlimited Press. 2006. ISBN 978-1-931882-61-4.

Fäth, Harald. *Geheime Kommandosache - SIII Jonastal und die Siegeswaffenproduktion: Weitere Spurensuche nach Thüringens Manhattan Project.* Schleusingen, Germany. Amun Verlag. 2000. ISBN 3-935095-08-2.

Georg, Friedrich. *Hitlers Siegeswaffen, Band 2: Star Wars 1947: Teilband B: Von der Amerikarakete zur Orbitalstation - Deutschlands Streben nach Interkontinentalwaffen und das ertse*

Weltraumprogramm. Schleusingen, Germany. Amun Verlag. 2004. ISBN 3-935095-33-3.

Good, Timothy. *Above Top Secret: The Worldwide UFO Cover-Up.* New York: William Morrow. 1988. ISBN 0-688-09202-0.

Good, Timothy. *Need to Know: UFOs, The Military and Intelligence.* New York: Pegasus Books. 2007. ISBN 978-1-933648-38-5.

Greer, Steven M., M.D. *Disclosure: Military and Government Witnesses Reveal the Greatest Secret in Modern History.* Crozet, Virginia. Crossing Point, Inc. 2001. ISBN 0-9673238-1-9.

Higham, Charles. *American Swastika: The Shocking Story of Nazi Collaborators in Our Midst from 1933 to the Present Day.* New York. Doubleday & Company, Inc. 1985. ISBN 0-385-17874-3.

Higham, Charles. *Trading With the Enemy: The Nazi-American Money Plot 1933=1949.* Lincoln, NE. Authors Guild Back-in-Print. 2007. ISBN 0-595-43166-6.

Johnson, Ian. *A Mosque in Munich: Nazis, the CIA, and the Rise of the Muslim Brotherhood in the West.* Boston. Houghton Mifflin Company. 2010. ISBN 978-0-15-101418-7.

Kampe, Hans George. *The Underground Military Command Bunkers of Zossen, Germany: Construction History and Use by the Wehrmacht and Soviet Army 1937-1994.* Atglen, Pennsylvania. Schiffer Military/Aviation History. 1996. ISBN 0-7643-0164-0.

Krüger, Henrik. *The Great Heroin Coup: Drugs, Intelligence, and International Fascism.* Trans. Jerry Meldon. Boston, Massachusetts. South End Press. 1980. ISBN 0-89608-031-5.

LaViolette, Paul. A., Ph.D. *Secrets of Antigravity Propulsion: Tesla, UFOs, and Classified Aerospace Technology.* Rochester, Vermont. Bear and Company. 2008. ISBN 978-159143078-0.

Loftus, John. *America's Nazi Secret.* Walterville, Oregon. TrineDay. 2011. ISBN 978-1-036296-04-0.

Bibliography

Manning, Paul. *Martin Bormann: Nazi in Exile.* Lyle Stuart. 1983.

Marrs, Jim. *Alien Agenda: Investigating the Extraterrestrial Presence Among Us.* New York: Harper Collins Publishers. 1997. ISBN 0-06-018642-9.

McClure, Kevin. *The Nazi UFO Mythos.* www.magonia.demon.co.uk/abwatch.naziufo. (In 12 parts).

Quigley, Carroll. *The Evolution of Civilizations: An Introduction to Historical Analysis.* Indianapolis. Liberty Fund.1979. ISBN 978-0-913966-57-0.

Quigley, Carroll. *Tragedy and Hope: A History of the World in Our Time.* Macmillan. 1964. (reprint by GSG & Associates, San Pedro, CA.) ISBN 0-945001-10-X.

Redfern, Nick. *Final Events: and the Secret Government Group on Demonic UFOs and the Afterlife.* San Antonio: Anomalist Books. 2010. ISBN978-1-933665-48-1.

Sauder, Richard, Ph.D.. *Underground Bases and Tunnels: What is the Government Trying to Hide?* Kempton, Illinois. Adventures Unlimited Press. 1997. ISBN 0-932813-37-2.

Schmidt, Michael. *The New Reich: Violent Extremism in Unified Germany and Beyond.* Trans. from the German by Daniel Horch. New York. Pantheon Books. 1993. ISBN 0-679-42578-0.

Simpson, Christopher. *Science of Coercion: Communication Research and Psychological Warfare 1945-1960.* Oxford University Press. 1994. ISBN 978-019510225.

Speer, Albert. *Infiltration: How Heinrich Himmler Schemed to Build an SS Industrial Empire.* New York. MacMillan Publishing Co., Inc. 1981. ISBN. 0-02-612800-4.

Steckling, Fred. *We Discovered Alien Bases on the Moon II: Revised Edition.* G.A.F. International. 1981. ISBN 0-942176-00-6.

Stevens, Henry. *Dark Star: The Hidden History of German Secret Bases, Flying Disks and U-Boats.* Kempton, Illinois. Adventures Unlimited Press. 2011. ISBN 978-1-035487-40-1.

Stevens, Henry. *Hitler's Flying Saucers: A Guide to German Flying Discs of the Second World War.* Kempton, Illinois. Adventures Unlimited Press. 2003. ISBN 1-931882-13-4.

Valle, Jacques. *Messengers of Deception: UFO Contacts and Cults.* Brisbaine, Australia. Daily Grail Publishing. 2008. ISBN 978-0-9757200-4-2.

Vallee, Jacques. *Passport to Magonia: on Ufos, Folklore, and Parallel Worlds.* Chicago: Contemporary Books. 1993. ISBN 0-8092-3796-2.

Vallee, Jacques. *Revelations: Alien Contact and Human Deception.* New York: Ballantine Books. 1991. ISBN 0-345-37566-1.

Valone, Thomas, Ph.D. *Electrogravitics II: Validating Reports on a New Propulsion Technology.* Integrity Research Institute. 2005. ISBN 0-9641080-9-0.

Wikowski, Igor. *The Truth About the Wunderwaffe.* Warsaw: European History Press. 2003. ISBN 838825916-4.

Yeadon, Glen, and Hawkins, John. *The Nazi Hydra In America: Suppressed History of a Century.* Joshua Tree, California. Progressive. 2008. ISBN 978-0-930852-43-6.

REICH OF THE BLACK SUN
Nazi Secret Weapons & the Cold War Allied Legend
by Joseph P. Farrell
Why were the Allies worried about an atom bomb attack by the Germans in 1944? Why did the Soviets threaten to use poison gas against the Germans? Why did Hitler in 1945 insist that holding Prague could win the war for the Third Reich? Why did US General George Patton's Third Army race for the Skoda works at Pilsen in Czechoslovakia instead of Berlin? Why did the US Army not test the uranium atom bomb it dropped on Hiroshima? Why did the Luftwaffe fly a non-stop round trip mission to within twenty miles of New York City in 1944? *Reich of the Black Sun* takes the reader on a scientific-historical journey in order to answer these questions. Arguing that Nazi Germany actually won the race for the atom bomb in late 1944,
352 PAGES. 6x9 PAPERBACK. ILLUSTRATED. BIBLIOGRAPHY. $16.95. CODE: ROBS

THE GIZA DEATH STAR
The Paleophysics of the Great Pyramid & the Military Complex at Giza
by Joseph P. Farrell
Was the Giza complex part of a military installation over 10,000 years ago? Chapters include: An Archaeology of Mass Destruction, Thoth and Theories; The Machine Hypothesis; Pythagoras, Plato, Planck, and the Pyramid; The Weapon Hypothesis; Encoded Harmonics of the Planck Units in the Great Pyramid; High Freqquency Direct Current "Impulse" Technology; The Grand Gallery and its Crystals: Gravito-acoustic Resonators; The Other Two Large Pyramids; the "Causeways," and the "Temples"; A Phase Conjugate Howitzer; Evidence of the Use of Weapons of Mass Destruction in Ancient Times; more.
290 PAGES. 6x9 PAPERBACK. ILLUSTRATED. $16.95. CODE: GDS

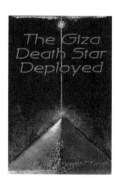

THE GIZA DEATH STAR DEPLOYED
The Physics & Engineering of the Great Pyramid
by Joseph P. Farrell
Farrell expands on his thesis that the Great Pyramid was a maser, designed as a weapon and eventually deployed—with disastrous results to the solar system. Includes: Exploding Planets: A Brief History of the Exoteric and Esoteric Investigations of the Great Pyramid; No Machines, Please!; The Stargate Conspiracy; The Scalar Weapons; Message or Machine?; A Tesla Analysis of the Putative Physics and Engineering of the Giza Death Star; Cohering the Zero Point, Vacuum Energy, Flux: Feedback Loops and Tetrahedral Physics; and more.
290 PAGES. 6x9 PAPERBACK. ILLUSTRATED. $16.95. CODE: GDSD

THE GIZA DEATH STAR DESTROYED
The Ancient War For Future Science
by Joseph P. Farrell
Farrell moves on to events of the final days of the Giza Death Star and its awesome power. These final events, eventually leading up to the destruction of this giant machine, are dissected one by one, leading us to the eventual abandonment of the Giza Military Complex—an event that hurled civilization back into the Stone Age. Chapters include: The Mars-Earth Connection; The Lost "Root Races" and the Moral Reasons for the Flood; The Destruction of Krypton: The Electrodynamic Solar System, Exploding Planets and Ancient Wars; Turning the Stream of the Flood: the Origin of Secret Societies and Esoteric Traditions; The Quest to Recover Ancient Mega-Technology; Non-Equilibrium Paleophysics; Monatomic Paleophysics; Frequencies, Vortices and Mass Particles; "Acoustic" Intensity of Fields; The Pyramid of Crystals; tons more.
292 pages. 6x9 paperback. Illustrated. $16.95. Code: GDES

SECRETS OF THE UNIFIED FIELD
The Philadelphia Experiment, the Nazi Bell, and the Discarded Theory
by Joseph P. Farrell

Farrell examines the now discarded Unified Field Theory. American and German wartime scientists and engineers determined that, while the theory was incomplete, it could nevertheless be engineered. Chapters include: The Meanings of "Torsion"; Wringing an Aluminum Can; The Mistake in Unified Field Theories and Their Discarding by Contemporary Physics; Three Routes to the Doomsday Weapon: Quantum Potential, Torsion, and Vortices; Tesla's Meeting with FDR; Arnold Sommerfeld and Electromagnetic Radar Stealth; Electromagnetic Phase Conjugations, Phase Conjugate Mirrors, and Templates; The Unified Field Theory, the Torsion Tensor, and Igor Witkowski's Idea of the Plasma Focus; tons more.
340 pages. 6x9 Paperback. Illustrated. Bibliography. Index. $18.95. Code: SOUF

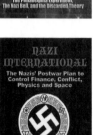

NAZI INTERNATIONAL
The Nazi's Postwar Plan to Control Finance, Conflict, Physics and Space
by Joseph P. Farrell

Beginning with prewar corporate partnerships in the USA, including some with the Bush family, he moves on to the surrender of Nazi Germany, and evacuation plans of the Germans. He then covers the vast, and still-little-known recreation of Nazi Germany in South America with help of Juan Peron, I.G. Farben and Martin Bormann. Farrell then covers Nazi Germany's penetration of the Muslim world including Wilhelm Voss and Otto Skorzeny in Gamel Abdul Nasser's Egypt before moving on to the development and control of new energy technologies including the Bariloche Fusion Project, Dr. Philo Farnsworth's Plasmator, and the work of Dr. Nikolai Kozyrev. Finally, Farrell discusses the Nazi desire to control space, and examines their connection with NASA, the esoteric meaning of NASA Mission Patches.
412 pages. 6x9 Paperback. Illustrated. References. $19.95. Code: NZIN

ARKTOS
The Polar Myth in Science, Symbolism & Nazi Survival
by Joscelyn Godwin

Explored are the many tales of an ancient race said to have lived in the Arctic regions, such as Thule and Hyperborea. Progressing onward, he looks at modern polar legends: including the survival of Hitler, German bases in Antarctica, UFOs, the hollow earth, and the hidden kingdoms of Agartha and Shambala. Chapters include: Prologue in Hyperborea; The Golden Age; The Northern Lights; The Arctic Homeland; The Aryan Myth; The Thule Society; The Black Order; The Hidden Lands; Agartha and the Polaires; Shambhala; The Hole at the Pole; Antarctica; more.
220 Pages. 6x9 Paperback. Illustrated. Bib. Index. $16.95. Code: ARK

PARAPOLITICS!
Conspiracy in Contemporary America
by Kenn Thomas

From the Kennedy assassination to 9/11, Thomas examines the underlying parapolitics that animate the secret elites and the war-ravaged planet they manipulate. Contents include: Octopus Redux; Previously unpublished interview with the girlfriend of Octopus investigator Danny Casolaro; Orgone; Wilhelm Reich: Eisenhower's secret ally against the aliens; Clinton era conspiracies; You Too Can Be a Researcher: How to use the Freedom of Information Act; Anthrax Terrorists; Media Mindwash; 9/11 Commission Omission, and much, much more.
340 Pages. 6x9 Paperback. Illustrated. $20.00. Code: PPOL

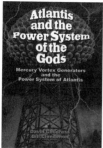

GRAVITATIONAL MANIPULATION OF DOMED CRAFT
UFO Propulsion Dynamics
by Paul E. Potter

Potter's precise and lavish illustrations allow the reader to enter directly into the realm of the advanced technological engineer and to understand, quite straightforwardly, the aliens' methods of energy manipulation: their methods of electrical power generation; how they purposely designed their craft to employ the kinds of energy dynamics that are exclusive to space (discoverable in our astrophysics) in order that their craft may generate both attractive and repulsive gravitational forces; their control over the mass-density matrix surrounding their craft enabling them to alter their physical dimensions and even manufacture their own frame of reference in respect to time. Includes a 16-page color insert.
624 pages. 7x10 Paperback. Illustrated. References. $24.00. Code: GMDC

TAPPING THE ZERO POINT ENERGY
Free Energy & Anti-Gravity in Today's Physics
by Moray B. King

King explains how free energy and anti-gravity are possible. The theories of the zero point energy maintain there are tremendous fluctuations of electrical field energy imbedded within the fabric of space. This book tells how, in the 1930s, inventor T. Henry Moray could produce a fifty kilowatt "free energy" machine; how an electrified plasma vortex creates anti-gravity; how the Pons/Fleischmann "cold fusion" experiment could produce tremendous heat without fusion; and how certain experiments might produce a gravitational anomaly.
180 PAGES. 5x8 PAPERBACK. ILLUSTRATED. $12.95. CODE: TAP

QUEST FOR ZERO-POINT ENERGY
Engineering Principles for "Free Energy"
by Moray B. King

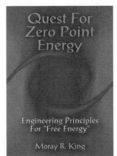

King expands, with diagrams, on how free energy and anti-gravity are possible. The theories of zero point energy maintain there are tremendous fluctuations of electrical field energy embedded within the fabric of space. King explains the following topics: TFundamentals of a Zero-Point Energy Technology; Vacuum Energy Vortices; The Super Tube; Charge Clusters: The Basis of Zero-Point Energy Inventions; Vortex Filaments, Torsion Fields and the Zero-Point Energy; Transforming the Planet with a Zero-Point Energy Experiment; Dual Vortex Forms: The Key to a Large Zero-Point Energy Coherence. Packed with diagrams, patents and photos.
224 PAGES. 6x9 PAPERBACK. ILLUSTRATED. $14.95. CODE: QZPE

DARK MOON
Apollo and the Whistleblowers
by Mary Bennett and David Percy

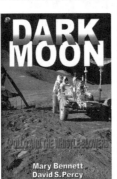

Did you know a second craft was going to the Moon at the same time as Apollo 11? Do you know that potentially lethal radiation is prevalent throughout deep space? Do you know there are serious discrepancies in the account of the Apollo 13 'accident'? Did you know that 'live' color TV from the Moon was not actually live at all? Did you know that the Lunar Surface Camera had no viewfinder? Do you know that lighting was used in the Apollo photographs—yet no lighting equipment was taken to the Moon? All these questions, and more, are discussed in great detail by British researchers Bennett and Percy in *Dark Moon*, the definitive book (nearly 600 pages) on the possible faking of the Apollo Moon missions. Tons of NASA photos analyzed for possible deceptions.
568 PAGES. 6x9 PAPERBACK. ILLUSTRATED. BIBLIOGRAPHY. INDEX. $32.00. CODE: DMO

LOST CITIES & ANCIENT MYSTERIES OF THE SOUTHWEST
By David Hatcher Childress
Join David as he starts in northern Mexico and searches for the lost mines of the Aztecs. He continues north to west Texas, delving into the mysteries of Big Bend, including mysterious Phoenician tablets discovered there and the strange lights of Marfa. Then into New Mexico where he stumbles upon a hollow mountain with a billion dollars of gold bars hidden deep inside it! In Arizona he investigates tales of Egyptian catacombs in the Grand Canyon, cruises along the Devil's Highway, and tackles the century-old mystery of the Lost Dutchman mine. In Nevada and California Childress checks out the rumors of mummified giants and weird tunnels in Death Valley, plus he searches the Mohave Desert for the mysterious remains of ancient dwellers alongside lakes that dried up tens of thousands of years ago. It's a full-tilt blast down the back roads of the Southwest in search of the weird and wondrous mysteries of the past!
486 Pages. 6x9 Paperback. Illustrated. Bibliography. $19.95. Code: LCSW

TECHNOLOGY OF THE GODS
The Incredible Sciences of the Ancients
by David Hatcher Childress
Childress looks at the technology that was allegedly used in Atlantis and the theory that the Great Pyramid of Egypt was originally a gigantic power station. He examines tales of ancient flight and the technology that it involved; how the ancients used electricity; megalithic building techniques; the use of crystal lenses and the fire from the gods; evidence of various high tech weapons in the past, including atomic weapons; ancient metallurgy and heavy machinery; the role of modern inventors such as Nikola Tesla in bringing ancient technology back into modern use; impossible artifacts; and more.
356 PAGES. 6x9 PAPERBACK. ILLUSTRATED. BIBLIOGRAPHY. $16.95. CODE: TGOD

VIMANA AIRCRAFT OF ANCIENT INDIA & ATLANTIS
by David Hatcher Childress, introduction by Ivan T. Sanderson
In this incredible volume on ancient India, authentic Indian texts such as the *Ramayana* and the *Mahabharata* are used to prove that ancient aircraft were in use more than four thousand years ago. Included in this book is the entire Fourth Century BC manuscript *Vimaanika Shastra* by the ancient author Maharishi Bharadwaaja. Also included are chapters on Atlantean technology, the incredible Rama Empire of India and the devastating wars that destroyed it.
334 PAGES. 6x9 PAPERBACK. ILLUSTRATED. $15.95. CODE: VAA

LIQUID CONSPIRACY
JFK, LSD, the CIA, Area 51 & UFOs
by George Piccard
Underground author George Piccard on the politics of LSD, mind control, and Kennedy's involvement with Area 51 and UFOs. Reveals JFK's LSD experiences with Mary Pinchot-Meyer. The plot thickens with an ever expanding web of CIA involvement, from underground bases with UFOs seen by JFK and Marilyn Monroe (among others) to a vaster conspiracy that affects every government agency from NASA to the Justice Department. This may have been the reason that Marilyn Monroe and actress-columnist Dorothy Kilgallen were both murdered. Focusing on the bizarre side of history, *Liquid Conspiracy* takes the reader on a psychedelic tour de force. This is your government on drugs!
264 Pages. 6x9 Paperback. Illustrated. $14.95. Code: LIQC

ORDER FORM

10% Discount When You Order 3 or More Items

One Adventure Place
P.O. Box 74
Kempton, Illinois 60946
United States of America
Tel.: 815-253-6390 • Fax: 815-253-6300
Email: auphq@frontiernet.net
http://www.adventuresunlimitedpress.com

ORDERING INSTRUCTIONS

✓ Remit by USD$ Check, Money Order or Credit Card

✓ Visa, Master Card, Discover & AmEx Accepted

✓ Paypal Payments Can Be Made To:
   info@wexclub.com

✓ Prices May Change Without Notice

✓ 10% Discount for 3 or more Items

SHIPPING CHARGES

United States

✓ Postal Book Rate { $4.00 First Item / 50¢ Each Additional Item

✓ POSTAL BOOK RATE Cannot Be Tracked!

✓ Priority Mail { $5.00 First Item / $2.00 Each Additional Item

✓ UPS { $6.00 First Item / $1.50 Each Additional Item
   NOTE: UPS Delivery Available to Mainland USA Only

Canada

✓ Postal Air Mail { $10.00 First Item / $2.50 Each Additional Item

✓ Personal Checks or Bank Drafts MUST BE
   US$ and Drawn on a US Bank

✓ Canadian Postal Money Orders OK

✓ Payment MUST BE US$

All Other Countries

✓ Sorry, No Surface Delivery!

✓ Postal Air Mail { $16.00 First Item / $6.00 Each Additional Item

✓ Checks and Money Orders MUST BE US$
   and Drawn on a US Bank or branch.

✓ Paypal Payments Can Be Made in US$ To:
   info@wexclub.com

SPECIAL NOTES

✓ RETAILERS: Standard Discounts Available

✓ BACKORDERS: We Backorder all Out-of-
   Stock Items Unless Otherwise Requested

✓ PRO FORMA INVOICES: Available on Request

ORDER ONLINE AT: www.adventuresunlimitedpress.com

Please check: ☑

☐ This is my first order   ☐ I have ordered before

Name
Address
City
State/Province   Postal Code
Country
Phone day   Evening
Fax   Email

Item Code	Item Description	Qty	Total

Please check: ☑

☐ Postal-Surface

☐ Postal-Air Mail (Priority in USA)

☐ UPS (Mainland USA only)

☐ Visa/MasterCard/Discover/American Express

Subtotal ▶
Less Discount-10% for 3 or more items ▶
Balance ▶
Illinois Residents 6.25% Sales Tax ▶
Previous Credit ▶
Shipping ▶
Total (check/MO in USD$ only) ▶

Card Number
Expiration Date

10% Discount When You Order 3 or More Items!